① "pattern" vs. "propositional - deductive"
theory

Theoretical thinking in sociology

WILLIAM SKIDMORE

Second edition

Cambridge University Press

Cambridge
London   New York   Melbourne

Published by the Syndics of the Cambridge University Press
The Pitt Building, Trumpington Street, Cambridge CB2 1RP
Bentley House, 200 Euston Road, London NW1 2DB
32 East 57th Street, New York, NY 10022, USA
296 Beaconsfield Parade, Middle Park, Melbourne 3206, Australia

First published 1975
Second edition 1979

Printed in the United States of America
Typeset by Huron Valley Graphics, Ann Arbor, Michigan
Printed and bound by BookCrafters, Inc., Fredericksburg, Virginia

Library of Congress Cataloging in Publication Data

Skidmore, William.

Theoretical thinking in sociology.

Includes bibliographies and indexes.

1. Sociology. I. Title.
HM24.S48 1979 301 78–74540
ISBN 0 521 22663 5 hard covers
ISBN 0 521 29606 4 paperback

First edition:
ISBN 0 521 20716 9 hard covers
ISBN 0 521 29932 3 paperback

To
JUNE AND MORLEY,
who cared and helped

Contents

Preface to the second edition

The main purpose of the second edition remains unchanged from the first. It is to provide a useful, substantial overview of the main branches of current sociological theory, while not resorting too much to minor detail. The author's hope is that anyone interested can get a working grasp of the subject in a manageable length of time. Further study will be easier when the main points have been established. This general objective determines the style and organization of the book. Each chapter can be read on its own, or the book can be read through as a unit. Of course, I hope that it will be read from front to back with no gaps between, but this is not absolutely necessary.

Each chapter is intended to describe an aspect of sociological theory in a way that unites the theory, its philosophical background, and research implications. These aspects, combined with the critiques that end the last four chapters, indicate strengths, weaknesses, and typical uses of various theoretical viewpoints. The contributions of significant theoreticians are relied upon heavily. The aim is to describe a theoretician's thinking by following out his logic from the challenge of initial questions to the resultant theory and its applications.

The first three chapters of the book concern the nature and importance of sociological theory, its enduring challenge and problems, and an introduction to the logic and organization of theoretical work in social science. Such material I consider crucial, rather than simply introductory, because it supports the thinking from which all theoretical questions in the social sciences arise and are answered. In Chapter 3, a distinction is drawn regarding the conceptual organization of theories. They tend to be: (1) hierarchically organized under general laws; (2) assembled into concatenated patterns; or (3) generalized perspectives. The procedures appropriate to understanding and using a sociological theory depend in part on what type of theory it is. The remaining chapters, which cover exchange theory, functionalism, symbolic interaction, and ethnomethodology, regard each as basically representative of one or another style of theorizing. Although there are overlaps in this system of categorization, it is most useful, because it derives from the conceptual foundations of sociological theory.

xiii

The basic plan of this edition is much the same as the first. But this edition differs by including a much expanded description of ethnomethodology, and eliminating the first edition's brief treatment of theory construction and formalization. Within chapters, significant reorganization has streamlined the presentation for easier reading, while retaining all substantial material.

I again gratefully acknowledge the graceful colleagueship of my friends at the University of New Brunswick, the reviewers whose comments have been important, and the support and help of my wife, Pat. I also thank Cambridge University Press for the opportunity to prepare a second edition.

W. L. S.

The Anchorage
June 1979

Preface to the first edition

Experience suggests that students of sociology at all levels have much in common. They need, on the whole, to be convinced that sociological theory is worth studying for its own sake, rather than as a requirement toward a degree. They need to know something about how to judge theory – how to tell good from bad in the conceptual world of sociology. They need, above all, to know the objective of theory: *to explain social order,* so that they can better see what the whole enterprise is aiming for and gauge progress.

When someone takes up the study of sociological theory, he does not want to be smothered in detail, nor to be insulted by superficiality. He seeks a substantial overview of theory, so that further work in the field can proceed according to solid preliminary understandings. Most students would also like to know the bearing of sociological theory on research, and to have concrete examples of how theory and research contribute to each other's success. Finally, to gain perspective, students ought to know that all theories are deficient in at least some respects, and that theoretical thinking includes a proper appreciation of critical remarks about each competing viewpoint.

Theoretical Thinking in Sociology attempts to speak to these requirements. The first three chapters consider the idea of sociological theory and its use, examine some methods of theorizing and some theoretical problems, and set out basic understandings from the philosophy of social science about the relation of evidence to theory, the logical structure of theory, and the methodological procedures appropriate to various theoretical styles. These first three chapters outline the distinguishing marks of the three kinds of theory to be described later on: deductive theory, pattern theory, and perspectives.

Chapters 4 through 6 examine these more closely. Chapter 4 describes deductive theoretical structure, using exchange theory as an example. Chapter 5 examines pattern theory, describing functionalism. Chapter 6 describes symbolic interactionism as a perspective. Finally, Chapter 7 outlines other activities of sociological theorists and returns to the question of social order by describing how ethnomethodology deals with this problem. These chapters are independent enough to be read separately, and in any order; but it is the author's hope that the book will be read through from start to finish, or at least that the first three chapters will be familiar to the reader before any of the following four. This is because the later chapters are intended as examples from active theory of the strengths, weaknesses, and thought styles that the first three chapters introduce. The book delineates the thinking of the theoreticians it discusses, not just their conclusions.

In writing any book, one incurs many debts, to teachers and students, to colleagues known and unknown whose ideas one has absorbed, to family. I wish to acknowledge the very considerable critical and editorial help given me by my wife, who has also typed the whole manuscript through twice. In addition, the University of New Brunswick kindly provided a grant to support the preparation of this book, and my colleagues in the Department of Sociology and Anthropology at U.N.B. maintained the usual congenial and encouraging atmosphere.

W. L. S.

The Anchorage
May 1974

1 Sociological theory

I. Introduction

Sociological theory is a richly rewarding subject to study. As one of the "social sciences" that emerged from the fascinating and important debates among philosophers and literary men about the origins and nature of society, sociology shares in the legacy left to the arts and humanities. Its theoretical ideas were shaped by the great intellectual debates about the nature and extent of human rationality, the growth and consequences of industrialism, social statics versus the inevitability of change, the relationship between human character and social structure. Broad organizing themes like these have always been the focus of interest for those who could produce subtle and compelling ideas. Sociology is privileged to have such a heritage.

And in addition to its humanizing foundations, sociology, like the other studies that strive for scientific knowledge about human affairs, has historically tried to provide firm empirical foundations for itself, as a kind of counterweight against its philosophizing tendencies. There has always been a drive among the best sociologists for clarity and "tidy-mindedness," in the spirit of scientific reasoning. Sometimes the scientific spirit seems to outweigh the humanistic elements in sociology, but often enough the scale is tipped the other way. No matter what the exact mixture, the scientific attitude, combined with a humanizing tradition, has provided an abundance of subtle sociological theory that in itself is a mental challenge, and which promises to be the intellectual basis for empirical research or social policy.

In this book, the separate branches into which sociological theory has divided itself are traced. Of course, these branches are not entirely mutually exclusive, but on the whole, generalized points of view about human society have tended to coincide with logically divergent means by which theories may be stated and their predictions and explanations given. It behooves us, therefore, to follow the thinking of some central figures in modern sociological theory as they attempt to unite their insights and hunches about human society with their rather enormous respect for data and scientific clearheadedness to produce sociological theory.

1

Theories come in various packages. Sometimes they are clearly and succinctly stated, or they may be implied by less precise arguments. Actually, most theoretical work is partially ambiguous and thus there is almost always room for interpretation concerning the exact meanings of any theory. There will be more about this as we progress in our descriptions of sociological theory, but for now it ought to be emphasized that seemingly detrimental ambiguity is very often a positive point. It is as a result of the mental work involved in analysis that we make advances.

The rise of sociology in universities and colleges has been accompanied by the more or less systematic study of sociological theory as such. But this was not always so. Formerly, what we know as theories developed out of someone's trying to understand some practical puzzle. Theories grew up around themes, which we might call theoretical problems. Subjects such as urban crime, the decrease in the birth rate, or the nature of social solidarity are such puzzles. Concern for issues like these actually transcends the immediate practical importance that gave rise to initial interest in them. Such issues formed the bases for systems of thought that came to be called theories, systems that went much beyond the problems that started them on their way.

The solution to a theoretical problem does not necessarily mean that the practical problem associated with it is also solved. Anyone who has ever noticed the number of theories of crime and the rising crime rate knows this. Theoretical problems have solutions in the sense that the ideas in a theory, their interrelations and implications, give answers to the theoretical problems. The problem of how to understand social class, for example, is solved in part by the generation of additional related concepts. When all these ideas are put together and systematized, the result might turn into the beginning of a more general sociological theory.

Theories initiated in this way might take many forms and exist in various states of relative consistency or inconsistency, clarity or obscurity. They could also be mixed with simple narration of fact or perhaps ideology. Therefore, it is sometimes hard to detect one precise meaning of a theoretical term, because it may be unclear whether its inventor means his reader to take the term as description, plan of action, or mainly for its usefulness in understanding something.

Sociologists sometimes give the name "theory" to such loose collections of ideas. But theories can take the form of precise statements of ideas, in which the concepts or processes posed by the theory are clearly and definitively spelled out. This, of course, is an ideal for many sociological theorists. Because this ideal state of affairs is not often reached in actual practice, we must expect to find working sociological theory somewhere between total precision and unsystematic looseness.

II. Theory and practice

At first glance, sociological theory sometimes seems a separate entity, something to master because, like the mountain, it is simply there. This attitude usually leads to frustration, because it is not based on a realistic grasp of what we can expect to get out of sociological theory. In general, the strength of theory is in its ability to bring a great deal of organized thought and information to bear on a specific problem, and thereby go far beyond unsystematic thought in detail and precision. Theories work out and hold ideas ready to be used at a moment's notice.

We may conveniently divide the ways in which a theory may address a theoretical problem into four categories and discuss them separately. It might be useful to think of these as the four ways in which theories are useful to sociologists. These are:

1 Theory may generate additional ideas in the course of solving a theoretical problem.
2 Theory may suggest models of the subject matter, so that a kind of schematic description results. Such description can be thought of as a pattern into which ideas may be placed for convenience and clarity.
3 Critical analysis of theories can produce new theory.
4 Theory may suggest hypotheses.

A. Theory can generate ideas

Thinking of theories as suggesting ideas more or less corresponds to the loose-construction approach to theory described earlier. Consider a single concept, which itself is not a theory. Social class, for example, may be felt or experienced, in some sense, but there is no theoretical meaning in the idea by itself. Only when the concept of social class is put together with additional ideas does it begin to be explained and accounted for, or to take part in explaining something else. Understanding social class has altogether to do with the meaning of social structure, social relations, power, privilege, obligation, authority, and many other ideas. In practical terms, this suggests that to understand social class, one is obligated to develop clear ideas of these related factors. In doing so, even more ideas probably will be suggested; each new step in this process requires a new search for clarity which usually brightens all the ideas, including the one at the center of it all – social class, in this example.

Ideas that seem to spring up around an initial thought do not do so at random. They develop principally because (1) the definition of one concept suggests another, or (2) some empirical observation suggests that an idea is needed. In the first case, we might say that the concepts with which we start imply logical relationships among them. Ideas could be generated in the process of ferreting out these relationships; for example, the idea that society is class stratified suggests that there is more than one class, and that the characteristics of these classes are not the same. Defining society in this way pushes us toward a logically consistent account of the various classes and their characteristics. Concerning empirical observation, we are asking a question of how well an initial idea seems to "fit" the facts. Again using social class as an example, it is possible in principle to have many concepts of class, only some of which will appear to describe something about real social classes. The ones that seem to do this will be preferred.

We see, in this example, that any definition of social class (whatever specific one we may care to choose) implies a division of something "social" into categories called "classes." Starting with an idea of "classness" we generated the need to know the relatedness of one class to another. In doing this, we also had to define social class so that there is a clear distinction between one class and another. "Classes" are thus becoming more distinctly defined as the theoretical work goes on and the question of their relatedness comes to the fore. The relatedness of these classes as they form a "social" unit is therefore of interest. The nature of this relatedness might form the basis of a more general idea about social structure.

In this example, we see that a theoretical approach to an idea leads quite naturally to the creation of other ideas that help clarify it and specify its relatedness to others. Something like this happens as theories develop logical structure, but before long, logically incompatible ideas will probably be discovered. Then such incompatibility will require the theorist either to change the ideas or to alter the whole theoretical structure in some way, hopefully resulting in a more coherent system that can incorporate all his thinking.

B. *Theory can suggest models*

There is no clear distinction between models and theories. A model is often confused with a theory, and sometimes the two terms are used interchangeably with no attention to the differences between them. In essence, theories without models explain directly; models explain by analogy.[1]

It will be useful to describe the concept of models before returning to the ways in which theory may suggest models and what is gained

---

[1] For a fuller description of models in science, see Abraham Kaplan, *The Conduct of Inquiry* (San Francisco: Chandler Publishing Co., 1964), Ch. 7.

when this happens. A *model* of something is, by definition, not the thing itself, but something else that has a *resemblance* to the thing of interest. It is precisely in the resemblances that the utility of models lies. A model is useful in pointing out elements of resemblance and in developing a better understanding of why the model resembles the reality. For example, everyone knows that a model airplane and a Boeing 747 are not the same thing. But in what ways are they similar? If the model flies, the air on the wings of the model holds the plane in flight. Because flight happens as a result of air on wings, the shape and structure of the wings and their relationship to the rest of the model plane are analogous in some ways to the flight of the 747. If we are interested in understanding the action of air on the wings of the 747, we might investigate that by observing the action of air on the model. But we could not do this to discover the cause of movement through air, because our model does not have jet engines. The model is analogous to reality in some important ways, and not analogous in others. The model is useless if we want to understand why the real airplane moves, but if we are interested in why it stays up, the model might be important.

Of course, in this example, we already knew that the model was not analogous with respect to the cause of movement (no jet engines) and this lack of correspondence between model and reality caused no difficulty. But, in social science, we sometimes build up models of reality, and then fail to notice the ways in which the models do *not* correspond to reality. Put another way, we might define parts of reality that are poorly understood as though they were analogous to the parts of a model, knowing that this is risky. In the field of economics, for example, the ways people allocate resources among hundreds of choices has long been a puzzle. Because the theory of spending must emphasize choice and choosing, one kind of model that has developed is Rational Man or Economic Man.[2] This model amounts to a series of assumptions about how choices are made, based on the principle of maximization of benefit. The main question about this model is, of course, whether it is true that real people always seek to maximize their own benefit when spending. Now, taken literally, the model is probably "wrong" in the sense that real people do not seem to spend on the basis of personal gain alone, and for no other reason. Obviously, they do not spend entirely for egoistic benefit; and they often spend unwisely. But remember, they do not spend chaotically, and they usually do spend with the objective of receiving value for money. And do not forget that what we are using is a model of the resource allocator, not a model of Emotional Man or Altruistic Man.

[2] The concept of rationality is not limited to use in economics, and we shall examine the concept in more detail, especially in Chapter 4.

Economic Man, as a model, is quite useful in emphasizing interesting aspects of economic behavior, even though this model is oversimplified and does not resemble "real" man in very many details. The intelligent use of a model like this involves understanding its analogous parts while not supposing that the model explains too much.

C. Critical analysis of theories

Models may suggest improvements or additions to theories. This process can be helpful when a theory is more poorly understood than a model. A theory may predict a certain relationship between two facts but say little about additional relationships among these facts and others. A model that seems to picture the relationship between the first two ideas may suggest by analogy the other theoretical relationships. A good example of this situation can be found in sociological theory. It is sometimes thought that the process of social change is analogous to biological evolution.[3] In fact, a very important branch of sociological theory in the nineteenth century (which is by no means outmoded today) said precisely this. Such theory uses our knowledge of evolution, a biological phenomenon, as a model for understanding social change. Among the things suggested by this approach to social change is that intense conflict may occur between discrete social units in the short run (individuals, classes, interests, etc.) but that the long-run result of conflict is not the destruction of society, but rather a reshaping, redirecting, and redevelopment of it. Note that this constructive conclusion was not suggested by empirical instances of social conflict; the idea of long-run benefit arose from the biological model.[4] It is not appropriate here to try to resolve the issue of whether social conflict is beneficial, but it is important to see where we got the idea of its being so. We used a model; the idea came from the model, not directly from observation. This analogy could go much further. We have already warned that in the absence of solid proof, the extent to which analogies may be taken is unknown. It would be important to know more precisely how "social evolution" resembles biological evolution, and if the resemblance is essential or superficial.

---

[3] A good short treatment of how this idea affected the work of William Graham Sumner and Lester Ward is found in Richard Hofstadter, *Social Darwinism in American Thought* (Boston: Beacon Press, 1944). The concept of evolution has been applied at many levels of generality. In a more recent work, Talcott Parsons uses the idea to help explain the pattern of world social development, in *Societies: Evolutionary and Comparative Perspectives* (Englewood Cliffs, N.J.: Prentice-Hall, 1966).
[4] The actual source of this material is a matter of controversy. It might have been borrowed by the natural sciences from political economy. The point remains, however, that in this example the idea of evolutionary change was borrowed by sociological theorists from the naturalists.

It should be emphasized that the desire to understand reality sometimes drives us to define it in terms of models. If we think that social
evolution is just a special kind of biological evolution, then we imply
that whatever is "social" resembles the biological world in essential
respects. This amounts to assuming a rather enormous analogy about
the social world in the terms in which the naturalist makes assumptions about the biological world. Done within reason, this can produce useful theory; but it can lead to absurdities as well. For example, it might be instructive to imagine society as a web of complex,
interrelated functional parts, such as a living body; but it is probably
absurd to attribute "life" to this web in anything like the physical
sense of life.[5] Models in sociology are usually better understood and
more complete than the social facts they are taken to represent.
Hence when the intention is to know reality by analogy through a
model, extreme caution is a must. We should always question the
extent to which models are really applicable. We can "learn" too
much too easily by making too grand an analogy.

D. Theories suggest hypotheses

In this discussion of models and theories, we have gone more or less
on the intuitive idea that a sociological theory is some kind of arrangement of ideas that "tells us something" about the social world.
But the particular way in which it does this may be important. One
way is for theories to produce hypotheses, although this is not the
only way.

A *hypothesis* is a statement about a relationship between two or
more ideas or classes of thing. This preliminary definition could also
be the definition of a scientific law, or just a guess. The important
difference between hypotheses and guesses is that the hypothesis is
somehow conceptually related to the theory from which it comes. The
tightest relationship between theory and hypotheses involves the deductive process; that is, hypotheses follow directly as a matter of
logical extension from the generalizations established within the theory.[6] A theory can generate hypotheses if it is applied to some specific theoretical or empirical problem.

For example, Durkheim[7] had a general theory concerning social

---

[5] When life is attributed to sociological entities, as in "the living city," this mistake is
  dangerously close.
[6] Deduction is often defined as reasoning from the general to the particular. Fundamentally, the deductive process follows the form of the syllogism: A major premise
  states a generality, a minor premise gives a statement of a specific case, and a
  conclusion states the relationship of the specific case to the generality.
[7] Tr. J. A. Spalding and G. Simpson (New York: Free Press, 1951).

solidarity and religious practices in mind when writing *Suicide*. Durkheimian theory holds, in general, that persons are entirely dependent for all aspects of life, including individuality, on society. Collective society gives identity, stabilizes against the buffeting forces of everyday life, and sustains the spiritual, as well as the material person. Society is represented in each person's mind by the "collective conscience," which may be concrete or abstract, depending on the state of societal development.

But how can a hypothesis be derived from Durkheim's theory? Wisely, Durkheim chose suicide as a problem with which to test his theoretical scheme. He reasoned if he could show a social influence on this, the most individual of individual acts, he would be a long way toward proving the point that society is of prime importance to individuality. But how to do it? It was easy to find statistical records to show that in certain places in Europe, at certain times, the suicide rate varied, went up or down, from the median level. Durkheim reasoned that if he could account for the changes in suicide rate entirely by reference to states of social solidarity, he would have his answer.

According to the generalizations in Durkheim's theory, the greater the social solidarity, the more likely it is that individuals will experience meaningful social support in times of stress, and the less likely, therefore, will be their suicide. Religion enters the picture at this point. Durkheim reasoned that the Roman Catholic faith provided stronger social solidarity than did Protestantism. This seemed to be so because Catholicism at Durkheim's time of writing tended to take a more collective and integrative approach to the individual, and it more often emphasized commonality and similarity to others. Protestantism, on the other hand, was much more individualistic. With their doctrines of direct participation in some of the sacraments, the emphasis on reading the Bible for oneself, and, in some cases, democratic control of church affairs by the congregation, the Protestant faiths were associated with a less tightly knit and less solidly integrated social system.

Here Durkheim had his answer. To demonstrate a relationship between social solidarity and individual behavior, Durkheim needed concrete indications of each. He had data about individual acts, par excellence – suicides. He wished to account for them. He had Catholicism and Protestantism with which to do it in terms of social solidarity.

His *hypothesis,* therefore, was that in areas of Europe where Catholicism was strong, suicide rates would be lower than in areas where Protestantism was predominant. It is important to spend a moment on what Durkheim's hypothesis meant. It meant, obviously, that he expected a relationship to exist between suicide rates and religious affiliation. But he did not guess this ad hoc. He derived it from a theory about something much broader and potentially important: the relationship between social solidarity and individuality. The fact that Durkheim's concrete prediction (his hypothesis) was by and large confirmed suggested that the theoretical scheme from which it derived also was valid. If his data had not tended to confirm his prediction, his theory of social integration would still be a theory, and the logic of predicting the distribution of suicides in Europe would still be intact.[8] However, it would not enjoy empirically derived evidence of its validity.

Durkheim's general theory of social solidarity and the individual suggests other hypotheses as well. For example, it implies the primacy of society in matters of morals and professional ethics. Durkheim did research in this field, again generally confirming his main theory.[9] More than one hypothesis can come from a theory. The number and variety of hypotheses derivable from a given theory are part of the measure of that theory's worth.

A hypothesis has not yet been differentiated from a scientific law. More detail will have to be postponed until the discussion of the structure of theories. But for now, if a hypothesis seems to be confirmed by experience over a wide range of events and in a wide range of situations, the hypothesis can be "elevated" to the status of a law. This means that those who work with and know a hypothesis in all its forms, and have sufficient confidence that its predictions are true, will begin to feel less of a need to test it constantly against experience each time they use it. They will instead begin to use the hypothesis as a principle from which to deduce new hypotheses. It will, thus, become a law.[10]

The statement of relationship between two ideas does not necessarily change its form when the statement ceases being a hypothesis and starts becoming lawlike. Neither would the form necessarily change if the statement were just a hunch. The distinction among hypothesis, law, and hunch lies in the state of logical relatedness and weight of

---

[8] This may seem confusing. Durkheim's hypothesis might not have been confirmed, but there are a variety of reasons why this might be: His statistics might have been wrong; he might have made a mistake in calculation; some other factor that had an effect on social solidarity might have influenced his results. Thus hypotheses are usually cautiously related to reality in terms of "weights of evidence" or "tendencies" to confirm or disconfirm a given hypothesis. Of course, all such errors that could have led to a failure to confirm Durkheim's hypothesis might have contributed to its confirmation as well.

[9] Emile Durkheim, *Professional Ethics and Civil Morals*, tr. Cornelia Brookfield (London: Routledge and Kegan Paul, 1957).

[10] A considerable literature in "the philosophy of science" has grown up, partly around the question of laws. See Kaplan, *Conduct of Inquiry*, Ch. 8, and N. R. Campbell, *Foundations of Science* (New York: Dover, 1957), Part I, for further discussion on laws.

confirmatory evidence that builds up between the statement of relationship and the rest of the story. If a statement of relationship is clearly and logically linked to a theory, it is a hypothesis rather than a guess. If the statement is supported by a quantity of evidence, it may be called a law rather than a hypothesis.

III. Types of theory and typologies of theory

Obviously, sociology has many theories. This does not mean that all but one of them are "wrong," or that any of them is "wrong." If theories have developed around problems, as has been suggested, they group themselves naturally into types of theories related to issues. But theories have a tendency to expand their scope: They suggest hypotheses that go beyond the initial point of interest for proposing theory in the first place. Thus over time, there has come to be an overlapping of theoretical "territory," so that now there are many theories that offer explanations of approximately the same phenomenon. This gives rise to the need to classify theories and sort them according to some rational criteria. The attempt to do this has sometimes led to problems and confusion.

One way to classify theories is to attach dates to them, according to the times in which they were first proposed or first came into relatively wide use. Then the theories can be discussed in temporal order. University courses in sociological theory that take a "historical" approach often do essentially this. The advantage of this procedure is to show repeatedly that a given idea has had the power to spawn other ideas, and that theoretical systems evolve as they are thought through again and again. By looking back over the course of time, new and different ideas can be traced to old ones.[11] A disadvantage of this approach is that it is sometimes difficult to grasp the reasons why theories change, rise, and fall.

Another scheme of classification used with some success is to group theories according to the country in which they were proposed and used most widely. This approach has led to some fairly stable classifications of theory, in sociology as well as in other disciplines. For example, German sociology of the middle and late nineteenth century tended to be distinguishable from sociology in England or France of about the same period. Probably the similarities among German theories resulted from common cultural themes or points of view shared by the German theorists. This is not to say, however, that German theories are all the same. Far from it. Nor is it to say

[11] The master at showing historical precedent for sociological ideas is P. A. Sorokin. See his *Contemporary Sociological Theories* (New York: Harper, 1928), *Sociological Theories of Today* (New York: Harper & Row, 1966), and *Fads and Foibles in Modern Sociology* (Chicago: Henry Regnery, 1956).

that theories produced in other countries did not resemble German theory. This happened. In fact, Durkheim's theory of social solidarity, developed in France, resembles German theories of folk spirit and cultural heritage. It could also be shown that rather similar ideas were in use in England at the time. Nevertheless, the national classification method has been used as a convenient labeling technique, and "German sociological theory" still has a reasonably precise meaning.[12]

A more defensible method of classifying theories is to analyze them according to their main ideas or assumptions, and to group similar ones, no matter when or where they were formed originally.[13] This method has the distinct advantages of showing the logical similarities of various theories, and of showing how a given theoretical group differs from another group on conceptual grounds. This approach is especially appropriate if we want a comparison of the usefulness of theories, as it shows more clearly what we can expect from a given group of theories. However, there is a danger in classifying theories according to main ideas. When theories are classified according to the similarities of their main ideas, concepts, predictions, and types of explanation, there is a temptation to regard all theories in one group as being the same. They normally are not the same, but the fact that certain similarities are emphasized, partly to satisfy the categorical approach, gives this impression. This often leads to the belief that there is one theory corresponding to the name of the category in which several theories are placed.

The most obvious example of this mistake is what is called "conflict theory." Several theories may be grouped together because of the fact that they all have something to say about social conflict. When differences among the theories are blurred, the result is the impression that the theories are similar in essentials. For example, Marx's ideas concerning social relations between classes in capitalist society are sometimes found grouped with Darwin's and with those who used Darwin's idea of natural selection to argue a basic conflict model of society. But we almost never see Marx's ideas grouped with those of Simmel, who also had a considerable amount to say about conflict. Similarly, Adam Smith's proposals could be considered a conflict theory just as well as a theory based on the variety and interdependence of human needs. Classification of Smith with Marx would emphasize certain things, whereas classifying Smith separately would emphasize others.

[12] Examples of this approach are: Howard Becker and Harry E. Barnes, *Social Thought from Lore to Science,* rev. ed. (New York: Dover, 1966), III, and Raymond Aron, *German Sociology,* tr. Mary and Thomas Bottomore (New York: Free Press, 1964).

[13] See Don Martindale, *The Nature and Types of Sociological Theory* (Boston: Houghton Mifflin, 1960).

Another classification of theory that has something to recommend it has been proposed recently. This scheme emphasizes that, to have a theory of something, the thing must first be precisely defined. In essence, the proposal is to group theories together that take a similar approach to defining "the social" and then examine similar theories to discover how they explain "the social." Theories that define and explain in similar ways are placed together for convenience; those that have substantial differences are placed apart.[14]

Any scheme of categories probably will not reflect the subtle changes occurring throughout the life of a productive theorist. This resistance to categorization leads to the last method of organizing the study of social theory, which is really no scheme at all. It is to study the work of men who have made substantial contributions to sociological theory, and try to become so familiar with their efforts that the knowledge gained provides sufficient background for us to say we know something about sociological theory in its entirety.

IV. Why theorize?

Is there an alternative to theorizing? This is a reasonable question, especially if one is uncomfortable about theory and wants to get on as quickly as possible to "the facts." But the truth is, we do theorize whether or not we realize it, and we do interpret facts in the light of theories that give facts their meaning. Sociological theory in the formal sense is simply a more thorough, more careful, and better-understood form of theorizing than the naive theory we all employ in everyday life.

Most people already know much sociological theory. The key terms of sociological theory often turn up in daily language. For example, one often hears people speak theoretically about "role," as in "the role of women today." What may not be understood in such usage, however, is that "role" is a key concept in several sociological theories. Used in the sense of functionalist theory,[15] "role" connotes a set of rights and duties accepted by a role-player who believes in the legitimacy of these rights and duties as defined and sanctioned by the system in which the person acts. "Role" in this context is given meaning by the webs of rights and duties. These collectively constitute a system that accomplishes something, has systematic effects, or functions (hence the term "functionalist theory"). Thus "the role of women" really connotes not only something about women, but something about the various roles of men and all the other roles with which

[14] Walter W. Wallace, *Sociological Theory: An Introduction* (Chicago: Aldine, 1969).
[15] Every functionalist is a bit different in emphasis and style. The exact meaning of "functionalism" is not settled. See Chapter 5.

someone playing the role of woman comes into contact. These interconnected roles are regarded in functionalist theory as constituting natural clusters, making up functioning groups. Thus the family is a set of legitimate relationships between two or more complementary roles defined by the functions of "family life," for example, mutually supporting and caring for persons of special relatedness, legally procreating, raising, and training children.

Alternatively, the term "role" is used in everyday language in quite another sense. If someone says he is "playing the role," meaning that he believes he is doing what others expect while he himself is not committed to the behavior, he is emphasizing the "self-presentation" or "impression management" meaning of the term "role."[16] This approach emphasizes the "self" as a conscious entity that uses symbols to convey meanings and impressions to others who, in turn, do the same. Here, the term "role" suggests the behavior at the front of a stage where a "presentation" is made, while the "other" is the audience. Behind the stage are all the production facilities making it possible for the stage-front action to proceed. Social organization, in this way of thinking, has not so much to do with the functional interdependence of roles in some system as it does with a kind of "negotiated order" in which each actor is working out his part as he goes along.

It is part of the job of sociological theory not only to point out different meanings, but in addition to analyze concepts and processes implied by sociological terms. Theory study emphasizes that it is in a conceptual and logical context that a term like "role" gains its meaning. Sometimes these contexts are enormously complicated, but rewardingly interesting and rich. A grasp of such systems of thought is gratifying and edifying in itself. In one way, this is what theorizing is for.

There is really no alternative to theorizing. If we did away with it, we would be left with a jumble of data and impressions that would only cry out for arrangement and interpretation. But how would we arrange it? If we had no idea of possible systems, no notion of how to start, we would really be powerless to give our raw material meaning. Facts and impressions gain meaning (and therefore sometimes imply the need for action) by their relatedness, their "theoretical" nature. Finding relationships among facts brings them into some coherent conceptual order. Thinking through such order, and explaining it, is the process of theorizing.

When these conceptual orders are grasped, it is possible to put them to work explaining. Discussion of the different meanings of

[16] See Erving Goffman, *The Presentation of Self in Everyday Life* (New York: Doubleday, 1959).

explanation will have to wait until Chapter 3, but for now, remember that explanation is the main goal of sociological theory. In essence, explaining means relating a conceptual problem or an observation to a theoretical context for the purpose of understanding. If no theoretical scheme is available, the desire to explain is really the desire to set things in order by inventing some scheme of relatedness that gives a convincing understanding of a problem. This is theorizing. If an existing theory fits a problem, the act of demonstrating this by logical analysis, or by marshaling empirical evidence is "explaining" the problem in theoretical terms.

But the utility of sociological theory does not stop at explanation. Knowing theory, one might be able to predict future events. Prediction is entirely a matter of theory because, strictly speaking, there can be no empirical data on the future – it hasn't happened yet. But what might happen can often be foretold with reasonable accuracy by consulting theoretical studies. These furnish explanations sometimes regarded as valid for explaining the future, because they seem to work in the present. Realistically, theoretical prediction is what would happen if the theoretical basis for forecasting were entirely adequate. There is considerable controversy about the validity of the claim that prediction in the social sciences is possible, but the fact is that attempts to predict and to control behavior are being made constantly. As government and business become increasingly committed to long-range social planning, community development, economic management, and so on, they rely increasingly on the ability of social scientists to use theories to suggest the results expected from expenditure or manipulation. This is not idle ivory-tower theorizing, and we ought to be keenly aware that such social prediction has its basis in sociological theory and explanation.

In addition to noticing the challenge and prospects of theoretical work in sociology, we ought to suggest a brief appraisal of the state of development now achieved, and come to a conclusion about possible development in theory in the near future. Sociological theory is in a constant state of change and reformulation. But this does not mean that, at some time, a theory will necessarily be achieved that explains everything, at which point additional development and interpretation will stop. As new problems arise and new needs press, theoretical accounts of the social process will be altered. Facts and ideas that seemed satisfactorily explained will again become a problem, as new emphases are required or new arguments arise. Thus theoretical work not only develops toward more subtle and accurate formulations; it also reshapes itself as it goes.

KEY CONCEPTS

theory	theoretical order
hypothesis	explain
model	predict
law	analogy

TOPICS FOR DISCUSSION

1 If a hypothesis does not describe observed reality, what is the implication for the related theory?
2 The same theoretical terms can have different meanings, depending upon the theories in which the terms are found. Discuss.
3 Is there one "conflict" theory? Why or why not?
4 What is the possible benefit of theoretical ambiguity?
5 What differentiates guesses, hypotheses, and laws?
6 What are the strengths and weaknesses of some various ways of classifying theories?
7 What would life be like if no one theorized?
8 What theoretical ideas or assumptions would you say are implied by everyday terms like "instinct," "conditioning," "free will," "system"?
9 What is an explanation?
10 How is it that a "theoretical problem" can be "solved" while the related practical problem remains unsolved?

ESSAY QUESTIONS

Describe how a practical idea like "human nature" really implies theoretical thinking, models, and concepts.

Examine the ethical questions involved in using social science to predict or control social events.

FOR FURTHER READING AND STUDY

Aron, Raymond. *German Sociology*. Tr. Mary and Thomas Bottomore. New York: Free Press, 1964.

Banton, Michael. *Roles: An Introduction to the Study of Social Relations*. London: Tavistock, 1965.

Braybrooke, David. *Philosophical Problems of the Social Sciences*. New York: Macmillan, 1965.

Goffman, Erving. *The Presentation of Self in Everyday Life*. New York: Doubleday, 1959.

Hofstadter, Richard. *Social Darwinism in American Thought*. Boston: Beacon Press, 1944.

Kaplan, Abraham. *The Conduct of Inquiry*. San Francisco: Chandler Publishing Co., 1964.
MacIver, Robert M. *Social Causation*. New York: Harper & Row, 1964.
Nettler, Gwyn. *Explanations*. New York: McGraw-Hill, 1970.
Ryan, Alan. *The Philosophy of the Social Sciences*. London: Macmillan, 1970.
Wallace, Walter W. *Sociological Theory: An Introduction*. Chicago: Aldine, 1969.

2 Key theoretical problems

The main goal of theory is to explain. But what is to be explained? It is not enough simply to suppose that because the explanation is "sociological," something "about people" will be explained. This chapter examines some issues connected with the question of what is to be explained sociologically and how to do it, as well as taking note of some of the problems involved.

These issues are listed as follows. In each case, the way a particular theorist resolves these problems has much to do with the form and content of the theory he eventually builds. The issues are:

1 The problem of how to conceptualize social orders and the related concepts, social stability and change. Are *different* theories needed to cover these two major ideas?
2 The problem of how properly to conceptualize the subject matter of a sociological theory. This is the polarity between the objective and subjective approaches.
3 The problem of the proper focus of sociological theory. How does the *individual* fit into sociological theory?
4 The problem of how to understand cause. The social sciences have great difficulty with the concept of *cause*. We shall discuss how to apply the scientific idea of cause and effect in sociological theory.
5 The problem of values. How, and to what extent, do theorists' values shape conclusions? Ought sociologists to try to keep values from influencing theory? This problem goes under the name of the "value-freedom problem."
6 The metaphysical problem of the repeatability of human events. Is there sufficient similarity between human actions to make theorizing possible?

I. Order, stability, and change

A. Order

The main problem for all sociological theories, and the main objective of theorizing in sociology at all times, is to explain social *order*. It is important to appreciate this, because confusion about the general objective of theory is usually at the root of specific confusions about specific theories.

Because of its central place in theoretical work in sociology, the idea of social order should be examined more closely. Theorists do not use the term in the sense of "law and order," where order is more or less identical with repression or conflict. Nor is "order" meant to denote authoritarian rule, such as orders barked by a drill sergeant, which are followed because of some strict penalty system. "Order," in the sociological sense, refers to any patterned action, or any regularity displayed in peoples' behavior. Social order is analogous to the order described by the periodic table of the elements in chemistry, or the observation that water runs downhill: Sometimes things behave in similar ways, patterned ways, in given situations. The main business of sociological theory is to conceptualize the circumstances in which certain behaviors result, and to discern the reasons why these circumstances are associated with these behaviors.

We must be careful not to speak of social order in a narrow and restricted sense. Order may be quite abstract, rather than directly observable. It may appear at one level of analysis and disappear at another. It may pertain to a given segment of a population or sample and not another. The idea of order in sociological work may be founded directly on some experience of orderly behavior, but when order is used as a *general* idea it indicates patterned events that are explainable, regardless of whether or not experiences suggest order to the naive observer.

Thus the idea of order itself is abstract, and covers much more ground than simply empirical instances of orderly behavior. Sociological theory, while it is trying to give reasonable accounts of concrete instances of sociological fact, is always developing toward a general statement on the causes and consequences of social order. This is because it is developing explanations of the general causes of order, and not just explaining instances of it. Theories always tend to become general statements, and they tend to expand. We noticed in Chapter 1 that theories might subsume diverse theoretical problems and explanations as they expand. As theorists cast their nets ever farther, giving reasonably consistent explanations of diverse behaviors, they broaden the coverage of their main theoretical principles, eventually producing "general theory."

What kind of order is there in society? This is a reasonable question, and one with several answers, because there are differing points of view on the issue. Society may exhibit many fairly obvious kinds of order. For example, the birth rate, which has important consequences for social planning, economic speculation, and so forth, can

Theoretical "causes" ordered

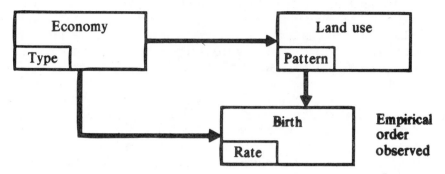

FIGURE 2.1

be seen to vary according to some influences. It is notable that the birth rate in most Western countries has been steadily dropping for the past ten years or longer. The reasons for this are complex, and have different effects in different places, but the main idea here is that the rate constitutes an example of order. How is this fact related to the general idea of social order? In the first place, one might want to see why in certain countries, the birth rate is fairly high, whereas it is rather low in other countries. How could such variation be accounted for? One answer is that some aspects of the belief systems might be an influence. Persons believing it is virtuous to have children may have them more often than those not believing this. Another explanation might be that some aspect of economy dictates it – much land to cultivate requires many sons. See Figure 2.1.

The point here is to show that when an instance of social order, birth rate in this case, is explained, the explanation goes beyond the instance itself, by suggesting that the things that account for this order are themselves ordered. For example, there may be some general relationship between type of economy and land use patterns, on the one hand, and birth rate on the other. This speculation suggests the possibility not only that birth rate exhibits order, but that the influences on it also are ordered in some way, and furthermore that there is something generally applicable about this relationship that might cover other social facts. Suppose the influence of a given kind of land use on birth rate, other things being equal, is always the same. This *similarity* of effect (given similar circumstances) is not observed directly, but abstractly grasped, because what we actually observe are instances of birth rate, but our explanation involves a *principle* that relates all birth rates to given causes. We have moved one step away from explaining our particular research problem and one step toward the "general level" on which all finished theory exists.

But what of the fact that in Western countries the birth rate is dropping? In addition to noting order in birth rates, and their possible relationships to characteristic patterns of land use, we are now introducing *order* in the form of a trend: Something is causing the birth rates to go from previously high levels to new lower ones. How is this accounted for?

Such a trend might be explained by showing that the causes of the previously high birth rate are collapsing, and that these are being replaced by something that results in a new, lower birth rate. In the example, the patterns of land use were hypothetically connected to high birth rate ("having much land to cultivate requires many sons"). But if this pattern of land use is changing, perhaps into one in which extensive mechanized agriculture is more important, and if the movement of sons from the land to the towns becomes more prevalent, would we not expect birth rates to drop? Could we not reasonably relate the changes in birth rates to some third trend, which might be called industrialization, mechanization, or urbanization?

Of course there is more to social order than birth rates, or other facts and figures. Consider, for example, the concept "authority" and how authority responds to sociological forces. Max Weber, in an important work on the nature of social and economic order, suggested that there were characteristic types of authority.[1] These types he related to the different reasons people have for following rules. For example, *zweck-rational* authority is that arising out of situations in which persons accept the authority of others because this acceptance brings them some rationally sought benefit. This is the sort of authority we give our doctors in matters of health. It is usually strictly limited to aspects of the relationship directly relevant to the objectives of those involved, and does not spill over into other areas. But "traditional" authority, on the other hand, is much different. We may accept the traditional authority of a chief or elder because either it has "always" been right to do so, or we can conceive of no reason not to do as has "always" been done. Typically, authority of this type is far more wideranging, covering more of the activities of those accepting it. It would be easy to relate such types of authority to types of social situations and to needs for efficiency or production. Doing so would predict that rational coordination (*zweckrational* authority) would come to characterize a society with extreme division of labor, and that societies with less of this might remain more traditional in authority patterns. Actually, Weber did something like this in his famous work on bureaucracy.[2]

[1]   Max Weber, *The Theory of Social and Economic Organization*, tr. Talcott Parsons (New York: Free Press, 1964), Ch. 1.
[2]   Ibid., Ch. 3, Part 1.

In the example of birth rates, we had something to count as our basic datum (births), but in the example using authority we have nothing so easily observed. Authority is an abstract quality, an aspect of a relationship in which one person gives directives and another takes them. And except in cases of compulsion, he who takes orders from authority does so with some degree of willingness. Abstractions such as "authority" are just as potentially orderly and just as important in sociological theory as things we can more easily see and measure. Most of the orderliness of sociological theory is the abstract kind, and must be understood in abstract terms. Most of the features surrounding things like authority, role, social structure, culture, and so on, are not visible directly. They must be inferred, and derived from the concrete order that we do observe.

Let us have an example to show this. In the previous chapter we used the role of women to show that the concept "role," which most people know well, was in reality a theoretical term. Now let us show that it is also an entirely abstract term. Recall that "role" involves a consideration of what may be called the duties of the role and the rights associated with it. Also recall that role implies the existence of other roles that have bearing on each other. What one woman considered duties, someone else could consider rights; what were the rights of one woman were the obligations of someone else. The relationship between these compatible sets of rights and duties is the important meaning of the term "role." But how do we observe a *relationship?* What one observes is *behavior.* We do not see the relationship composed of rights and duties; we see only what we can use as data from which to *infer* the relationship. We see concrete behavior that we may take as evidence – but we do not see the orderly relationship as if it were itself observable.

Most of what sociological theorists propose as the causes and consequences of social order have this abstract character. This is not radically different from the situation in other disciplines that make use of theory, but it is often harder to grasp in sociology. Because we are so used to social relations, we tend to think about them as more concrete than they are and to look in vain for concreteness about things that are by nature abstract. Thus we have an order to account for – usually an abstract one. See Figure 2.2.

B. Stability and change

Sometimes we think of change as the opposite of order, but it is important to distinguish among change, stability, and chaos. The term *change* applied to social arrangements means some kind of alteration in patterns of social relations. If there were no patterns at all, there

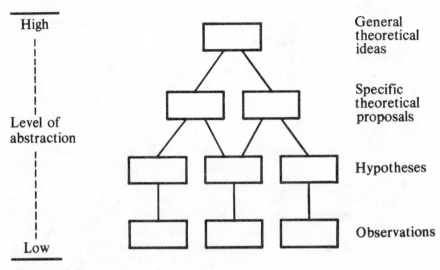

High

Level of
abstraction

Low

General
theoretical
ideas

Specific
theoretical
proposals

Hypotheses

Observations

FIGURE 2.2

would be no change, but chaos instead. Thus it is true to say that change is a kind of order. In the example of decreasing birth rates, given previously, change was taking place, but it was not chaotic – it was orderly change.

Any sociological theory can account for change if it is capable of accounting for stability. This contention is not universally recognized. Some argue that separate theories for stability and change are needed. The alternative view, however, is that any theory that accounts for stability in social relations does so by pointing out the orderly forces making things "stable." Stability is taken as something remarkable, a kind of dependent variable. The question in the mind of the theorist accounting for it is: Why should this aspect of social relations be patterned in this way, and not in any other of the possible ways? Now when he has satisfactorily answered this question, he has built up a theory about social relations that accounts for things as they are. But, at the same time, the theorist has produced to the best of his ability, a theory that can account for change, in exactly parallel terms. This is so because, according to his analysis, stability is obtained because of a certain relationship of social elements; in the absence of some of these, or if one or more of them is altered, the theorist must predict social change as the result. Moreover, this would also be the case if a theorist started by trying to explain social change. If he did, in fact, explain change by citing basic processes and facts of social life, he would be faced with the problem of explaining stability: Every appearance of stability would be a special problem, to be accounted for by the adaptation of his theory of change.

For example, an old and important branch of sociological theory explains social stability in terms of shared values. It puts particular emphasis on the centrality of broadly held values, and considers the moral acceptance of these a key factor in shaping society. This explanation in the simplest terms says that when there is substantial consensus on values among the members of a society, there results a morally based social system. The stability is explained by the consensus. Now this kind of thinking can just as easily explain change, by resorting to the same key term, "value consensus." By showing imperfect consensus, or failure of consensus, the prediction is reversed, and the theorist must expect change instead.

The same argument holds in reverse, of course. Suppose a theory posits change as the major fact of all society, and that it located the reason for this change in a continuing struggle among the oppressed to become "free." This theory would immediately be faced with the fact that all are not presently "free," and the next step would have to be the suggestion of a reason why. Clearly, this theory would need to identify constraints that prevented freedom, thus bringing in a form of "anti-change agent." However unexpected this might be, such a theory would eventually do it; it would have to give a theoretical account that included stability, even though the theory emphasized change initially.

With this discussion of stability and change in mind, it should now be possible to see more clearly the roots of the controversy among sociologists about whether or not separate theories are required for explaining stability and change. As long as change and stability are seen as facets of a more abstract orderliness, and as long as we regard both change and stability as effects that have causes, it will be possible to derive theories of both change and stability from the same basic theoretical material. It is the orderliness of social events to which sociological theory is addressed, and not to particular manifestations of it. Stability and change are aspects of a broader orderliness to which sociological theory is addressed. It is important to recognize this, and not to make the mistake of regarding social change as the opposite of social order.

II. Subjective and objective

The subjective–objective dichotomy is very old, going back in the history of thought far beyond the foundation of sociology. It is still with us. This dichotomy suggests that there are two fundamentally opposite ways to understand man and his social organization. One is the *objective* way. This views man and human society as basically similar to other aspects of the physical world. This suggests that even though man may be complex and intricate, in principle his actions are explainable in the same way as any other aspect of the natural world. Defining human behavior objectively leads to two sets of concepts, one set defining social relations in objective terms and the other set giving the explanation of these relations in terms of objective forces. This kind of objective thinking, for example, leads some psychologists to conceptualize all human behavior in terms of physical process (e.g., stimulus and response), and to suggest that this idea, if rigorously applied, could explain all human activity, including social organization and culture.

The objective viewpoint can also be taken in a slightly less scientific sense, but the kernel of meaning remains the same. When someone suggests that objective forces outside the control of individuals are at work, he is suggesting the reality of these forces. But he may not be saying in addition that these forces are properly thought of as aspects of the physical environment. For example, we might take the existence of social classes as an objective fact; the class system may be concretely real enough, but it is probably not possible to explain its existence in purely scientific objective terms.

There is good reason to seek objectivity in the study of human behavior. Objective things, in principle, can be measured, counted, observed, and correlated according to their behaviors. This is an advantage to a social scientist who wishes to make the strongest possible empirical case for his theories, and to use observable facts to do it. There is also a formidable argument that there is no alternative to the objective approach. We know nothing about behavior that we do not learn by treating it as objects of our senses. There is a cliché that "talk is cheap." The confirmed objectivist classifies any nonobjective contention about behavior as "mere talk," and pays little attention to it.

For example, some would argue that human behavior is dependent on states of mind or on attitudes. But do these things exist? Is there "mind"? If so, what is it and where? What does the "mind" do that cannot be understood entirely in terms of objective physiology and chemistry? Even though at present we do not have an explanation of "mind" in these terms, the objectivist will point to examples of research on animals suggesting that the "emotions" can be controlled and explained by electrical impulses in the brain. He will point to the advances in genetic research that make it possible to produce animals and people having predictable traits, once thought of as matters of upbringing.

What of the concept of "attitude"? Is attitude more than a convenient fiction, a word for the "stuff" that seems to be in the mind? There have been many clever attempts to objectify attitudes and to measure them. But these attempts have met with only limited success. We do not always act the way our attitudes suggest we "ought" to act. Does this mean that a theory of human behavior based on attitudes is based on a fiction? In Chapter 6 we shall read about the basic split in the symbolic interactionist school of theory that developed because influential interactionists took different positions on this question.

Problems like these have led some to abandon research into the "mental" or subjective aspects of human behavior and to concentrate entirely on the objective. But a problem soon arises if this is done. Exactly what is *entirely* objective about human behavior? The no-nonsense answer is that very little of it makes much sense when considered only objectively. Perhaps population or migration studies offer an exception to this, as long as all we wish to know is what people do, and not why they do it. For example, we can use census and immigration data to draw up statistical pictures of age distributions, sex and occupation characteristics, and the movement of people from place to place. When we ask the theoretical question, "Why are these objective things the way they are and not otherwise?" pure objectivity does not carry us very far. As soon as an answer to one of these questions comes in terms of will, choice, belief, value, and so on, we are out of the realm of objectivity and face to face with human motives, which do not respond well to objective research.

Thus it is that the *subjectivist* position gains its strength. It argues that social behavior must be understood in human terms that are fundamentally different from objectivist ones, and that it is fruitless to try to reduce this humanistic knowledge to objective science. A subjectivist might start with the will, as Tönnies did,[3] and develop a theory of types of social organization based on types of will. Or, following Weber, he might wish to understand types of social organization by reasoning from characteristic motives for following rules.

To some, it sounds almost subversive to suggest that there is anything wrong with the subjective view. Persons studying human society often want to understand it in terms that seem uniquely applicable to humanity. But as the objectivist would argue, there is in principle no way of verifying subjective statements about human society. Verification implies a public demonstration of truth. But the very essence of subjectivism is that it is the conceptualization of inner experience, which may be described to others, but never demonstrated. Often,

[3] Ferdinand Tönnies, *Community and Society,* tr. Charles P. Loomis (New York: Harper & Row, 1963).

subjectivist theory takes the form of the "ideal type." Consider Weber's idea of bureaucracy as an example. Weber's intent was to understand bureaucracy as a form of social order and to show why it was growing in importance. He found bureaucracies had several characteristics that tended also to define them as bureaucracies. He built up an ideal type (a mental construction) describing "ideal bureaucracy" according to these main features.[4] He then explained the activities of persons and of organizations as though their views and motives fit those of his ideal type. Note that he did not try to verify the ideal type. He did not "prove" the theory. Instead, he used it as a guide to discover something in particular cases. The ideal type, based on subjective criteria developed through description, was not verifiable, but only useful. And the usefulness of it was not in its "rightness" or "wrongness" but in Weber's ability to describe his experience in a meaningful way.[5]

All sociological theory, formal or not, must take account of the subjective–objective polarity. We cannot get around it, and if we take a stand on one side or the other, we are open to criticism from the opposite side. Probably the best plan is to understand the reasoning on both sides and be able to use whichever kind of theoretical attitude seems appropriate. But a final word about consistency. If we slip from one side to the other of the subjective–objective polarity in an effort to "explain everything," we shall eventually find that the resulting mixture we develop as a "theory" will be muddled, and more confusing than enlightening. It is better to settle for a clear explanation of some of the truth than a confused account of "all" of it.

III. The place of the individual in sociological theory

Precisely what is the domain of sociological theory? Is it to confine itself to society per se, or may the individual be the focus of interest, or perhaps some combination? It is not as easy as it might appear to make a theory adequately and convincingly treating both society and the individual. It will become obvious in later chapters that, depending on which we emphasize, or how we combine the two, we come out with quite different social theories. In fact, the controversy between exchange and functional theorists around which Chapters 4 and 5 are organized, may be regarded as arising over disagreement about the place of the individual in social theory.

Of course the goal should be to develop an acceptable theory that handles the individual and society equally well. But the problem often

---

4   Max Weber, *Max Weber on the Methodology of the Social Sciences,* tr. Edward Shils and Henry Finch (New York: Free Press, 1949), Ch. 2.
5   Weber, *Theory of Social and Economic Organization,* Ch. 3, Part 1.

is that theories explain one in terms of the other. This might be done simply or subtly, but the problem remains. For example, the belief is not unheard of that society controls, shapes, and directs the individual. In extreme form, this argument leads to the conclusion that virtually whatever society wishes to make of us, it can. The individual has no power of resistance. Thus schooling is sometimes criticized with the allegation that it "conditions" individuals, meaning that the experience of school (which represents society in the larger sense) forms students so completely that they evidently have no ability or judgment except that given them at school.

Perhaps there is truth in this social-determinist argument. Certainly young people experience a very considerable amount of social formation. In a sense, the society molds and shapes attitudes, behaviors, morality, and so on. It is easy to see that this process continues throughout life, for "fitting in" is often the prime requisite for a rewarding and comfortable social life.

But can we say that society has all power of constraint and formation over the individual? Are we not insulting the intelligence, ability, and judgment of individuals when we say that individuality consists basically of doing what we are told? If we take this objection seriously, we see that it implies the negation of most of the previous argument, for if individuality consists of abilities, reason, judgment, and character not entirely attributable to society, then we have demoted society from its theoretical position of omnipotence over individuality.

We might go further in this vein, arguing that, indeed, the whole idea of society is just a fiction. Instead, there are only individuals, people of uniqueness and character, who find it necessary for a variety of reasons to get along together. The "getting along" we call "society," but the operative force is really individuality. Theoretically speaking, whatever we may wish to explain about society can be explained by making reference to the quality, character, or activities of individuals. This is an appealing argument, for every person likes to feel this is true in his daily life; he wills his own actions and formulates his attitudes.

But now all that we thought before about socialization and the shaping force of society comes back to haunt. If we take a very individualistic viewpoint, how can we adequately explain the "facts" about society that previously seemed true? These include the presence of society itself in the lives of individuals – how society forms, controls, and molds. If, as individualists, we have trouble accounting for the influence of society's dictates, as we surely will, then we might feel the need for an intermediate position on the society – individual polarity.

Actually, it is overly simple to conceive of this distinction as a polarity. In fact, there is no continuum on which we might be able to find the midpoint, combining features of individualism and sociologism[6] in just the right proportions. Remember the previous caution: Mixing compatible ideas will lead to a conceptual muddle. So it is here. A given idea of "society" will imply compatible ideas about individuality, but normally not what the "individualist" has in mind when he regards all social relations as arising out of individual uniqueness. Similarly, the individualist will have a hard time giving a convincing account of "society." No amount of mixing terms that imply each other's negation will produce an acceptable theory containing adequate accounts of each.

Keeping in mind the difficulty caused by "individuality versus society" in sociological theory, some additional points concerning concepts and method should now be made. We often speak in terms of "levels" of analysis in sociological theory. Usually, this term refers to some abstract segment, such as society, or some intermediate, for instance, primary groups or institutions. Depending on the level, some aspect of the society–individual problem is probably being emphasized. This usually means that some other aspect of the question is being ignored. Thus we might wish to know the "functional prerequisites" of society, that is, what things must social organization accomplish for society to exist? This is a macrosociology question, or one at the "level" of society. In other words, the question pertains primarily to the society, and although all kinds of questions about individuality come into it, they are in effect being set aside. Similarly, theories of face-to-face interactions in specific situations usually take almost no account of society as such. The "situation" may be relevant, as may some aspects of the individuals participating, but this analysis is mainly at the "level" of the individual. Sociologists slide up and down a scale of levels, depending on what they wish to emphasize and explain. The advantage of doing this is that the problem at hand can be made fairly clear; the disadvantage is that what is said at one level may mean absurdities at another.

We can bring together aspects of the individuality–society problem with the objective–subjective question to show another difficulty facing sociological theory. How do we observe, measure, or count anything uniquely pertaining to society without reducing this to individuals? If we wish to determine something at the level of society, we ought to focus our methodology there. But society defies direct observation at its own level. We can only infer "facts" about society from the behavior of individuals, even though we may not believe that the behavior of individuals is primary. This methodological individualism

---

[6] This is a term sometimes used to designate a point of view emphasizing collective factors in the explanation of individual acts.

that is forced upon us sometimes makes us adopt a subjectivist approach to society – one that we may not wish to take. If society is an objective reality, in principle as real as anything else in the natural world, yet it is not directly observable, the necessity to infer a knowledge of society leads away from objective methods. Society is in our experience only as an inference, not as an observation – it demands to be considered subjectively. On methodological grounds we cannot be strict objectivists where society is concerned, even if we want to be objectivists as theoreticians.

This problem of method can become a wedge driven between types of sociological theory; the resultant gap is bridged only occasionally. One side, emphasizing methodological concerns, has tended to neglect things that are not directly observable; hence it has tended to settle on the individualistic side of the individual–society question. The other side, less concerned about objective methodology, has tended to be impressed more with the substance of society, and hence has taken the society side of the polarity.

IV. Function and cause

The words "function" and "cause" are very troublesome in sociological theory. They are often confused with each other, so that when one person says "function," a listener may somehow hear "cause," or vice versa. There is a large variety of mainly philosophical descriptions of what "cause" really means. One is that cause does not exist except in the minds of those who believe they see causes in action.[7] Another says that despite the problems with the concept and verification of cause, we still cannot seem to do without the idea.[8] Some descriptions of sociological methodology use the idea of cause without explaining it, arguing that there are ways of inferring cause from statistical procedures.[9] Concerning function, it has been claimed that "functional analysis" is really the only method in use in sociology and anthropology.[10] "Function" also has a variety of meanings, but the main point of trouble with it for sociologists arises when it is confused with "cause" – as in the contention that the way society works *is* the reason society exists.

Common usage of "cause" is not very precise, even though some precision was introduced by Aristotle, who was interested in the term

[7] Bertrand Russell, "On the Notion of Cause," in *Mysticism and Logic* (London: Allen and Unwin, 1963), pp. 132–51.
[8] Robert M. MacIver, *Social Causation* (New York: Harper & Row, 1964), Part 1.
[9] Hubert M. Blalock, Jr., *Causal Interferences in Nonexperimental Research* (Chapel Hill, N.C.: University of North Carolina Press, 1964).
[10] Kingsley Davis, "The Myth of Functional Analysis as a Special Method in Sociology and Anthropology," *Amerian Sociological Review*, XXIV, no. 6, pp. 757–71.

in its strictly logical sense.[11] He showed that "cause" usually means one (or more, simultaneously) of these:

1 that for the sake of which – the purpose
2 that in which – assumptions, concepts, or the logical context
3 that by which – the technique of making something happen
4 that out of which – the material context; the stuff from which an effect springs

If we mean the first type of cause, we say, in effect, that a purpose, or some end state of things guides current behavior. If behavioral scientists use cause in this way, they probably use the terms "cause" and "intention" synonomously. This involves mentalistic assumptions – cognition, and so forth. If cause is meant to suggest intention on the part of a whole society, however, problems arise. How can a society, as such, intend, wish, seek goals?

The second type of cause has to do with the logical necessity of drawing certain conclusions, given certain premises. For example, the sum of two and three is five; hence five is "caused" by the addition of two and three. Five is the "result" of the logic involved in "two," "plus," and "three." It is sometimes tempting to think that because some behavior seems to be related logically to a principle or social "law," the behavior necessarily is "caused" by the principle. Such fallacies dog the steps of those who wish to package their sociological theory in propositional form. See Chapter 4.

The third type of cause has to do with making something manifest itself, given that it is possible to do so. If we ask, "What were the causes of the French Revolution?" we might actually mean, "What were the techniques by which the revolution was brought about?" Social science that is based solidly on the concept of "process" often uses "cause" in this sense. It tends to focus interest on concrete interactions in an effort to show "what leads to what."

Aristotle's final type of cause suggests the setting, the material context. When explaining purely abstract human relations, the social scientist often ignores this, but theories emphasizing some feature of either "human nature" or social life as an inevitable starting point can use "cause" in this way.

It should be clear by now that when one seeks a sociological explanation for the cause of an event, he could have a variety of questions in mind. A theorist's choice out of this variety has much to do with where and how he seeks his causes, and how he constructs his theory or evaluates someone else's. Does he pay particular attention to logical structure, to techniques and principles, to the specific situation in

[11] Aristotle, *Organon: Analytica Posteriora*, Book 2, Ch. 11, in Richard McKeon, ed., *Basic Works of Aristotle* (New York: Random House, 1941), pp. 170 ff.

which the theory is applicable, or does he look for a theory that explains in terms of a unity or an evolving structure with some overall purpose? Actually, as one would expect, sociological theory has developed around each of these usages of "cause."

Cause-as-purpose has been particularly troublesome for social science. Strictly speaking, cause-as-purpose and "function" do not mean the same thing, but they have a way of getting entangled with each other. Basically, "function" means "to have an effect," and generally is used to denote the sustaining mutual effect of related social structures. These can be roles, groups, institutions, or perhaps other units of analysis (as we shall see in Chapter 5), but in functionalism the idea is always to discover the relationships among structures and to see how these relationships form some kind of system.[12]

We may wish to know why a given set of structures have clustered together in the way they have and not otherwise. We are asking a question about the nature of the total cluster, and also about the functions of each unit in this cluster. This is perfectly proper to do, and it is legitimate to construct a functional theory here. If we answer the question about the nature of clustering structures by saying that, in order to operate as a total cluster, some specific arrangement of structures is required, the question has been answered *causally* by reference to the required state of relations of the structures. They are so clustered in order to enable each to perform adequately to maintain the whole. The end purpose is a "cause" of the structuring. But how could the structures have "known" this in the process of clustering? This question is not satisfactorily answered by sociological theory alone, but some suggestions may be made via example. One popular solution to this dilemma is to say that "evolution" toward the most satisfactory state of organization is a natural process, and that it will work to determine which functional arrangements persist. Another solution is to posit some kind of life for social structures that will inevitably lead them to seek compatibility. Cultural arguments have been proposed saying essentially that common values and beliefs will lead people to common behavior patterns, and that the result is a workable, functional unity. No matter which tack we take, for present purposes it is important to note the relationship of functional analysis to the concept of cause. If we try to explain how a functioning whole (society) came to be so impressively interdependent, we have to dream up some theoretical concept (evolution, rationality, insight, culture) that gives a causal account of the "cooperation" among the structures of society.

[12] Robert Merton, "Manifest and Latent Functions," in *Social Theory and Social Structure* (New York: Free Press, 1957), pp. 19–84.

V. Sociological theory and values

Because sociology is one of the disciplines that try to explain aspects of human life, it is natural that sociologists should be sensitive to discussion about the values and moral questions involved in theorizing. In general the argument for "value-freedom" in sociological theory has run as follows. In order to discover what "is," it is necessary for the sociologist to bring no personal prejudice about social relations to his study. This does not mean that sociologists should not be moral people, but for purposes of description and theory, if one wishes to know what is, then one must observe, describe, and theorize dispassionately. If disinterestedness is not maintained, what one believes "ought" to be may get in the way of what "is"; dogma would interfere with thought.

This position on value-freedom arose, curiously perhaps, among those who took a subjective approach to sociological problems. It has since been taken over largely by the objectives; but in the beginning it was felt that if proper understanding of society required inferences and an interpretive appreciation of abstract human relations, value-freedom was essential. If accurate information about human relations were obtained only in this way, the observer would have to hold his own feelings in check, "bracket" them, for the duration of his observation and theorizing. Certainly, any sociologist could freely comment from a moral standpoint like anybody else, but he had no right to impose his values in the conduct of sociological analysis. Because all data gathering was subjective in nature, if there were no value-freedom the sociological enterprise would surely break down into mere controversies of opinion. For the objectivist, the sociological theorist who wanted to describe and theorize about only what was strictly observable, the value-freedom position took the form of seeking the best methodological tools available. He needed techniques that would actually measure the things he wanted to measure, and not fool him by measuring something else. This is an impersonal form of the same hope voiced by the subjectivist.

As long as the point of theorizing remained explanation alone, the question tended to rest. If the intent of theorizing was not overreached, then the problem of being biased could be solved by men of goodwill if they simply tried hard. At least, so it seemed. But this kind of argument eventually leads to a new attack on the proper goal of theorizing, one that blurs the distinction between explaining something and altering it.

The attack on value-freedom tends to point out that explaining things as they are puts emphasis on the forces leading to stability and status quo, and to direct attention away from what perhaps might be possible by way of improvement. Indeed, if the status quo is taken too seriously, runs this argument, it may appear that there is no alternative possible. At times, people who argue in this vein have also impugned the motives of sociological theorists, arguing in effect that value-free interpretations are surreptitious efforts to justify society as it is and keep it that way. A less personal version of the same line of attack points 'out that sociological theorists who are intimately familiar with a given society will have biases peculiar to that society they are not aware of, but that nevertheless influence what they tend to see and explain. Hence the attack on value-freedom usually ends up, for one reason or another, by advocating a knowingly biased viewpoint in sociological analysis, not an unbiased one.

What alternatives to value-freedom are there? One option is for the sociologist to become frankly normative about what he says. By subtly changing the objective of theory from explanation per se to "criticism," one can present things in a different light. This does not mean that the critic fails to explain. He must do that, and thus explanation remains the first intent of sociological theory. But by "critically" explaining, he shifts the emphasis from what "is" to what might have been or what could be. By making one's biases clear and open, one's explanation takes on a reformist tinge. Matters needing reform are clearly indicated by the points at which the sociologist's opinions differ from what, in fact, exists. Done in this way, the no-value-freedom option accomplishes the same thing as the value-freedom approach, but with a different emphasis.

Alternatively, the sociologist not wishing to be value-free could turn sociological theory into propaganda – arguing that existing theory is only a tool of the status quo, and that new theory, which might make different assumptions and come to different conclusions, will pave the way for new modes of social organization. Such theorizing could promote social reform, or it could support some movement or dogma that might not have the good of society as a whole as an overriding intent.

The value versus value-freedom controversy need not involve politics, although politics often arise. Indeed, taking a value stand for or against something one is studying can clarify things that might remain obscure otherwise. Many who try to understand poverty, for example, have felt that a clear sympathy with those in poverty is an advantage. Also, it is often argued that to understand a culture, it must be experienced from "the inside." This involves taking onto one's self the values, beliefs, and themes of that culture, to experience these things personally. It is in this vein that black sociologists sometimes argue that none but other blacks can adequately interpret the experience of being black.

There is a lingering problem behind the controversy. What is "explanation"? If the objective of theory is simply to explain what people do, and to deduce these explanations from descriptive data organized into concepts, then the value-freedom problem does not really arise. This is because no matter what one's values with regard to the subject matter, the same results will obtain. If, on the other hand, to explain means not only to derive explanations but also to "understand" or to have "insight," then the value problem will arise. When it does, the distinction between theory per se and bias is blurred. One becomes intentionally biased, then, at the risk of prejudicing the accuracy of his results. But this risk is sometimes worth the price in terms of the quality of insight rendered possible.

VI. History and sociological theory

The final problem to be considered in this survey of theoretical muddles is whether or not theory is really possible. Because we are sociologists and not historians, we have all taken a decision on this matter. It is well, however, to understand the decision we have made, and to understand some of the reasons why this decision is open to question.

When we propose to draw up a theory about something, we assert that it is possible to conceptualize it in general terms – that our subject matter has essential qualities that, in principle, link it to other aspects of human relations. And thus it is automatically alleged that the theory is applicable to any events of the same type as those that led to the theory's being formed. It is alleged and not proved, remember, but nevertheless the allegation remains.

The problem here is simply this: We cannot know, and will never be able to find out, the exact extent of the similarity between events. Because of this inability to know just how much similarity there is, we can never be certain that one situation resembles another sufficiently, or in essential ways, so that the generality covering one event actually covers more than just one. The only solution to this problem – and it is not a final solution – is to keep testing theory in various settings so that the supposed similarities assumed in general statements may gain more support.

If it is not true that one event can resemble another in essential or sufficient ways for a class of events to be established, then theory building is useless, because, in principle, a theory could apply only to one case. There would be absolutely no way to know how one case differs essentially from the next. This possible uniqueness of human events is the reason for comparing sociological theory with history. History is the record of unique events, together with theory occasionally borrowed piecemeal from the other sciences. In general, historians describe what happened, and account for it by narrating what happened earlier – by describing previous situations. Sociology, on the other hand, is fundamentally theoretical, relying on historical-like data only for its information. The emphasis of history is not theoretical in this sense. The difference is that theoretical sociology arrives at general conclusions about types of events whereas history does not.

Now it is true that some historians have developed theories of history. There is nothing sacred about the boundaries between departments of learning. But the point is that whenever anyone asks a question about the reason why a class of social events occurs, not about one event alone, he is asking a theoretical question that demands a generalizing – a theoretical – answer.

Drawing up a defensible and enduring list of the classes of things that may be sociologically explained has been one of the continuing headaches in sociology theory. The headache could be taken as evidence that the historians are right: It is not possible to have a social theory in the first place. Nevertheless, we need and use classes and categories, and thence comes the support for them. "War," "revolution," "bureaucracy," "family," – all of these are names of things that are identifiably of a type. Although it is hard to define the types precisely, they are social forms in terms of which we order our thinking, and in terms of which we often try to theorize about causes and functions. These types of social relations, and many more, are the objects of all sociological thinking. They are the classes of events about which we make the assumption that it is defensible to produce generalizing theory.

Thus although we recognize that the assumption of similarity is not without its critics, we make the assumption and proceed to theorizing. And although we recognize that there are philosophical questions about the existence of essential similarities, we provisionally decide the issue in the positive when we make the decision to study sociological theory and to theorize. Making the opposite decision denies our obvious and natural tendency to think in types and explain by categories.

In summary, it should be emphasized that all of the problems examined in this chapter (order–change, objective–subjective, individual–society, function–cause, values, and uniqueness) are not simply past issues involving social theory. They are problems still very much alive. As appealing solutions are worked out and found wanting, new approaches are tried. These and other issues are the stuff of which controversies and dialogue are made; they make sociological theory change, grow, and advance.

KEY CONCEPTS

social order	role	value-freedom
social change	chaos	levels of analysis
abstract idea	value	ideal type
subjective	function	individuality
objective	causation	teleology
class of events	stability	
uniqueness of events		

TOPICS FOR DISCUSSION

1 What do we mean by saying that we wish to "explain social order"?
2 Can the same sociological theories be used to understand both social stability and social change?
3 What is the difference beween objectivity and subjectivity?
4 Could the future of society be the "cause" of its present state?
5 What might we mean by saying that X is the cause of Y?
6 How does the historian depend on the social theorist?
7 In what ways does the sociologist use the data found by historians?
8 How do we know that one event resembles another enough to be "like" it?
9 What properties of sociological theory cause it to change and develop?

ESSAY QUESTIONS

If we "know" something because we ourselves believe it is true, is it necessarily "objectively" true?

What are the relative merits of maintaining value-freedom in socio-logical analysis?

Describe the ways the terms "cause" and "function" might become confused in sociological theory.

What are some of the things that a sociologist might be interested in explaining that one might call aspects of "social order"?

What is the controversy between the free-will concept of the individual and "sociologistic" accounts of society?

Why, when we attempt to deal with "classes of events," must we do it theoretically?

FOR FURTHER READING AND STUDY

Isajiw, Wsevolod. *Causation and Functionalism in Sociology.* New York: Schocken Books, 1968.

MacIver, Robert. *Social Causation.* New York: Harper & Row, 1964.
Merton, Robert K. *Social Theory and Social Structure.* New York: Free Press, 1957.
Rudner, Richard. *Philosophy of Social Science.* Englewood Cliffs, N.J.: Prentice-Hall, 1966.
Russell, Bertrand. *Mysticism and Logic.* London: Allen and Unwin, 1963.
Stein, Maurice, and Arthur Vidich (eds.). *Sociology on Trial.* Englewood Cliffs, N.J.: Prentice-Hall, 1963.
Tiryakian, Edward A. *Sociologism and Existentialism.* Englewood Cliffs, N.J.: Prentice-Hall, 1962.
Tönnies, Ferdinand. *Community and Society.* Tr. Charles P. Loomis. New York: Harper & Row, 1963.
Weber, Max. *Max Weber on the Methodology of the Social Sciences.* Tr. Edward Shils and Henry Finch. New York: Free Press, 1949.
The Theory of Social and Economic Organization. Tr. Talcott Parsons. New York: Free Press, 1964.

3 Types of theory in sociology and the problem of verification

I. Introduction

In Chapter 2 we saw that the would-be theorist of social behavior faces a bewildering array of problems. If attacked systematically, the task of the social theorist might become easier. But it would take a long time, and perhaps no final solutions would be reached after all. Actually, theorists have either tended to ignore certain problems of explanation to focus on others, or they have tried to solve their problems as they went along. The results have become a collection of varied literature. This body of literature takes different logical forms and embodies different views on the task of explaining social phenomena. In this chapter we discuss some of these kinds of explanation, with special attention to their logical forms. We must also ask how one goes about confirming a theory that is written in one or another of these forms. How could evidence be related to a theory so that the theory might be "proved"?

II. Explanation, an ideal

It has been stressed that the objective of sociological theory is to "explain" social relations. Of all the other uses that sociological theory might have, whether as an aid in social policy, or as material of academic interest only, it loses its justification to the sociologist if it fails to explain something sociological. This objective is an ideal and is, in absolute terms, out of reach. We can never completely explain anything, nor does it appear that we can explain without raising questions about procedure and adequacy. This is probably advantageous. If we did possess that final sociological theory that made all social action scientifically understandable, life might be explained, but far less interesting.

If a final social theory, explaining everything completely and adequately, is impossible, we can make significant advances. It is precisely because we can formulate the idea of a complete explanation that we are able to advance. The idea of a perfect explanation defines the boundaries of our work, and provides the criteria by which real achievement is judged.

III. How explanations have been judged

In general, the notion of an ideal explanation raises three distinctly different but related questions, and gives three different criteria by which to judge real attempts.[1] In no particular order, the three are:

1 Which theories most closely approach the formal or logical purity of the particular type of explanation in use?
2 Which theories explain most clearly and with widest scope the largest amount of observable or interpretable data?
3 Which theories most completely bring our curiosity to rest?

It might appear that a theory particularly impressive on one of these criteria would automatically be good on all of them, but it is not so. For instance, in an earlier day, much social evil was explained by the supposed presence of witches. The theory of witches, as we can call it, said in effect that certain people were possessed of the devil, and hence were in a particularly effective position to do evil. Such a theory, in its day, was well suited to bringing curiosity to rest, and it did explain an amazing amount of otherwise unexplainable data. But witch theory does not stand up very well from a logical point of view, although the realization of this was a long time in coming.

Similarly, we can take the somewhat more subtle case of a theory that does rather better on logical grounds, but that is not very satisfactory as an assuager of curiosity. Such a theory is the "opposites attract" thesis of Winch.[2] He says that persons having complementary psychic needs tend to marry each other, and that persons having strengths and weaknesses along parallel lines do not marry. Winch has offered evidence to show that this is so, but the "reasonableness" of the theory is not demonstrated. The theory does not satisfy.

It might seem that logical minds would tend to be satisfied by logical theory, but this does not seem wholly true either. For example, one might consider individuals to be "satisfaction maximizers" who always strive to reduce cost and maximize reward in social interaction. Many interesting deductions from this theory are possible, some of which are supportable by evidence. But this theory does not satisfy us that it is an explanation of human action. We probably feel something *human* is left out, although that something is hard to specify.

Clearly, then, although the ideal explanation is yet to be found, it is a great help in that it clarifies the purposes of explanation. But one further point needs to be made. There is no reason why an

[1] Nettler deals with the ways explanations are judged at some length in Gwynn Nettler, *Explanations* (New York: McGraw-Hill, 1970).
[2] Robert F. Winch, *The Modern Family,* 3rd ed. (New York: Holt, Rinehart and Winston, 1971).

explanation must fulfill all the criteria. A completely logical system like arithmetic need not refer empirically to anything. And indeed, pure mathematics does not empirically refer to anything. Neither does a curiosity-satisfying theory require logic to perform its services. There are no rules to follow that will yield an explanation serving equally well on all three criteria. When we actually do have a somewhat logical theory that satisfactorily explains empirical phenomena, it must be regarded as a valuable creation, and not the result of some kind of routine application of rules for explanation.

IV. Description and explanation

What divides *description* from *explanation,* and how are the two related? These questions are central to the study of any theoretical subject because they highlight the different kinds of terms involved in theory. They also point to some of the applications of models (see Chapter 1).[3] We turn first to the types of terms in theories, and then to a general statement of how description and explanation are related. Then we shall be ready to describe types of theory in sociology.

A. Observational terms

Obviously, a description of an event is not the same thing as the event itself. But a description can call forth images or understanding of that event.[4] This may sound trite, but in fact it is crucial. Terms which do this but take no part in the explanation of events are called *observational.*[5] These are the terms that label events or facts for conceptual use. They are names. For example, consider the term "person" as in "This person has $100,000." Now "person" might have all kinds of theoretical and spiritual implications to a psychologist or a theologian, but as an observational term, it simply labels the thing that possesses the $100,000. "Persons" can be explained many ways, from various viewpoints and toward various ends, but when the term is used simply to designate something without further intent, it is observational.

---

[3]   A particularly good discussion of scientific terms and their relation to usage is found in Mae Brodbeck, "Models, Meaning and Theories," in Mae Brodbeck, ed., *Readings in the Philosophy of the Social Sciences* (New York: Macmillan, 1968).

[4]   It is impossible here to go into just how a symbol can do this, but an excellent treatment of the philosophical issues involved is found in Susanne K. Langer, *Philosophy in a New Key* (Cambridge, Mass.: Harvard University Press, 1951).

[5]   There is some variation in the words that name the kinds of terms used in scientific theory, but from context it is usually easy to tell which kinds of terms are meant. The usage here follows that of Abraham Kaplan in *The Conduct of Inquiry* (San Francisco: Chandler Publishing Co., 1964), pp. 56 ff.

B. Constructs

It is important to understand that many of the things we say we observe, we really do not observe. These cannot be designated by observational terms. Chapter 1 discussed the word "role" in another context, and the same term can serve to point out the difference between observational terms and constructs. It is common to speak of observing someone's role. Usually, this means we observe a series of specific behaviors over some extended time or in various situations. These specific acts could be labeled with observational terms, but in no sense could we say that we observed the role of a person in the same way as we observe Blossom the cat sitting on the windowsill. "Role" refers to the abstract coherence among the specific activities we observe. The word "role" is a *construct*. Constructs make reference to observable things, but are not themselves the names of those things. Another example is the word "government." We are always speaking of "government" as if it were something to be observed directly. This example is instructive because there is a difference between the traditional British and American usages of the word. The American usually says, "The government is. . ." He uses the term to designate an entity, a monolithic structure that acts and has a state of being. But the British tradition is more accurate. It says, "The government are. . ." designating a group of men with specific powers. The construct "government" refers to the concerted actions of men, but it does not name the actors or the actions. It names the mental construct of collective action, taken from a given point of view.

Similarly, the basic idea of all sociology, "society," is a construct, and not an observational term. "Society" may be real enough. It may even have its own unique explanation and behave according to its own historical laws, as some theorists have suggested.[6] But the word "society" does not refer to something we observe. The subject matter of sociology is the collective representation of individually observable acts taken together as an abstract construct. It is this construct, and related ones that grow up around it, which "behaves" and is explained by sociological theory.

1. Primitive terms and analogies

Constructs in the social sciences may be divided in a way that brings out the important distinction between *primitive* terms and *analogous* ones. This distinction relates to the use of models in sociological theory. A "primitive" term is rooted in an observation that is directly

---

[6] What usually goes under the name of "the philosophy of history" is the work done in philosophy relating general abstract principles to total societies.

germane to the construct itself. For instance, the primitive term "society" refers to a collective construct of individual behaviors, things we all see everyday.

But not all constructs in social science are like this – in fact, a great many are not. Consider, for example, the idea of force. We often speak of "social forces" as though there were stresses and strains in society, almost irresistible pressures directing peoples' lives. But realistically, there is nothing we could observe to produce the construct "social force" in the same way that we could observe individual action and conceive the idea of "society." "Force" as used in social science is not primitive to social science. It is primitive to physics, where it has a specific physical definition and may be calculated quantitatively.

Terms like "social force," in legitimate use in social science yet not primitive to it, are called "analogous" terms.[7] It may be unclear to which field a term is really primitive. For example, "evolution" is an ambiguously primitive word. Often, it is used to designate a biological process of change by adaptation to environment, but "social evolution" was in use two hundred years ago to designate orderly social change.[8] Biologists use "evolution" today as though it were primitive to biology, but actually it might be a grand analogy to a human social process.

(a) Types of analogies in social theory. It is useful to know the difference between primitive and analogous constructs in social theory. Knowing this makes it easier to understand how constructs relate to observations. Also, the basic explanations proposed in some theories are analogies. They have their root meaning in some other science or branch of knowledge. In the history of sociology, many theories have grown up around analogous explanations. Consider, for example, Table 3.1, which separates types of theory according to the analogy proposed for the main explanatory idea.

(1) Mechanical analogy. It was noted earlier that the term "force" is an analogy to physical principles. When it is used in sociology as "power" or "coercion," the dynamic ideas are actually analogies to what we mean when speaking of levers and pulleys, pressures and

[7] The meaning here is similar to that in a treatment of theories of social order in P. Meadows, "The Metaphores of Order: Toward a Taxonomy of Organization Theory," in Llewellyn Gross, ed., *Sociological Theory: Inquiries and Paradigms* (New York: Harper & Row, 1967), pp. 77–103, but the categories and conclusions are different from Meadows'.

[8] See J. W. Burrow, *Evolution and Society* (Cambridge: Cambridge University Press, 1966).

TABLE 3.1

Type of analogy	Main explanatory ideas
Mechanical	Force, equilibrium
Logical	Interests, rationality
Moral/ethical	Consensus
Biological	Species survival, vital principles

containers.[9] "Coercion" theory suggests that a "force" exerted in some social fashion will cause some entity to "move" in something like the physical sense of "change position." Obviously, sociological force does not mean this at all. We are familiar with the mechanical analogy and therefore the sociological use of the term "force" is not usually a problem. But it is useful to know how we get ideas such as social force in the first place.

(2) Logical analogy. A more subtle but nonetheless important analogy in daily use in social science is the logical one, in which "interests" and "rationality" play a large part. Pure logic and mathematics have basically two sets of terms, those that designate entities and those that designate operations. Hence "$2 + 3 = 5$" has no empirical meaning, because 2, 3, and 5 have no empirical referent. They are definable logically as part of a mathematical system. In this example the operations are the plus and equals signs. The expression tells us that, regardless of empirical significance, when we do a logically defined operation called addition on two abstract things called the numbers 2 and 3, we have a result called 5. The reason we automatically have this result is that 2 plus 3 is *by definition* in a state of equality with 5. Hence $2 + 3 = 5$ is "true" not because it refers to anything in the world that is empirically true, but because it is true by definition.

Now consider the concepts "goals" and "rationality."[10] Goals are the things people want, or what they would consider rewards, together with the things they wish to avoid. It would be in their interest to get what they want and avoid what they do not. "Rationality" may be defined as the mental insight that can be applied to one's goals. If a

---

[9] The terms "power" or "coercion" are not the names of specific working theories, but points of view. See P. Cohen's treatment of the typologies of theory in social science in his *Modern Social Theories* (New York: Basic Books, 1968), Ch. 2.

[10] Both of these terms, when applied to human behavior, are somewhat ambiguous. Part of the ambiguity is caused by their being used in a great many different ways by different writers, but to illustrate the point about logical analogies to sociological theory, this ambiguity need not detain us.

man has rationality and uses it, he can see what rewards a certain action will bring him or what he can avoid by acting.[11] If he had perfect rationality, he could see precisely what to do in each situation in order to maximize his gains and minimize his losses.

Now consider the concept of "goals" as analogous to the numbers in the example from arithmetic given previously, and consider rationality as analogous to the plus and equals signs. If a given set of goals is combined in a certain way (by "perfect" rationality), a given outcome is assured, in just the way that 5 is assured by the addition of 2 and 3. The outcome for the perfectly rational man is sure to be the best possible maximization of his pleasure, and the greatest avoidance of all the things inconsistent with his goals. This is a true statement in just the same way that "2 plus 3 equals 5" is true. It is true by definition. The perfectly rational man can always be expected to behave in ways that will serve his interests in the best possible way.

All this becomes a very elegant sociological theory, if we put aside the difficulties related to real rationality and real goals. All we need do is assume that persons have goals, which does not seem hard to do, and to assume that they behave rationally. Now all the theorist does is reconstruct the rational process used by the individuals he is explaining. He could reconstruct the mutual influences of various persons' activities, always from the standpoint of the assumption that persons rationally seek their own goals. In this way, a full and complete explanation of all action and an utterly infallible prediction of future outcomes can be set down. Obviously it is only possible to theorize this way if persons have rational goals and never behave nonrationally. Unfortunately, they do not seem to do so, or at least not often and consistently enough to make this theory work well.[12] Nevertheless, the logical analogy turns up rather prominently in exchange theory. See Chapter 4 for more details.

(3) Moral/ethical analogy. Perhaps the moral and ethical analogy is easier to grasp intuitively than the logical one. It may be a novelty to think of morality as having theory connected with it, but so it has. Briefly, moral theories propose certain duties we have to each other by virtue of our being bound together in common profound experience. Usually, these duties, like kindness, brotherhood, and the Golden Rule, are duties of such a nature that they cannot easily be made laws of the state. Nevertheless, moral theory argues that we all depend on each other to behave according to these rules because life would be unlivable if we did not.

---

[11] Defining "rationality" with precision is beyond the scope of this chapter, and not of any great usefulness here.

[12] Charles Dickens brought home this point in his novel *Hard Times* (London: J. M. Dent, 1907).

It is important to emphasize that such duties are not legal ones, and that they cannot be readily enforced. Only through their being voluntarily accepted as proper, legitimate requirements of human life can they have any influence. The common acceptance of moral prescriptions gives them their utility as regulators of conduct.

The analogy to sociological theory should now be easy to see. If something about the rules of social conduct places them more or less outside the realm of enforceable strictures, then there must be at least a minimum voluntary acceptance of these rules as the basis of social organization in general. Social organization may be too complex to be accounted for otherwise than by saying that it substantially depends on individual acceptance of defined prescriptions. Such a sociological theory emphasizes acceptance of rules and consensus just as moral theory does. In fact, in an earlier era, this seemed so obvious that what we call sociology was often combined with economics and political science, as well as law, and referred to as "moral science." Modern sociological functionalism, as well as aspects of symbolic interaction theory, are closely tied to the moral/ethical analogy.

(4) Biological analogy. Biology has provided one of the richest analogies for sociologists. This is because there is great similarity between physical and social notions of complex functioning whole structures with interconnecting links of influence or causation. There is some confusion, however, concerning what the unit of analysis ought to be when sociologists use the biological analogy. This has caused much confusion in sociological theory. Sometimes the body of a living being is used, as when we speak of "the body politic," meaning the collection of "political people" making up society. This analogy uses the general idea of a body composed of parts operating so as to service and complement each other. This kind of theory emphasizes these interconnections, and considers a thing explained when they are made clear. For example, it is obvious that the rest of the living body needs the stomach because of the important functions carried out there; similarly, the stomach and all the rest of the organs need the heart, and so on. It is a matter of some disagreement what the usefulness of the appendix is, and hence this organ remains unexplained in the body.

Although the issue is no longer important in academic biology, we might point out that the principle of "vitalism" still appears in sociological theories based on biological thinking. In an earlier time, biologists were troubled that the explanation of all the parts of the body in terms of all the other parts still did not yield them an explanation of "life." As with Frankenstein, it might be possible to hook up the proper connections among parts, but it still was not possible to make this collection of parts "live" as a body does. Hence came the idea, which is no more than an assertion of what seemed obvious, that biological organisms operated on some "vital" or living principle that was not explained simply in terms of the interconnections of parts.

The sociological use of biological thinking has somewhat declined, but much of the substance of it still exists in modern sociology. The analogy to the body suggests a specialization and functioning among the institutions of society. For example, it is no surprise, from this point of view, that the educational and economic institutions of Western society are closely linked. It is precisely this that would be predicted from the biological analogy: As the organs of the body are linked in complementary function, so the institutions of society are similarly linked. This analogy suggests that if we were to examine closely and fully enough all the institutions of a society we would find similar connections among them.

But what of the vital principle? Do societies live, as bodies live? Taken literally, it is absurd to suggest this, but the suggestion has been made. When we say that a society "grows" or "develops" or "adapts" we hark back to the vital principle. We are saying that the organized collection of institutions called a society has the ability to perform functional tasks. When we say that "the whole is greater than the sum of its parts," we are suggesting that the details of the functional interconnections among institutions and persons in a society do not amount to a full explanation of the "living" society. Something analogous to the "vital principle" is left out of this. This something accounts for the difference between the sum of the parts and the whole. Defining that "something" remains a problem.

Using this biological analogy suggests a rather harmonious cohabitation of the parts that perform interdependent functions; but when we take not the body but the species as the level of biological analogy, this picture changes. It is among the first principles of evolution that a species is set in an environment that must sustain it. Hence there is a natural antagonism based on competition for survival among the individual members of a species. For a species to "adapt" to its environment, individuals born into that species who cannot get along produce no offspring, and their characteristics are lost. But this is for the good, because those who succeed (having natural characteristics favorable to life in the environment) tend to produce offspring and pass on their favorable traits. As a result, the species as a whole is strengthened and becomes "adapted" to the environment.

Turning this thinking to sociological use produces quite a different picture from the harmonious one suggested previously. The "normal" relations among segments of society are now intensely competitive. This suggests that if persons were left to their own devices, there would be no concern for those who cannot survive, and indeed to care for such persons is bad for the "species," because it tends to perpetuate nonadapting types who would otherwise die out. In short, the sociological analogy drawn from this version of biology suggests that human society will as a whole tend to become strong as long as it promotes competition and insofar as it rewards the winners and leaves the losers to suffer the consequences. Human societies tend to weaken their natural adaptiveness when they extend help and kindness to the weak, support sick and foundering institutions, and so on.

Put in these terms, a biological analogy to human affairs sounds unbelievably harsh and inhumane. But the fact is that we use a form of it every day, and think it perfectly proper to do so. If we say, for example, that the patterns of work and leisure or the standard expectations of sexual morality will "have to change" to fit new conditions, we mean that the "progress" of society (analogous to the species) depends on these old patterns' being thrown out and new ones put in their places. When we accept new technology as a "more efficient" way of handling goods and services, we recognize our "struggle for survival" in our environment. A recent example of this is the advent of container technology in the handling of seagoing shipping. Containers have put hundreds out of jobs in dock work throughout the world, but there has been no very serious opposition to this. It was regarded as appropriate that this should happen.

2. Primitive terms, analogies, and descriptions

We can now return briefly to the topic of sociological descriptions and draw some conclusions from the discussion of analogies. Descriptions of social phenomena may be in "primitive" terms. These terms have their root meaning in sociology itself, and hence imply sociological examples and sociological explanation. But it is more common to describe social action by making use of analogies; this involves taking over the primitive terms of other fields and turning them into "constructs" for sociological use. This type of borrowing goes on in the world of science all the time, but it has a built-in danger: The description that emerges may also contain a hidden explanation, and we might not wish this explanation at all. An example to which we can return to illustrate this is that of society's being like the animal body. It might be like the body in that certain identifiable parts are related in a complementary way; but it is another question whether or not this body "lives" or carries out any of the other biological functions common to animal bodies. The fact that we have tended to project explanation into a descriptive analogy, not stopping at a description alone, shows the powerful influence the terms of a description may exert over the explanation of a phenomenon. The terms of a description derive their richness of meaning in the context in which they form and take root. Some of this contextual meaning inevitably colors description. It is up to the theorist to determine whether this is a good thing or not.

It is partly for reasons like this that the language of the social sciences deserves so much attention and invites so much criticism. Most sociological terms carry an excess baggage of meaning which their users may not intend, or even be aware of.

C. Explanatory terms

Recall the difference between observational terms and constructs. Observational terms denote things we can see; constructs denote things we do not see. *Explanatory* terms have yet another referent, theory itself – the web of concepts and processes that forms an explanation.

Consider two examples of explanatory terms. First the term "Protestant ethic." Max Weber developed this as part of his thesis on the rise of capitalism in Renaissance Europe.[13] Briefly, the term denotes a psychological turn of mind derived from Calvinist theological doctrines and applied to the worldly pursuit of economic enterprise. To Weber, it did not mean crude economic egoism, as we sometimes find the term degraded to mean today. It meant a complex psychological orientation toward life. This orientation derived partly from the concepts of a "calling" (being especially called by God to work in some specific way) and the related ideas of stewardship and election. "Stewardship" in Calvinist theology implied that there could be no "ownership" of goods in a permanent sense here on earth, because in the end all was owned by God who had originally created everything. All that man did was to become steward or caretaker of certain goods during his brief time on earth. "Election" refers to the theological tenet that God, being omniscient, already knows which persons will join him in heaven; and all the rest are damned. This choice is beyond the control of man.

To Weber, the sociological importance of this complicated theological doctrine was that it tended to foster a specific kind of orientation toward everyday work and leisure among those who believed it. Such persons took their "calling" seriously. It was no light matter to be called by God to a specific task. It was natural to wish to perform in the task to the best of one's ability. This was not a haphazard business either, because to be a steward of the Lord's goods required

[13] *The Protestant Ethic and the Spirit of Capitalism*, tr. Talcott Parsons (New York: Scribner's, 1958).

careful attention and performance. Neither could one waste God's goods. Extravagance and self-glorification using God's creations would be a sin. Equally important to recognize is that one could not influence the Lord's choice of election by good works. Election and damnation were already set. Men could have no ulterior motive in behaving properly here on earth. Weber argues in *The Protestant Ethic and the Spirit of Capitalism* that this kind of orientation to the world could not help but foster economic abundance and the growth of capitalism. It emphasized thrift, diligence, and thorough, rational achievement. It discouraged extravagance, wastefulness, self-glorification, and chaotic expenditure.

It should now be obvious that the term "Protestant ethic" refers to a complex set of ideas about man's relation to his world and to God. The "Protestant ethic" does not refer to an observation, as an observational term would, not to a construct that indirectly has its basis in observation. It refers to something we might call a "theory" of the relations between man and God, specifically the psychological impact of these relations. The term has *other ideas* as its only referent. These are arranged and interconnected so that the whole complex forms a meaningful completed thought.

Weber used "Protestant ethic" as an explanatory term, and it is its function in an explanation that we emphasize now. When we suggested that the requirements for the growth of capitalism were coincident with the tenets of the Protestant ethic, Weber was "explaining" the growth of capitalism. Note that he was not "describing" the growth of capitalism with the Protestant ethic. He was emphasizing that capitalism required a complex set of attitudes based on peoples' relationship to God, and the place this relationship had in their daily work. It is this relationship, argued Weber, that explains the phenomenon of the rise of capitalism in Western Europe. The term "Protestant ethic" refers to a set of ideas and not to something actually or potentially observable.

An even more abstract example of theoretical terms gaining their meaning only from theoretical contexts is provided by Freud. It seems legitimate to use this example, because so many people use words like "ego," "superego," "id," "projection," "trauma," and so on, in daily language. But the fact is that these terms "mean" nothing, if what we are looking for is physical referents. The id is not to be found inside the body or out. Nor is the ego, and a projection has nothing to do with physical or social events per se. These terms have all their meaning locked up in the conceptual context we might call "Freudian theory." It makes no sense to talk about the superego unless it is described entirely in terms of its relations with the id, the ego, and so on.

In what sense does Freudian theory "explain"? It does not explain by making much use of observational terms, by relating observations to theory directly. Explanation here is to suggest the proper interpretation that observed events deserve. Once one is familiar with "Freud's theory," it is possible to interpret actual events as though they fit into the pattern created in the mind of the observer by "Freud's theory."[14] The utility of this exercise is, of course, that an explanation of the interpreted events is the result.

The Protestant ethic and the Freudian examples emphasize that truly theoretical terms have *systemic* meaning. They derive their meaning from the system of ideas in which they are imbedded. A full definition of such terms using only observables is impossible. Kaplan suggests that the relationship between observables and theoretical terms is that the observable "marks the occasion" for the application of a theoretical term, and so it is.[15] When we know "Freud's theory" sufficiently to apply it to something, the application consists in recognizing the occasions on which particular "Freudian" concepts and processes are appropriate, as decided on the basis of "Freud's theory" itself. The terms of the theory have "systemic meaning" relating them to the entire theoretical system in which they are found and defined.

V. Description and explanation: a summary

After describing the types of terms that appear in all theory, we are in a position to sort out the differences between description and explanation. It ought to be obvious that an empirical discipline like sociology cannot do without a firm basis in description. Description labels events with words and sentences; these create mental images. Description is thus the first step toward explanation. Constructs are the terms that help to generalize observations into a form more widely applicable than the particular event in question. For example, although we do not observe roles, but only actions, we still talk about "role" because we are interested in the coherence of various acts. It is at yet another level of abstraction that we actually explain what we observe and conceptualize. Theoretical-level terms have systemic meaning, and impart this meaning to particular explanations. They do this by pointing out the theoretical relatedness between observed behavior and constructed ideas. Perhaps it appears that sociologists have dreamed up an abstract complicated way of thinking about

---

[14] It should be noted that Freud's ideas developed and changed. There is, therefore, no single theory.
[15] Kaplan, *Conduct of Inquiry*, p. 57.

simple things. But the fact is that normal everyday thought follows much the sort of course described here. Philosophers of science have broken down such normal processes to show what people actually do with their minds when they explain.

VI. *Types of theories*

Even though all theories use similar kind of expressions, the forms taken by various theories differ markedly. The reason for this is not necessarily that different theories have different subject matter; more often theorists have simply chosen to present ideas in various styles. What formal types of theories do we have in sociology?

In Chapter 1, a rough typology of theories was suggested, stemming from the kinds of "packages" theories arrive in. It is now time to improve this typology and divide it into three parts. One word of caution. It has been emphasized that explanation, in a full and final sense, is an ideal not yet reached, and perhaps not reachable. Do not mistake the most thoroughly worked out theory in terms of clarity and precision for the one that explains the most. Neither should one take any single theory as belonging entirely to one single stage of precision. As we shall see later, theories vary in ambiguity or precision, no matter what stage of precision they are in. We have to take theories as we find them.

We can easily identify three types of theories in sociology.[16] The first two types are more precisely defined in the literature than the third. These types are:

1 deductive theories
2 pattern theories
3 perspectives

The first two, though very different in logical form, are far more toward the logical and rigorous end of the scale than is a perspective. In fact, perspectives are sometimes not considered theories at all. The word "perspective" is sometimes used to designate a looser set of ideas or point of view. But because perspectives and theories are both employed for the purpose of explaining social events, perspectives are considered here to be one type of theory.

A. *Deductive theories*

Fairly recently in the long history of science, philosophers and scientists themselves have turned their attention partly away from their

---

[16] This typology is adopted because it closely parallels the theories in use in modern sociology, but it is also based on the philosophical explication of theoretical forms. Cf. Kaplan, *Conduct of Inquiry,* Ch. 8; Quentin Gibson, *The Logic of Social Enquiry* (London: Routledge and Kegan Paul, 1960), Chs. 10, 11.

other work and tried to reflect on the methods by which ideas are organized into theories, and the ways these theories produce explanations.[17] This attention to the theory of a subject, taken as an area of study in itself, has given rise to the field called the philosophy of science.

The philosophy of social science has not yielded one standard account of the way social scientists go about their theorizing. There is disagreement among the philosophers on what scientists do, and there is also disagreement among the scientists. Nevertheless, the theoretical form that enjoys a position of "near orthodoxy"[18] is the *deductive* type. This type relies on general laws–true statements that are broadly applicable.[19] Laws may be more or less general, according to whether or not they can be deduced from other laws. The laws that cannot be deduced from any other laws are the most general ones, and occupy the "highest level" of generality. Laws are statements. They set down the relationships among aspects of their subject matter. They thus unite two or more theoretical ideas in an orderly way by stating the general relationship between them. For example, economics contains what is often called the law of supply and demand, which is actually two laws combined. It contains a law of supply and a law of demand. The law of supply states a general relationship between the market price for an item and the amount of the item that will be produced in a free market. The law of demand states the relationship between the market price and the amount of the item demanded. These two laws can be combined because they share the common term "price."

Theoretical laws must be *general* statements. A statement of a specific relationship (say, between the supply and demand in a specific market for a specific item) is not a law, because the statement is intended to hold good only for one specific instance. Thus laws do not relate specific observational terms together. Only constructs can be used in making laws. "Men like women" is in the form of a law; "Oren likes Vesta" is not.

Several things have been suggested to characterize the logical meaning of laws. The argument that seems to claim the most for laws says that they refer to *causes:* hence the name "causal laws." This argument says if a law states a relationship that is always observed

---

[17] In the social sciences, this kind of attention to the philosophical side of the subject is older than in the natural sciences. Part of sociology (if not all) has never been as far removed from metaphysics as the physical sciences became.

[18] This is the way Alan Ryan puts it in *The Philosophy of the Social Sciences* (London: Macmillan, 1970), p. 46.

[19] For an extended treatment of the logical status of laws, see Ernest Nagel, *The Structure of Science* (New York: Harcourt Brace and World, 1961), Chs. 4, 10.

between two classes of events, the law is making a generalization about the causes of events:

(events of type *X*)   cause   (events of type *Y*)

But we saw in Chapter 2 that "cause" is highly problematical in the social sciences. This seems especially so if events of type *X* and type *Y* are human ones in which the actors can visualize the consequences and take steps to avoid or change them. Thus, although the "casual law" approach is relatively clear-cut philosophically speaking, it is the hardest to justify in social science.

What else might the laws express? They might express a "causal nexus," or a "constant conjunction." Observations leading to the expression of a law do not produce evidence for cause, since cause is not observable. But still, it might be possible to think of laws as expressing, in general terms, a state of affairs in which events of two classes are always found in a specific relationship to each other. We might write this as follows:

(events of type *X*)⇌(events of type *Y*)

The arrows do not indicate that *X* and *Y* "cause" each other, but rather that the complex relationship between these two types of events always takes a certain form.

Alternatively again, laws may not express cause at all. A common noncausal form is the "statistical law." It is based on a number of observations. Used this way, the general form of the law states that in the presence of events of type *X* and certain conditions, events of type *Y* probably will be associated.

The meaning of the term "law" making the weakest claim is in the "lawlike proposition." This asserts that, at best, it is a risky business formulating laws; we do not achieve one hundred percent validity, nor do we achieve the highest level of generality. It is far better, says this argument, to make less logical distinctions between laws and other general statements.

If there is uncertainty about the statements laws make in deductive theory, there is far less confusion about the function of the laws in a deductive theory. Laws come at the top of the deductive pyramid. They are the statements at the highest level of generality and have the widest scope; from them intermediate statements and hypotheses are deduced. Figure 3.1 diagrams this.

Deduction is reasoning from general statements at high levels of generality to specific statements, or hypotheses, at lower levels. Hypotheses are about observables and actual events. When deduction is properly carried out, the hypotheses will be in the same logical form as the laws, but the hypotheses will refer to specifics.

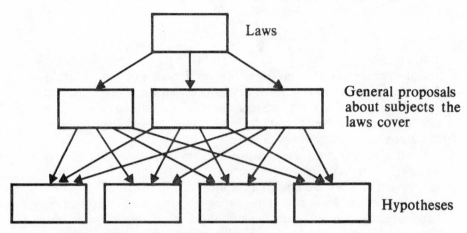

Arrows indicate deductive pattern

FIGURE 3.1

A well-known proponent of deductive theory building in sociology is George Homans, about whose work more will be said in Chapter 4. As an example of general laws explaining specific events, let us examine one of his "laws," which he prefers to call "general propositions." It reads:

> The more often within a given period of time a man's activity rewards the activity of another, the more often the other will emit the activity.[20]

The statement takes the form, X is in specific relationship to Y: It says that in a situation of social interaction, where one person "rewards" another, the rewarded activity will increase in frequency. Let X symbolize the rewarding activity of one person, and Y the rewarded activity. Let r represent the relationship between these two general categories of action. In this case, r signifies some direct function; as X increases, so does Y. In symbols, we now read the Homans general proposition as follows:

X r Y

Using words in place of symbols, we read: The rewarding activity of one person is related to the rewarded activity of another person by some direct function.

[20] George Homans, *Social Behavior: Its Elementary Forms* (New York: Harcourt Brace and World, 1961), p. 54.

Now it should be possible to find instances of Homans's "law" in real life. Let us imagine we notice a child brushing his dog, Pudgie, and receiving praise for this from his family, praise that the child regards as rewarding. Also imagine that Pudgie-brushing behavior becomes more frequent and that it is constantly rewarded. We have here an instance that appears to conform to the general relationship between activity and reward proposed by Homans.

But what if we cannot find an instance of some generality proposed as a "law?" We still have a theory, we still have a hypothesis. There are several reasons why one might fail to find the hypothesized relationship; only one of these is that the "law" is "wrong." Hence we cannot simplistically argue a theory that looks empirically wrong is no theory.

We can now summarize some points about deductive theories, and draw some things together before going on. Deductive theories consist of statements, arranged in a hierarchical order, so that those at the top of the order are the most general. These are statements of relationships often called laws. Beneath the laws are lower-level statements. Strictly speaking, one law and one hypothesis must be considered a theory from the logical point of view. But in fact, theories that follow this type of hierarchical organization usually contain more than one law, and have a great variety of hypotheses. It is, in fact, the ability of the laws to explain a wide variety of hypotheses that gives deductive theory its utility and elegance. Theories general enough to be given serious consideration in sociology implicitly contain nearly all the hypotheses possible about the phenomenon to which the theory is addressed.

Up to this point, certain important details have been neglected that must now be brought into line. Deductive theories must contain statements of limiting conditions. Our hypothetical law (X r Y) says in effect that "All X have a specific relationship with all Y." What must be added or implied is the additional statement, "This is so under certain conditions." The common phrase "other things being equal," is a way of saying we expect laws to produce empirically true hypotheses under conditions that gave rise to the laws. As theories are used and tested, the exact nature of these conditions should become better known.

And how is it that deductive theory explains? Puzzling observations are explained when they fit a hypothesis as evidence confirming it. It is then that discrete facts are recognized as instances of some general pattern. This pattern is expressed by the laws and conditions made plain in the theory. When this is seen once, it will be easy to imagine other instances following similar patterns. If such instances are actually found, they help confirm the theory, and bring added aspects of the study into theoretical order.

Early in this chapter, three different criteria for judging theory were offered. The first was that the theory must approach the appropriate logical form of explanation in use. We now know the logical form for a deductive explanation. The second criterion was that the theory must explain a number of observable phenomena. We now know that deductive theory in science contains laws that have considerable support, wide empirical application and produce hypotheses that fit facts. The third criterion, that the theory be capable of bringing curiosity to rest, has no logic as such. To the extent that deductive theories can bring this about, they can be satisfying intellectual toys.

The heavy emphasis on deduction has permitted us to neglect an important consideration about deductive theories that has nothing to do with deduction. This is the question of where laws come from. We have taken their existence as given. The fact is that there are no formal rules for deriving laws from observations or constructs. There are rules for deduction, rules that when followed will always produce logically "true" hypotheses from given laws, but the laws themselves are harder to justify. This accounts in part for the controversy about just what types of statements laws actually make. In fact, laws come from two main sources. One of these is from other subjects, by analogy. The previous discussion of sociological analogies can now be seen for what it really is: a description of one source from which to draw general insights that might be transformed into sociological laws. These we can try to verify by experiment and observation; for example, the "law of evolution" can have not only a metaphorical meaning in sociology, but in principle it might have a scientific meaning, too. The second source of laws is observation itself. When we, along with many others, see something occurring under specified conditions so often that it appears to be a very reliable regularity, we may cautiously suggest its occurrence under those conditions as a general rule, and then begin to treat it as a law from which to make specific predictions.

B. Pattern theories

Pattern theory does not emphasize formal deductive reasoning. Nevertheless, a different aspect of deduction characterizes pattern theory's organization.

In *pattern* theory, the vertical dimension is less important than what we might call "lateral" logic. The statements that describe the pattern, and the constructs making up these statements, are logically connected and defined in terms of each other. With reference to the whole system, each idea in it has an explanation. Hence the system "makes sense" as a set of ideas. The practical application of such a system of ideas consists of "seeing" relationships between the theoretical terms and reality. With pattern theory this "seeing" has no clearly specified methodology, unlike the situation with deductive theory. Application of pattern theory is a matter of insight.

We might compare the insightful application of pattern theory to reading a novel. In a novel, there are no real people. The characters are all constructed in the author's imagination. Nor is real action reported. This again is invented. Nevertheless, novels have the power to invoke actual experience and illuminate the activities and feelings of real people in real situations. A novel does this by giving the reader an insight into situations and patterns of action. The system of ideas, behavior, and characters in a novel does not describe anything to be found in actual life. But novels contain systems of ideas and images that have the power to highlight, emphasize, and systematize real experiences. Reading them, we can feel that we have read of "real" experience.

It is in this sense that "Freud's theory" does its work. No one believes in the material existence of the "ego." Nevertheless, in Freud's story of the psyche's workings, the processes involving ego form a pattern with internal coherence and a kind of sense. Application of pattern theory consists of knowing when and how to relate real experience to certain aspects of the pattern. The concepts in this kind of theory become appropriate on certain occasions in reality, and on these occasions we invoke the pattern as an explanation of reality.

Pattern theories have a natural tendency to become "closed systems," because their concepts gain meaning from the pattern itself. In Chapter 1, we saw that theories have a tendency to expand and become general theory rather than remain at a low level of generality. With pattern theory, a logical tendency to closure contributes to this. Insofar as they are able to achieve internal completion and coherence by connecting all parts together in a system of related definitions, pattern theories become sufficient within themselves, or "closed." Parsons says of his theory that it

> is a body of logically interdependent generalized concepts of empirical reference. Such a system tends, ideally, to become logically closed, to reach such a state of logical integration that every logical implication of any combination of propositions in the system is explicitly stated in some other proposition in the same system.[21]

Being logically closed, yet intended for general use, it must cover "everything."

---

[21] Talcott Parsons, *Essays in Sociological Theory*, rev. ed. (New York: Free Press, 1954), p. 212.

Pattern theories, having this tendency to become logically closed, contrast sharply with deductive theories, which are often called "open." At the "bottom" of deductive theory, there is room to accommodate new observations or to incorporate new hypotheses as these seem appropriate. Deductive theory has little trouble in handling novelties. Similarly, at the "top" of deductive theory, there is almost always room for another general principle. This is not so with pattern theories, which make "sense" by being tightly integrated, logically closed, and highly general.

1. Reductionism: changing the form of a theory

Theories tend to compete for territory and status. If there is more than one theory about something, all sorts of questions arise about the breadth, scope, and importance of each one in comparison with the others. This is quite natural, and in part has led to a debate in sociology known as the *reductionism* controversy.[22] Briefly, it has been argued that the theories of different branches of social science are, in principle, reducible to other, more basic theories. Thus "sociological theory" (that which has as its subject the behavior of groups) is reducible to "psychological theory." Psychology explains the individual; because groups are composed of individuals, it can be claimed that we need no sociological theory. Of course, the biologist or geneticist might carry on this argument, saying that psychology is really reducible to biology or genetics. The physicist could argue that everything is a matter of physical mechanisms of atomic behavior – that these account in the end for biology, psychology, and sociology.

In an oblique way, each of these arguments would be right. Insofar as there are crucial dependencies among the social and biological sciences, the bases for reduction exist. But if the theory of groups was reduced to the terms of atomic mechanisms, it would be so unwieldy and cumbersome, and perhaps trite, that it would be of no use. The levels on which theory operate are partly a matter of utility and convenience, and partly produced by observation and conceptualization.

This ties up nicely with the discussion of the difference between pattern and deductive theory in sociology. We noted that pattern theories were concerned less with hierarchies of deductive statements and more with well-defined, systematized arrangements of explanatory terms. We also saw that the deductive theoretician regards something as "explained" when it is deduced from a set of general princi-

---

[22] Although "reductionism" is a general name for the reduction of any theory, in recent sociology the strongest claim for reductionism was made by Homans in "Contemporary Theory in Sociology," in R. E. L. Faris, ed., *Handbook of Modern Sociology* (Chicago: Rand McNally, 1964), pp. 951 ff.

ples. Now it is possible to turn pattern theory into deductive theory simply by adding a set of general statements on top of a pattern.

There have been notable attempts to destroy sociology by reducing its theory to psychology. The argument runs that if there is no truly sociological subject matter, but only the psychology of individuals, then there is no real theory in sociology. In defense, sociologists have tended either to ignore the charge, or to derive uniquely sociological theories and generalizations. This has led back to Durkheim's dictum that "social facts," not reducible to individual facts, are the subject matter of sociology. Similarly, social theorists have sought to use analogies to biological and economic theory giving expression to phenomena that are not reducible to individual behavior.

C. Perspectives

Perspectives are separated from pattern and deductive theories not by matters of kind so much as by matters of degree. Perspectives are collections of ideas that are important as "sensitizing" agents. They point out important isolated aspects of reality. But perspectives are usually less internally coherent. In general, perspectives resemble pattern theory more than they do deductive theory.

For example, "symbolic interactionism," which is discussed in Chapter 6, is usually called a perspective. A perspective like this points out certain things of special importance when explaining social relations. Interactionism invites us to pay particular attention to the "self" as it is formed, changed, stabilized in interaction. There are several factors that, from this perspective, are important to self-formation and self-stabilization. These include the maintenance of self-definition, defense against disconfirmatory or confusing evidence, utilization of symbolic communication to achieve social integration, and so on. The perspective provides a language in which to have discourse about this kind of thing, but it does not tell specifically what to say in that language.[23]

There are several other sociological notions that might be called "perspectives." Indeed, the term lacks precision partly because what some call a theory, others call a perspective. If all we want to know is a theory's general suggestions and general explanations, we are taking it as a perspective. Theories can be used as perspectives; however, notions lacking logical coherence and specificity cannot be turned into theories without additional effort.

Perspectives sensitize us to the social environment, and suggest a

[23] A. M. Rose's *Human Behavior and Social Process* (Boston: Houghton Mifflin, 1962) is a book based on interactionism. Although Rose attempts a "systematic summary" of interactionism, the summary does not constitute a theory.

language in which to describe experience. Also, they may specify certain general processes. When Marxism is taken as a perspective, it suggests a general process of conflict between naturally opposed groups. We need not ask too searching a question about the nature, origins, kinds, and conditions of conflict (that is, we need not have a theoretical statement of it) in order to understand Marxism merely as a perspective based on conflict.

VII. Verification of theories

We expect our theories to depict reality as it is, and to produce accurate predictions. Because this is the case, *verification* of theory is of central interest. Verification is the business of finding out which theories, or which aspects of one theory, are right. "Right" means, broadly speaking, having the ability to produce accurate theoretical descriptions or to give hypotheses that predict experience: "Right" theories come true. Verification is the process of finding out when and why a theory is "right."

A. Verification of deductive theories

When we deduce a hypothesis from a theory, the hypothesis is logically "true." By deductive thinking, we simply apply theoretical generalizations to a specific case and produced a hypothesis. We add nothing, observe nothing, subtract nothing–we simply deduce. Now the question is whether or not this logically true hypothesis is empirically true. Does the hypothesis, which states a logically derived relationship between ideas, describe an actual relationship?

The obvious way to decide is to go and look, and this is exactly what sociologists do. And what is the conclusion if, on looking, the sociologist finds what the hypothesis told him to expect? Would he regard the hypothesis as confirmed and would the theory be confirmed as well? Or is only the hypothesis confirmed? Or is anything confirmed?

The sociologist would probably conclude that the hypothesis had been "confirmed," but he would bear in mind the following factors:

1 The hypothesis could have been confirmed by "chance"–he might have seen a chance association and not one that normally occurs.
2 The hypothesis was "true," but for different reasons than those depicted in its theory–the hypothesis might predict the truth, but the theory could still be "wrong."
3 The hypothesis was "true" because of unsuspected factors–important additions to the theory might need to be made before a crude hypothesis can depict essentially important parts of reality.

Now imagine that the sociologist, hypothesis in hand, looks around and decides that his hypothesis does not seem "right." Something logically "true" appears empirically "false." What is his conclusion? He might conclude the theory is "wrong," and so he should – but he ought to bear in mind that his observation might be inaccurate.

Note that when the sociologist finds his hypothesis confirmed, he is in a deeper quandry than when it is not confirmed. It is far easier and less risky to decide that a theory is "wrong" when it gives false hypotheses than to decide a theory is "right" when it gives true ones. There are several reasons why a hypothesis might appear true when it is in fact false. Spurious confirmations of hypotheses can result from wrong observation, chance, intervening factors, and so on. On the other hand, when a hypothesis turns out to be empirically false, it does not matter what spurious factors are at work. The hypothesis failed, and hence the sociologist must go back to the theory to make adjustments. It is easier to say that a theory is "wrong" than to say that one is "right."

This seems like an impasse. We can only come to final conclusions about deductive theories that are "wrong." It is not possible to say with certainty that a consistently good producer of "right" hypotheses is actually a "correct" theory.

Although the topic being discussed is supposed to be verification of theories, we have demonstrated that it is not possible to "verify" deductive theories, but it is possible to "falsify" them. In fact, this is the way scientists tend to look at the verification problem. The whole process of "verification" is one of comparison among competing theories. Theories are eliminated by falsification until there remain only the ones that are yet unfalsified. We work with this residue of unfalsified theories until evidence builds up that they, too, are false. Hence the theoretically minded sociologist does not regard a theory as he would a certain fact. A theory is always tentative, and the closest we can come to a final conclusion about unfalsified theory is to say that it seems at the moment to be true.[24]

Falsifications are not usually as clear-cut as this description suggests. Theories produce a wide range of hypotheses, and it is probable that a single theory will give some that are better than others – some empirically true, some empirically false, and those that turn out to be false may highlight necessary alterations to the theory. The philosophical problem of verification is actually the question of what decision to make about a theory based on comparative falsification of its several hypotheses. Such judgments remain tentative. If you have

[24] See Karl R. Popper, *The Logic of Scientific Discovery* (New York: Harper & Row, 1959).

ever wondered why a science can carry on for a long time with false theory, this is part of the reason.

Another aspect of verification, one that is concerned more with the logic of application than empirical truth, is the question of whether a theory is really falsifiable at all. If it is not, then there is no possible way of deciding that it is not empirically true. If there is no way, in principle, to come to this conclusion, then we can never know the empirical usefulness of such a theory. Thorstein Veblen's idea of an "instinct of workmanship" in *The Theory of the Leisure Class* provides an example.[25] If we wish to try to verify whether or not such an instinct exists, how would we go about it? Veblen says that it does, but that as affluence grows, a person tends to waste money and leisure as a sign that he has "arrived" socially and that work is no longer necessary. But we wish to try to verify Veblen's theory. On examination, we see some people working diligently, and some conspicuously consuming goods and engaging in wasteful pursuits. What do we conclude? That Veblen was right? How can we? People may work for many reasons, only one of which might have anything to do with Veblen's hypothesis of an instinct to do so. Also, if people are endowed with an instinct for workmanship and creative effort, how could they so easily abandon this instinct when they get money ahead? The fact is, Veblen has given two contradictory hypotheses about man's nature: He (1) instinctively works and creates, and (2) wastes time and conspicuously destroys creation. When we see someone doing one of these, Veblen appears right; when we see someone doing the opposite, Veblen again appears right. In fact, we cannot conceive of anyone doing anything that could not be given a Veblenesque interpretation. There is no possible observation that could falsify Veblen's theory. We can never know, therefore, if the theory has any empirical truth or not.

A word of caution. Theories that are not falsifiable seem to cover a great deal of ground, as the preceding example shows, and to do so with amazing facility. Sometimes these may seem to be the best theories. But the fact is that another theory, similarly lacking in falsifiability but different in every other respect, could do exactly the same. Then there would be two sets of unfalsifiable but opposite hypotheses, neither of which could be judged according to empirical value. Science would be no better off for having the two, just as it is no better off for having one or the other.

What makes a theory falsifiable? A theory must refer to observables, either directly or indirectly. Generally speaking, a theory must yield hypotheses that are specific and be clear about the conditions under

[25] New York: Macmillan, 1899.

which to expect its hypotheses to hold. Vagueness is the enemy of
falsifiability. For example, Marx may have predicted that revolution
will occur in capitalist societies, given certain general conditions. But
what exactly is the revolutionary condition, and what exactly is a
revolution? Can Marxian principles be applied to "green revolutions"
or revolutions in morals? Overgenerality and vagueness make Marxian
theory difficult to apply with precision, and therefore hard to falsify.

Similarly, theories must clearly give the conditions under which
their hypotheses are not applicable. Only with this knowledge can a
practitioner tell the exact circumstances in which to search for proof
of a theory's predictions.

B. Verification of pattern theories

Strictly speaking, pattern theories are not "verified," but "interpreted." We saw that deductive theories are "open" at the bottom.
They give hypotheses deduced from general laws. By contrast, with
pattern theories we have no such convenient hypothesis-producing
machine turning out logically true hypotheses. Instead, we must interpret the theory in relation to situations we wish to have explained. To
interpret it means simply this: to know the theory well enough to be
confident that observed facts are similar in nature to those conceptualized in the theory–that they "fit" it. To put it another way, we
must use a theory of sufficient clarity and precision that anyone familiar with it would, as a matter of common sense, see that the descriptive and explanatory content of the theory had an interpretive application to a real situation.

Of course, there are limits to this kind of interpretive understanding
of a pattern, and again the analogy to the novel makes this clear. We
do not expect children to read novels for the meaning, but they can
understand the story. The difference between children and ourselves
is that our experience with life makes episodes in the novel stand out
as meaningful. We see their application. We interpret the novel in the
light of experience, getting a level of meaning above that of the story.
We interpret pattern theory in a similar way. We see the story. But
beyond that, we see the implied or explicit reasoning that brought the
story about. In novels we know the difference between fantasy and
"real life" simply because we realize one kind of story is not perti-
nent to what we experience, but that the other is.

A pattern theory is a kind of reconstructed picture of reality describing clearly the relationships among its parts. Application of this
kind of theory means "seeing" the reality on which the concepts and
processes are based. By reference to such a theory, one can develop
ideas about relationships and processes to be expected in reality.

We can seek these real relationships either mentally or empirically. If we do it mentally, we interpret what we actually see in terms of the theory, trying to cover every aspect. If a theory gives a reasonable and definitive picture of what we know by experience, then we consider this to be evidence of the "truth" of the theory. We can proceed more empirically, by allowing theory to guide us toward expectations. An example of this is found in the treatment of motivation in sociology and psychology. Motivation is something that no one will ever "see"; it is entirely conceptual. Now when we seek correlations, for example, between motivation and achievement, we are seeking these correlations not because we have evidence suggesting they should be there, but because a theory suggests they should be.

As with the deductive model, it is much more sound to proceed on the basis of falsification than confirmation. We saw that the principle of falsification added strictures of clarity and specificity. This applies equally to pattern theory. But here the problem is compounded. Because the whole pattern is a closed coherent picture of reality, it should contain an account of just about everything we see. Hence, by nature, pattern theories are less susceptible to falsification than deductive ones. This is both a blessing and a curse. The blessing is that pattern theories are capable of extremes of internal coherence and elegance that are intellectually very exciting. The curse is that they are less restricted in reaching these limits and can more easily drift away from useful application.

VIII. Conclusion

In this chapter, we survey terms and styles of explanation now in use in social science. It is emphasized that explanation is more than just "making clear." It is an exercise contained by a more or less formal structure of concepts having specific relationships. Such sets of concepts have, to some degree, the power to bring our curiosity to rest, to do it logically and coherently, and to pertain to reality. We note that doing one or another of these things does not necessarily give a theory high value, but it is in doing them simultaneously that theories gain their staying power. It is worth noting again that explanation, although it must remain the prime goal of social science, is an ideal, probably never to be reached ultimately. We do not have, and may never have, theories that maximize all the criteria of theoretical performance to the fullest. Thus, because of the need for accurate prediction and explanation, and the intellectual importance of coherent, reasonable thought, theoretical work is never complete and should never be regarded as finished. It is changing and developing, and it is worthy of particular attention for its own sake.

KEY CONCEPTS

observational term	systemic meaning
construct	deduction
theoretical term	hierarchical order
primitive term	concatenated theory
analogous term	deductive theory
true by definition	perspective
empirically true	laws
general proposition	"other things being equal"
falsifiability	reductionism
verification	interpretation

TOPICS FOR DISCUSSION

1 What is the difference between a pattern theory and a deductive theory? Could we have theories of both types pertaining to the same subject?

2 What is the difference between primitive terms and analogous terms?

3 What are some of the kinds of analogies in use in sociological theory?

4 How could a descriptive analogy disguise an explanation?

5 Describe how a hypothesis could be "logically true" but "empirically false."

6 What are some of the things one might be referring to when one speaks of a "law" in science?

7 What is the difference between verification and falsification?

8 What differentiates a pattern theory from a perspective?

9 How did the example of the "spirit of capitalism" illustrate systemic meaning?

10 "Society" is said to be a construct. Why?

ESSAY QUESTIONS

How is a deductive theory verified?

Compare deductive- and pattern-type theories with specific attention to their logical structure.

If we deduce a hypothesis from a theory and find it "true" empirically, what can we say about the theory from which it came?

Describe the ways in which the biological analogy has entered sociological description and explanation.

What does the phrase "other things being equal" have to do with deductive theory?

What do we mean when we say we have observed a person's role?
Name some primitive terms from sociology and describe why you
    think they are primitive to it.
Discuss how a theory may be taken as a perspective, and tell what
    additional information and analysis are needed to transform the
    perspective into a theory.

FOR FURTHER READING AND STUDY

Brodbeck, Mae (ed.). *Readings in the Philosophy of the Social Sciences.*
    New York: Macmillan, 1968.
Gibson, Quentin. *The Logic of Social Enquiry.* London: Routledge and Ke-
    gan Paul, 1960.
Gross, Llewellyn (ed.). *Sociological Theory: Inquiries and Paradigms.* New
    York: Harper & Row, 1967.
Kaplan, Abraham. *The Conduct of Inquiry.* San Francisco: Chandler Publish-
    ing Co., 1964.
Langer, Susanne K. *Philosophy in a New Key.* Cambridge, Mass.: Harvard
    University Press, 1951.
Nagel, Ernest. *The Structure of Science: Problems in the Logic of Scientific
    Explanation.* New York: Harcourt Brace and World, 1961.
Popper, Karl R. *The Logic of Scientific Discovery.* New York: Harper &
    Row, 1959.
Ryan, Alan. *The Philosophy of the Social Sciences.* London: Macmillan,
    1970.

4 Exchange theory

I. Introduction

In this chapter we begin to inspect a working theory in sociology—
exchange theory. A word about the name of this theory. As "exchange" implies, this theory concerns the exchange among individuals of valued objects or sentiments as a basis for social order. The
exchange in question usually does not pertain to tangible things.
Rather, it commonly involves intangibles such as esteem, liking, as-
sistance, and approval. Exchange also applies to the avoidance of
something such as pain, expense, embarrassment, and the like. And
sometimes exchange involves opportunities, advantages, or some
comparative aspect of human relations. In general, the idea of exchange is very broad and inclusive, not limited to the giving and
receiving of concrete things.

In the discussion of exchange theory, we encounter the *deductive*
approach to sociological theory. Chapter 3 explained how a theory
could be built hierarchically with lawlike principles, from which hypotheses about actual observations could be deduced. One of the modern
founders of exchange theory in sociology, who is currently its main
proponent, George C. Homans, decided to organize his theory this
way. In studying exchange theory, there is an opportunity to see
deductive theory building applied to sociological subject matter.

II. Sociological use of the term "exchange"

As with most ideas, the idea of exchange in social science has a long
and varied history. Indeed, an idea as simple as giving and receiving
is probably as old as man himself, but the review of it here will go
back only as far as the eighteenth century. In the eighteenth century,
a new wave of critical thought about the nature of social order accompanied changing economic and social conditions. Although there had
been extensive commerce among European nations for some time,
the mid-eighteenth century saw the reorganization of economic enterprise that was to culminate eventually in what is referred to as the
Industrial Revolution.[1] This meant that trade and manufacturing,

---

[1] No date can be placed on the Industrial Revolution; historians are not agreed.

standards of value, organization of production and of markets, accounting procedures, wage labor, and so on, were important topics in the minds of thinking men of the time. It was bound to occur to somebody, sooner or later, that perhaps the forces that kept economic markets relatively stable and functioning were specific manifestations of principles accounting for social order in general.

There was great advantage in this kind of theorizing. It seemed down to earth and, in principle, was based on observable activities. The idea behind an economic market analogy to general social order was basically this: Individual decisions about buying, selling, trading, and carrying, made in the course of commercial activities, were special cases of more general decisions about daily life; these general decisions could be understood in the same way as economic decisions. The question, "What am I going to get out of this?" took on a theoretical meaning. It seemed possible to apply concepts from the economic theory of the time to all social transactions and emerge with a general theory of social order.

Some other occurrences about this time, and on into the nineteenth century, reinforced the emerging conceptual basis of exchange theory. As industrialization gained ground, the existing legal systems of Europe were not equipped to handle it and its consequences. At first, there was no regulatory law to control hours of work, minimum wages, conditions of employment, superannuation, benefits to families, and the like. Nor was there law yet applied to monopolies, business practices, factory location, and so on. In general, until reform movements caught up to the pace of the rapidly expanding Industrial Revolution, there was an era of free-for-all competition that emphasized extreme individualism. This individualism could be both good and bad. It allowed the free run of genius to build up capital, develop new techniques, and alter industrial practices. It also allowed a free hand to employers, employees, and competitors in exploiting and undercutting each other in irresponsible, even lethal ways.

It was primarily an interest in market economics, which emphasized the concept of exchange, that thrust the idea of an entirely free individual into the forefront of social thought. Later on, the theory of evolution, as popularized, emphasized a struggle among individual members of a species in a limited and sometimes hostile environment. The theory of evolution added credence to the existing emphasis on the individualistic, freely competitive picture of social order then developing.[2]

It is this legacy of social history and theory that exchange theory carries with it today. Who exchanges what, in exchange theory? The

[2] See Dorothy Marshall, *Industrial England, 1776–1851* (London: Routledge and Kegan Paul, 1973).

answer is always that persons, individuals, exchange things. The unit of analysis is the person and not the collective, the society, the group. What does he exchange? He trades what is uniquely and privately his to give, whatever that might be. What does he get for it? He tries to get whatever he might personally happen to want. We do not, in exchange theory, imagine that a group of people must share common values to form a society. From exchange theory's point of view, persons of quite different tastes and propensities can live side by side in the same society if they can provide for each other the services and amenities each one happens to desire.

The period of extreme individualism as a way of life was actually rather short, although the political and social philosophy accompanying it lasts to this day. Extreme individualism engendered a reaction, a move toward collectivism, a banding together for common good and mutual aid. This collective action was bound to need a philosophical and theoretical justification. These theories were forthcoming.

We are the intellectual heirs to these exciting times in the eighteenth and nineteenth centuries. Sociology has gravitated, at one time or another, toward either the individualistic or the collectivistic pole of a theoretical continuum. The years from approximately 1937 to the late 1950s were dominated by sociological theory emphasizing structured relations, specification of roles, and perhaps a tendency toward collective determinism. (There is a great deal more about this in Chapter 5 on the theories of the functionalists.) Exchange theory, in its present form, is actually a return to the spirit and principles of extreme individualism – a reaction to structuralism and functional theory of the 1940s and 1950s.[3] The emergence of exchange theory in the 1950s and its development in the 1960s can be viewed as another chapter in the continuing debate about the proper theoretical way to picture the individual-in-society, a question first raised in a modern fashion by the coming of the industrial age.

Modern exchange theory also owes a deep debt to experimental psychology. As a well-defined position among the schools of psychology, experimental psychology bears remarkable similarity to the main features of individualistic social theory. It emphasizes the concrete behavior of specific individuals or, more often in this field, experimental animals. It takes this individualistic viewpoint in combination with considerable emphasis on the concept of motivation – the apparent eagerness of individuals to act for reasons of their own. However, private motives may sometimes be manipulated. Experimental psy-

---

[3] Modern exchange theory (from the 1950s onward) arose partly as a critique of sociological functionalism. See Alvin Gouldner, "Reciprocity and Autonomy in Functional Theory," in Llewellyn Gross, ed., *Symposium on Sociological Theory* (Evanston, Ill.: Row, Peterson, 1959), pp. 241–70.

chology is a branch of "learning theory." It suggests in general that persons' actions can be shaped, controlled, and therefore predicted by manipulating environments, especially the things that reward or punish. In experiments, it is possible to control these rewarding and punishing qualities fairly precisely; and in real life, it seems possible to observe such things, applying the same principles of explanation outside the laboratory as inside it. Thus it is possible to observe a subject as he learns to cope with or master his environment and conceptualize the subject's response to the rewarding or punishing features of it.[4]

The experimental psychology tradition bears considerable similarity to the philosophical movement called hedonism. Not much detail is needed here, except to point out that experimental psychology is based on more than just experiments with animals. Hedonism as a philosophy affirms that individuals are capable of discriminating between pleasure and pain and that naturally they will always try to avoid pain and gain pleasure. As a philosophy, hedonism was largely applied to the problem of how to organize the world so that all could experience pleasure and minimize pain and so that one person's pleasure did not entail another's pain. It was thought that this pleasure-and-pain principle was a basic law of human affairs, and that it would be senseless to expect people to behave as if it were not. Experimental psychology makes somewhat the same assumption in postulating that we can always expect persons to discriminate among stimuli and act on the basis of whether they find them rewarding.

We have now built up a sketch of the intellectual background on which exchange theory draws. Briefly recall the objective of theory so that we can see more clearly what these intellectual foundations were bound to produce. The aim of sociological theory is to explain social order. Exchange theory's purpose in sociology is to build upon a set of basic principles, drawn from consistent and complementary lines of thought (economic individualism, experimental psychology, and hedonistic philosophy), by which to give a coherent and workable general explanation of social order.

III. A general statement of the principles of sociological exchange theory

As with all sociological theories, it is difficult to separate particular theoretical works from the generalities of the theoretical model. Exchange theory is no exception to this. This chapter considers the works of George Homans and Peter Blau. In addition, other contem-

---

[4] Of particular importance to this movement in psychology was B. F. Skinner, *The Behavior of Organisms* (New York: Appleton-Century-Crofts, 1938).

porary contributions, comment, and critical material will be reviewed. But first, in order to highlight the main ideas, a generalized description of exchange theory is presented.

A. *The unit of analysis*

The unit of analysis, the thing to watch when observing, and the thing that plays the main part in the explanation of order, is the *individual*. Exchange theory does not ask preliminary questions about subjects like institutions, public opinion, or cultural commitment. Nor is the group per se the main focus, although exchange theory usually ends up saying something about groups, institutions, sentiment, and so forth. Exchange theory does not remain focused on the individual. However, it begins there because it intends to examine the social interchanges persons have among themselves that account for order and change. By focusing on individuals as a starting point, its practitioners hope to learn something about the nature of groups. In exchange theory, groups are understood as serving the ends of their members. Hence there is no justification for assuming that groups have special identities of their own, have a nature not derived from their members, and so on.

B. *Motive*

Exchange theorists assume that persons have their own private desires and ends-in-view. Everyone may need certain things, but this does not make these things "common goals." We all need food, but food is not a common goal in the same sense that victory is the common goal for an army that organizes and disciplines itself toward that end. Assumed here is the premise that persons are egotistically motivated by their private and unique goals and wants. The exchange theorist persists in viewing motivation as a private and individual matter, although he may see culture as having a hand in it. But no matter what, motivation is expected to be in the direction of gaining wanted commodities, pleasure, satisfaction, and the like, and nothing else.

What about the altruist? How does exchange theory account for the person who gives his money to charity, or risks his life to save a drowning man? Certainly these activities entail loss and risk, something seemingly contrary to the assumption. The usual way this kind of problem has been handled is to point out that giving away your goods to help others imparts a sense of emotional satisfaction, even if it does mean a money loss. Remember that the rewards involved in exchange theory can be of any type whatsoever, and emotional reward might offset money loss. Similarly, it might be worth the risk to dive in and save a drowning man. The payoff for such an act is recognition and self-satisfaction, to say nothing of the enormous debt the saved man would owe his rescuer in gratitude and esteem. It is also worth remembering, if you are considering rejection of exchange theory right now, that the altruist is much in the minority in human affairs, and if exchange theorists simply wrote him off as unexplainable, there would be a very large amount of nonaltruism left to explain.

C. Profit

We have assumed persons act egotistically to gain pleasure or satisfaction. With all persons doing this, no one can act in a vacuum. All will have to give as well as get. They must, because to disregard the other person is to deny him his reward. In the absence of mutual satisfaction there would be no social interaction at all. Because of this give and take, as the exchange theorist sees it, there is always some cost involved in gaining reward. Cost is normally defined as the effort required to gain satisfaction, plus the potential rewards forgone as a result of the specific choice. This last point requires some attention.

We might be interested in explaining why Bill and Pat went to the movies instead of going out to eat. Of course, the date is going to cost them something, no matter what they do. But this simple example is complicated, if we really try to understand the concept of "cost." First, there is the relative price of eating and of watching a film. But it is perhaps also important to Bill to impress Pat, and taking her to a B movie might be decidedly less effective than treating her to dinner in a good restaurant. Also, consider the fact that he cannot take her to eat in common clothes; he might have to spend more time and effort (not to mention money) dressing for this occasion than for a trip to the cinema. Without going any further, and without considering the viewpoint of Pat in any way, we see that an array of possible rewards and costs is set before Bill. The exchange theorist regards Bill as being aware of these rewards and costs (in principle Bill is aware of *all* of them). Being so informed, Bill makes his choice.

Now what are his costs? They are the actual costs of what he did – take Pat to the movie – plus the forgone rewards he would have obtained had he taken her to dinner. Why does dinner come in again? It comes in because his efforts with Pat would have been advanced by taking her to dinner, but he chose not to do this. He lost the benefits of that activity, and he must count them in with the costs of doing what he chose to do. Bill did, however, get something out of his decision. He went out with Pat, which is bound to have been of some benefit to him, and he did not have to pay as much to do it, either. On his calculations, what he got for his pains was a good return on effort, and what he lost by not taking her to dinner would not have been worth that much more, anyway. If we can say the preceding is true for Bill, we might say that, all things considered, he made a *profit* on the movie date. In more formal language, he maximized his reward and minimized his cost. His profit is determined by comparing reward and cost; it is the difference between them. Profit accrues when reward is greater than cost. Bill might have gained higher rewards from the dinner date, but he would have had higher cost, too. The difference, taken as profit, was not as great in the case of dining, and so he chose the films.

D. Voluntarism

It should be evident that exchange theory emphasizes the type of social action we might label *voluntary*. It views everyday behavior as responsive to individual desire and calculation; it assumes a large degree of freedom of choice for actors. How could it do otherwise? If a person had no choice about action, it would make no sense to speak about comparing rewards and costs of alternatives. In sociology, we sometimes emphasize the constraints placed on persons by outside forces, but exchange theorists never overemphasize these. In exchange theory, that leads to an absurdity. The absurdity lies in conceptually denying the individual powers of decision. There is considerable choice in human affairs, and no matter how dominant culture may appear, it is never so complete as to specify totally the actions of people.

E. Social approval

One more thing should be pointed out about human exchange systems – the apparent importance of approval as a general satisfier and motivator. Up to now, little has been said about the things that reward people. Reward is a cornerstone of the theory of social exchange, but no one has really specified what it is. In fact, exchange theorists are reluctant to be too specific about this, because to do so would be to construct a set of categories of reward that would then require justification. Exchange theory avoids this because of its emphasis on individuality and voluntarism. The things that reward people may be unique to them. Categorizing rewards would violate a basic assumption about individuality.

But it does seem that we can discover generalized rewards, and the most powerful one is *social approval*. In everyday terms, this is the "liking" people seem to seek and enjoy in social relations. Persons prefer others who like them and approve of them, and shun those who are disapproving or critical. Furthermore, this is not always a conscious, calculated matter. Experimental evidence suggests that persons will respond to approving aspects of their environment even when they are concentrating on something else and are completely unaware of subtle approval. As the term implies, social approval can take many concrete forms. It is the apparent regard of the approver that makes the encounter a rewarding one.

IV. *General theory of social order based on exchange fundamentals*

Thus far we have discussed individuals and their motivated acts. But the sociological theorist's aim is to explain the nature of groups. And describing individuals who exchange does imply a picture of group action. Whom would we expect to associate regularly? Those who can substantially reward each other. Those who require rewards that can be gained in interaction will regularly associate with those who provide them. How will they do it? They will establish "rates of exchange" among the things they trade (tangible or not). Associated with these rates of exchange will be the relative costs of producing rewarding actions and the relative availability of them. Usually these dynamic forces lead to varying amounts of esteem distributed among the members of a group. Similarly, we might account for other aspects of "group structure." To exchange theorists, group structure means the dynamic interplay of individually derived forces at work in the group.

Viewing social approval as a generalized reward, we can predict roughly that mutual social approval will be high among people who regularly associate freely together. And we can suppose that if social approval is all a person has to offer, it alone will be sufficient to attract at least some others and that, in a group, all persons will gain at least some approval. But there is one thing about social approval that makes it inadequate as an explanatory concept for much of what happens in groups. Social approval does not usually cost much to give, and it is in never-ending supply. When we approve of someone, we do not thereby reduce our stockpile of approval, making it more costly to approve of him next time or to approve of someone else. From an exchange viewpoint, mere approval is exceedingly cheap as a commodity. This means that while social approval as a general reinforcer can explain some association, other rewarding qualities of persons, such as knowledge or skill, remain crucial. A general reward such as social approval, which costs little or nothing, will probably not elicit other scarce resources in the give and take imagined by exchange theorists.

A. Ranking and value

Suppose we wish to investigate the *ranking* schemes found in groups. We might observe a particular group in which there is a definite hierarchy of persons (there usually is). This "pecking order" may be indicated by who defers to whom, whose word is least often questioned, who sits at the head of the table. All these aspects of ranking within the group are components of the general social order evident in the group. To explain ranking using exchange, we employ the ideas of value and scarcity. Social approval is not usually the only basis for high rank. It is too readily available to be valued highly. But many exchange commodities are rare; something may be highly sought after and be in short supply, perhaps hard to produce. This comparatively scarce yet wanted item will be *valuable* in the comparative sense in which we are using the term "value."

In order to understand rank ordering in a group, let us compare two men. One is highly capable of rewarding the other with witty and intelligent conversation. He might possess wisdom, and his delivery is easy and agreeable. The other person, however, is not so witty, and usually can think of the perfect comeback only after the opportunity to use it is long past. However, this latter one is able to give approval to the witty man. Now we shall undoubtedly see the wit and charm of the first outrank the simple approval proffered by the second. It does so because it is a scarce commodity, not easily attained. It is worth something to have a man like that around, whereas the more simple-minded are "a dime a dozen." The supplier of charm and wit is of special significance for the enjoyment of all, and his presence will be sought ahead of the others. That is, he ranks high in that group.

B. Value is comparative

Obviously this is a very simple example. Groups are usually far more complex, involving a wide array of valuable activities that cannot all be produced with equal facility by any one person. This array of rewards becomes the basis of the *comparative* ranking system in our sample group. How does one kind of reward come to outrank another? Those that are comparatively the most valuable, because they are of most service yet hardest to get, will "cost" the most. This cost, perhaps in terms of social approval, goes to the providers of these valued things and becomes observable as their esteem within the group.

C. "Explaining" the group

What else do we usually want to know about groups? One of the stock-in-trade items that sociologists research is *conformity* to rules.

How do standards apply? We might be tempted to say that group standards apply universally and that deviation is likely to be disapproved, no matter who deviates. But alas, it is not so. Group standards apply differentially and, as we shall see, this may be a good thing. Let us continue our example.

First, recognize that conformity to group standards might be a source of satisfaction in its own right. Doing what others expect of us without being forced is what we usually mean when we talk about moral behavior or "socialized" activity. But most exchange theorists would not stop at this as an explanation. We must explain, they say, why these commitments arise.

Note that we are not looking for a single reason to account for all the conformity among group members. It is a basic principle of exchange theory that individuality implies private motives. Hence the conclusion left to us is that conformity to norms gains individuals something. That something may vary from person to person. But whatever the happy results of belonging may be for a particular person, there is at least one way of obtaining them: by conforming to group standards. Conforming behavior is an outward sign of belonging, an advertisement to the other members and to outsiders that the benefits of group membership ought to be conferred on the conformer.

According to this, the person on the receiving end of group benefits would always be the most conformist-minded. If he is giving mostly social approval and getting something more scarce and harder to obtain in return, the balance at this juncture seems to be in his favor. We might expect those benefiting most in our group to be the most conformist. If a real situation were this simple, exchange theory would predict precisely this. But it might also be true that persons in the lower ranks are receiving less benefit from group membership than those of more importance. In relation to what they give they may be getting good measure, but compared to others giving more, they may be getting less. Hence their commitment to the success of the group could be less. And because of this lesser commitment, the standards of the group might be less important to those in the lower ranks. This would be especially true in the light of another of our basic starting points – that reward is calculated on a comparative basis. If another group were competing for the loyalty of our lower-ranking members, it would probably draw off some of their commitment, lowering their willingness to conform to the first group's standards.

Under conditions of least competition for group loyalty and best return for effort, we would expect the lower ranks of a group to be the most committed to it, but under changing conditions and competitive loyalties, we might have to modify our prediction. But what about those higher up? Do we expect them to be regularly conformist or eccentric? Here again, rank itself interacts with the tendency to conform to rules. Remember that when we started out analyzing this group, we thought that rank was roughly related to contribution to group satisfaction. But rank itself can become a kind of license to deviate. As many people suspect, activities that would be punished or disapproved in ordinary group members are tolerated or even welcomed among "higher-ups." This tolerance of deviance can be thought of as being "bought" as a privilege. It is part of the reward of high status, which, in turn, derives from contributions to the group. Of course, there will be limits. Deviation cannot be total, and it might be only trivial. Alternatively, extreme commitment to group practices often goes with high rank, and this rewarding commitment can form a counterweight to deviance, as in the case of the country landlord who is always prominently placed in the parish church on Sunday morning.

This general discussion of conformity to group standards implies a particularly interesting question for exchange theorists. How are norms changed? How do certain ones fall into disuse and pass away, whereas others become prominent? We might regard this as a question about *innovation*. In principle, everyone is in a position to innovate, but for different reasons. Those in the lower ranks might be less committed to norms, especially if they have alternative groups to belong to, because their rewards for membership are comparatively less. Also, their contribution to the group is probably less. These persons will have a certain freedom, simply because less is at stake, both on the contribution and payoff sides. It might be easier for such persons to change the rule and make it stick simply because for them the removal of group rewards is not that crucial; they might be willing to take the risk. Similarly, there is a built-in freedom to innovate for those who contribute very heavily to group satisfaction, because their pleasure will often be considered imperative to ensure their continued performance.

Now, in a perfunctory way, we have discovered some links between important aspects of group process and structure: ranking as it might develop, conformity to standards, norm change and innovation. We should review in more formal terms how we went about discovering these things. They were found by starting with a set of assumptions concerning the nature of individual motivations. These led to explanations of individual acts. Combining gave a theoretical account of some aspects of group structure. A minimum of assumptions were made about groups themselves. But we made assumptions; we did not reach our conclusions by observation only. Our assumptions were about individuals. Manipulation of these assumptions led to hypothetical ideas about the behavior and characteristics of groups. This is a typical line of argument for exchange theorists: working upward from individual-level analysis to group-level conclusions by a smooth process of transition. Later in this chapter, we shall describe some of Blau's work on exchange structures, which is essentially this kind of theorizing.

V. Deductive exchange theory – G. C. Homans's propositions

So far, the background of exchange theory has been sketched, its viewpoint and some of its main ideas have been introduced, and the way exchange theory might be applied to some aspects of groups has been suggested. We turn now to exchange theory according to one of its main proponents, George C. Homans. In particular we are concerned with the extent to which Homans explains social order by deductive theorizing and how he employs his exchange propositions to do so.[5]

Homans has been particularly explicit about exchange theory. He reasons as follows: We can only explain aspects of social order and change by referring to some small number of general propositions from which the particulars we wish to explain may be deduced. The general propositions must therefore be statements of broad scope. Furthermore, these statements ought to be about individual actors and ought to be propositions about motivation and the ways people respond to their environment.[6]

Homans has written widely, but it is useful to focus on two particular works and briefly consider their relationship. The books are *The Human Group*[7] and *Social Behavior*. *The Human Group* is a descriptive book. It is largely a review of research in social relations, and it contains a good deal of data, but the book is not particularly strong on "explanation." It says a lot about "what" but not much about "why." *Social Behavior*, on the other hand, contains more theory and correspondingly less description. It contains more "why" and less "what." We might view *The Human Group* as the foundation

---

[5] The following works contain Homans's theoretical contributions to exchange theory: "Bringing Men Back In," *American Sociological Review*, XXIV (December 1964), pp. 809–19; "Contemporary Theory in Sociology," in R. E. L. Faris, ed., *Handbook of Modern Sociology* (Chicago: Rand McNally, 1964), pp. 951–77; *The Nature of Social Science* (New York: Harcourt Brace and World, 1967); "Social Behavior as Exchange," *American Journal of Sociology*, LXII (May 1958), pp. 597–607; *Social Behavior: Its Elementary Forms* (New York: Harcourt Brace and World, 1961; rev. ed., 1974); "Theory of Social Interaction," *Transactions of the Fifth World Congress of Sociology*, IV (Louvain: International Sociological Association, 1964), pp. 113–25.

[6] Homans's work on this is *The Nature of Social Science*. He often cites as his mentor in this regard Richard B. Braithwaite, *Scientific Explanation* (New York: Harper & Row, 1953).

[7] New York: Harcourt Brace Jovanovich, 1950. This book is actually functionalist in inspiration, although Homans has used its contents in another way.

material from which the inductive process sprang, and *Social Behavior* as the deductive link in the chain where the explanatory propositions are stated. Hence *Social Behavior* is where we find Homans's exchange theory most fully developed.

A. The propositions

We now give the propositions as Homans has done, with explanation and comment but not criticism. Critical material will be included later in this chapter, together with an assessment of the general success or failure of exchange theory.

From the first edition of *Social Behavior,* Homans's first proposition is:

> 1. If in the past, the occurrence of a particular stimulus-situation has been the occasion on which a man's activity has been rewarded, then the more similar the present stimulus-situation is to the past one, the more likely he is to emit the activity, or some similar activity, now.[8]

In the revised edition, Homans renames this the "stimulus proposition" to emphasize his intention to link human behavior with environmental stimuli. It is restated thus:

> 1. If in the past the occurrence of a particular stimulus, or set of stimuli, has been the occasion on which a person's action has been rewarded, then the more similar the present stimuli are to the past ones, the more likely the person is to perform the action, or some similar action, now.[9]

Let us take these propositions apart. First, Homans's reference is to some person's past. As in learning theory, a person's past is of particular importance to his present behavior. According to the proposition, the past is composed of situations in which the person was either rewarded or punished. Some aspects of the past have bearing on the probability of behaving in similar ways now. Homans expects that history is, at least in some gross way, repeatable. When one of the situations in which a person has been rewarded recurs, behavior of the kind displayed in the previous situation will be repeated. This is really no different from expecting Strong the dog to walk on his hind legs in response to rewards given by his master. Strong and master created the original situation, and now the master can control things by reminding Strong of the rewarding aspects of the previous situation. The emphasis of Homans's proposition is on the individual's response to pleasing circumstances and his willingness and ability to emit voluntarily behavior of this kind again.

[8] Homans, *Social Behavior,* p. 53.
[9] Ibid., rev. ed., pp. 22–3.

2. The more often within a given period of time a man's activity rewards the activity of another, the more often the other will emit the activity.[10]

The revised edition labels this the "success proposition," and restates it as follows:

2. For all actions taken by persons, the more often a particular action of a person is rewarded, the more likely the person is to perform that action.[11]

Of special interest here is the fact the Homans has introduced the time element. We more easily count frequencies of actions than infer strength of feeling. The propositions say there is a direct relationship between the frequency of rewarding behavior and the frequency of response to the reward. This proposition combines two of the things Homans is especially interested in, reward and activity, and states the kind of relationship he expects between them. In form, this statement fulfills the requirements of a general proposition for deductive theory.

3. The more valuable to a man a unit of the activity another gives him, the more often he will emit the activity rewarded by the activity of another.[12]

This proposition is called the "value proposition" in the revised edition, and is rewritten as follows:

3. The more valuable to a person the result of his action, the more likely he is to perform the action.[13]

These propositions give the expected relationship between value and activity. Individuals have their own ideas about what they value, and values are not the same to all people. The theory forecasts a direct relationship between frequency of activity achieving valued reward and the degree of value the reward carries. If it is extremely important that a person obtain the goodwill of his roommate at all times, he will be at particular pains to behave so that this is forthcoming. Because the person cannot do everything at once, there may be times when he has to choose between pleasing his roommate and doing something else that might also be of benefit. In situations like that, if the relative values of pleasing the roommate is greater, then this is the activity our friend will choose. The greater the number of alternatives outweighed by pleasing the roommate, the more often roommate-pleasing activities will be attempted; as the proposition says, the more often we can expect the behavior.

Here exchange theory is stated in terms of units that appear measurable or countable. Although it is hard to measure value (something

[10] Homans, *Social Behavior*, p. 54.
[11] Ibid., rev. ed., p. 16.
[12] Homans, *Social Behavior*, p. 55.
[13] Ibid., rev. ed., p. 25.

about which more will be said later), and it is not entirely clear how to measure units of activity, the proposition is still given in what might be called observational terms. It says there should be a direct relationship between strength of rewarding activity and frequency of activity gaining the reward.

It may appear that propositions 2 and 3, the success proposition and the value proposition, are saying the same thing. However, proposition 2 gives a general relationship between reward and activity gaining the reward, whereas proposition 3 says something additional. It introduces the concept of value and says, in effect, "Proposition 2 is true, and also, the more valuable the activity discussed in proposition 2, the more it will take precedence when there is an alternative."

   4. The more often a man has in the recent past received a rewarding activity from another, the less valuable any further unit of that activity becomes for him.[14]

Proposition 4 is named the "deprivation–satiation" proposition in the revised edition of *Social Behavior,* and appears thus:

   4. The more often in the recent past a person has received a particular reward, the less valuable any further unit of that reward becomes for him.[15]

This proposition might appear to contradict some of the others, especially propositions 2 and 3, the success and value propositions. But it does not contradict them. Notice especially that Homans has limited himself to the recent past in these propositions and that he is giving a general statement about the extra amount of activity he expects once the rewarding exchange is in progress. That is what is called a marginal statement – it is describing the effects of additional units of activity. For example, suppose a student goes to talk with his professor and finds the encounter stimulating. He would, according to proposition 2, return to visit the professor again. But he does not come back in quite the same condition as on his first visit. He is probably somewhat more informed now and, also, the professor may already have presented his most striking insights during the first meeting. The student may find that the second visit, although probably still rewarding, is not as rewarding as the first. If "visit to the professor" is the unit of activity, then unit 2 is less valuable than unit 1. Unit 3 will probably be even less rewarding, in comparison to the previous two. Proposition 4, the deprivation–satiation proposition, leads us to expect the value of these visits to decrease continually. As soon as the value of professor visits drops below whatever the competing alternative may be, the visits should stop, and the more valuable unit of activity should take over. Proposition 4, the deprivation–satiation proposi-

---

[14] Homans, *Social Behavior,* p. 55.
[15] Ibid., rev. ed., pp. 28–9.

tion, is the sociological exchange equivalent of the "law of diminishing returns" of economic theory.

> 5. The more to a man's disadvantage the rule of distributive
> justice fails of realization, the more likely he is to display the
> emotional behavior we call anger.[16]

Homans argues that it is possible to establish a rate of exchange
among traded behaviors and sentiments. In general, the investments a
person makes in an exchange, calculated in effort, commitment, time,
and the like, ought to be compensated by payoff in direct proportion.
If we invest heavily, we feel entitled to considerable reward. Additionally, we do not expect those who have not invested heavily to
receive a large measure of reward. Now if we happen to entangle
ourselves in an exchange with a person whose investments are small
in comparison to his rewards, especially at our expense, our sense of
distributive justice is outraged, and we display anger.

Some important additions are made to exchange theory by the distributive justice idea. Remember the comparative nature of value.
Exchange is a highly individualistic theory, true enough; but persons
in exchange relationships do not limit their comparisons to only those
in exchange with them. Going rates of exchange between other people
become our own standards. And though we need not assume other
people's values, they do influence our choices.

Also in connection with the idea of distributive justice is the time
dimension. Without distributive justice, one might imagine that exchange theory took no notice of the continuing nature of interaction.
Without it, it might seem that particular exchanges make up little
dramas unto themselves, which people play out for what they are
worth, and then abandon. But the emphasis on investment suggests a
time dimension; the present may be payoff for past services. In times
when the old, the hale, and the young huddled around the same stove
to keep warm, we usually found grandfather nearest the fire. This was
probably not because he had worked the hardest that day, or earned
the most for the family. Rather, grandfather "deserved" to be made
comfortable in his old age because in the past he made sacrifices for
all and underwent hardship for the family's benefit. In exchange theory terms, he made heavy investments in a lifetime series of exchanges with family members, and he is now in a position to expect
distributive justice to come into play, giving him reward.

The first four propositions were cast in terms of Homans's basic
theoretical ideas: units of activity, frequency of activity, rewards for
activity, value of activity. With the fifth proposition he introduced
distributive justice. This always seemed more difficult than the other

---

[16] Homans, *Social Behavior,* p. 75.

propositions. Distributive justice is not clearly linked to the theoretical terms of the previous propositions. In the revised edition of *Social Behavior,* Homans divided his distributive justice proposition into two and discarded the term itself. The idea remains the same, but the new propositions are expressed in terms more similar to the others. These new propositions are called the "aggression–approval" propositions. Part one says:

> When a person's action does not receive the reward he expected, or receives punishment he did not expect, he will be angry; he becomes more likely to perform aggressive behavior, and the results of such behavior become more valuable to him.[17]

This proposition introduces an additional theoretical term, "expectation," and suggests that expectation of reward must be satisfied or displeasure will follow. This seems simple enough. But additionally, if reward is not up to expectation, aggression results and such aggression, Homans says, is gratifying. Perhaps this is Homans's way of stating the getting-even idea found in the original distributive justice proposition.

The second part of the aggression–approval proposition states the same ideas in positive form:

> When a person's action receives reward he expected, especially a greater reward than he expected, or does not receive punishment he expected, he will be pleased; he will become more likely to perform approving behavior, and the results of such behavior become more valuable to him.[18]

B. The deductions

After Homans's presentation of the propositions, we would expect to find some examples of deductive theorizing. Several deductions, forming an array of hypotheses, should follow at this point. Homans himself does not provide them. Although he has been attentive to deductive theory and its logic, he has done little about derivations from his main propositions. His real concern is to illustrate the propositions thoroughly. But this does not mean that derivations are impossible. In fact, there are quite a number.

The deductive format encourages the production of hypotheses by logical inference from abstract starting points. Such inference can be the demonstration that a particular hypothesis follows directly from a general proposition in one step. This would indeed be logical inference, but it would also be rather trivial. The deduction would be obvious to most people and the production of such a hypothesis

[17] Ibid., rev. ed., p. 37.
[18] Ibid., p. 39.

would be exceedingly easy. But intermediate steps performed on Homans's propositions can yield a greater number of hypotheses that
would not be obvious. If they were all followed up, these hypotheses
could occupy any number of researchers for quite some time.

In *Social Behavior,* first edition, Homans gave at least twenty-three
such hypotheses, although he did not formally deduce them. As an
example of how the propositions may be employed to derive an implicit hypothesis, one of Homans's own theoretical statements is
given next. This statement is not directly derivable from any single
propositions in one step; we must combine some propositions.

> When the costs of avoiding interaction are great enough, a man
> will go into interaction with another even though he finds
> Other's activity punishing; and far from liking him more, he will
> like him less.[19]

Examine proposition 2, the success proposition. It says we should
expect a direct relationship between rewarded activity and the frequency of that activity. The directness of the relationship implies that
the less a man's activity is rewarded, the less frequently we should
expect this activity. This suggests that even activity that would normally be considered punishing might still be valuable. Consider, for
example, the "least of evils" condition. Homans's statement suggests
that when this occurs, a man will enter such a relationship, even if it
is punishing. This is so because he will be cutting his costs, when
compared with his other more punishing alternatives.

Now it is necessary to examine the relationship between "liking"
and the general propositions, because Homans is talking about liking
in his hypothesis; but "liking" is not a theoretical term found in the
propositions. Consider proposition 3; Homans names it the value
proposition. If an exchange ensues between persons in which liking,
or "social approval," is the currency paid in exchange for some activity, this proposition tells us to expect a direct relationship between
reward, liking in this case, and the activity that fetches it. As in
proposition 2, this direct relationship suggests that in cases where
activity leads to disliking, the expectation is that such a relationship
will entail less activity, eventually reaching zero and breaking off.

Combining these propositions, the derivation is that the unfortunate
individual Homans describes makes a cost-cutting deal with someone
because it is in his interest to do so (the success proposition), even
though he is unhappy with the results. This interaction that allows
him to avoid an even worse fate causes him to assume an interaction

---

[19] Homans, *Social Behavior,* p. 187. This statement is also derived somewhat differently in a commentary on Homans's logic by Ronald Maris in "The Logical Adequacy of Homans' Social Theory," *American Sociological Review,* XXXV (December 1970), p. 1074.

pattern he dislikes. The value proposition indicates that the more he participates in this activity, the more he will be motivated to break off the relationship because of his not liking it. But this is precisely what he cannot do. In fact, he is forced to maintain some level of participation in this relationship, enabling him to avoid the worse fate.

But why will he like this predicament less and less, instead of simply simmering away at a stable level of dislike? From proposition 4, the deprivation–satiation proposition, we see that satiation entails an inverse relationship between activity and reward. The benefits derived from avoiding the worse fate will become less valuable as time goes on. The dislike built up in the relationship will eventually come to outweigh the benefits of avoiding greater costs; "liking" will continuously decrease.

Homans's hypothesis said we should expect less liking between parties to this interaction, not more, and that the amount of liking between them would decrease. By combining the meanings of some of the propositions, which in themselves do not describe such situations, we can account for this statement. This is so despite the fact that the statement is not derived directly from any of the propositions in one step.

In principle, it is possible to examine the implications of the five propositions and, by substituting some equivalent terms or inverting the form of the statements, to derive many more hypotheses.[20] In fact, it would probably be possible to produce several hypotheses never before given. These would be logically "true" if we made the correct inferences. It would be up to the researcher to discover whether the statements were empirically true.

C. The institutional and subinstitutional in Homans's theory

We may now leave the more technical aspects of Homans's theory in order to consider some other features. Emphasis on the individual and the concepts of reward, cost, activity, and so on, have kept the discussion focused directly on the individual, or on a two-person group. Homans spends considerable time talking about his hypothetical characters, Person and Other, and how they get along with each other. But sociological theory commonly addresses units of more than two persons. Homans does go beyond Person and Other to give an exchange account of institutional and subinstitutional levels of social life.

Homans says that institutions are based on the same principles of exchange as interpersonal behavior, but that institutions are more complex networks of exchanges. The complexity is related to special-

[20] Maris derived forty statements that were logically possible extensions of Homans's propositions and the corollaries accompanying them. Ibid., pp. 1069–80.

86   *Exchange theory*

ization of activity and indirectness of exchange. By specialization, he means that tasks once done by one person are broken up and segments are performed by many different people. As a result of this, the beneficiaries are indebted to several persons, whereas before they were indebted to only one. Also, there may be many beneficiaries. Institutional arrangements stabilize these complex exchanges among many persons related by their participation in divided tasks.

Moreover, basic activities of institutions are not random, according to Homans; they must fulfill certain "needs" that are common to all.[21] This point would seem to be a departure from Homans's previous meanings of "rewards." He had emphasized that rewards are entirely the private concern of the person rewarded. Indeed, Homans made quite a point of liberating individuals from commonly held value positions – it was a cornerstone of his emphasis on individuality. But in his explanation of institutions, he modifies this stand.

Concerning institutions, he says there must be a basic and common "repertory of human nature" that causes certain emotions and needs to be rather constant. To support this view, he cites anthropological literature to show that there are various institutions in quite diverse societies that all fulfill similar needs. This appears to amount to the contention that "human nature" is not so wideranging as the extreme individualistic position suggests. Homans says:

> Cultures cannot pick up any old sorts of behavior and hope without more ado to carry them on generation after generation. What they pick up must be compatible with some fundamental reportory of human nature, though the compatibility may, of course, be complex.[22]

These fundamentals of human nature Homans later categorizes as "primary rewards."

But according to Homans, these cannot account for the growth of institutions by themselves. Because not everybody responds to these fundamental propensities,[23] persons sometimes apply secondary rewards to bring nonconformists into line. Here Homans is no longer thinking of primary rewards, but of generalized rewards such as social approval and money. In short, the argument is that secondary reinforcers are employed in support of primary ones, where the primary ones alone are not capable of ensuring collective commitment to institutional norms.

To illustrate his approach to institutions, Homans explains the norm of expressing grief.[24] He says that those who feel genuine grief

[21] Homans, *Social Behavior*, pp. 381 ff.
[22] Ibid., p. 381.
[23] Ibid.
[24] Ibid.

on certain occasions do so not because of any outside inducement, but because of their "nature." But not all who "should" feel grief do. Those who do not are induced to behave as if they did by the application of secondary reinforcers, such as the loss of esteem that would accompany a failure to express grief at appropriate times. For such people, the expression of grief is not motivated by feeling, but by the desire to gain the benefits of conformity. True grieving is a more basic sentiment than the wish to maximize gain, but gain is a partial explanation for the widespread acceptance of norms regulating the expression of grief.

And why, according to Homans, do institutions endure? It is because of the complexity of institutionalized exchanges, and because values are "handed down" to younger generations.[25] Complexity means a series of exchanges that are all related and that are therefore not easily altered. The decision to change behavior with respect to one institutionalized role probably entails alterations in other relationships. Receiving pay for a service is a useful example to illustrate this. If one is paid for working in a firm, he must attend to his relations with the paymaster, in addition to those with the foreman, the work group of which he is a part, the firm in general, and the industry as a whole, to say nothing of his desire to maximize profit and minimize costs. Such complicated situations hem us in not because they are inflexible but simply because the exchanges all influence each other. This complexity gives any particular social arrangement an inertia or staying power. It is important to recognize that Homans is not drawing a distinction in kind between interpersonal and complex institutionalized exchanges, but only pointing out differences in degree.

VI. *Exchange and the social psychology of groups: Thibaut and Kelley*

J. Thibaut and H. Kelley in *The Social Psychology of Groups*[26] adjust the focus of exchange theory somewhat, but they do not depart from the general idea very far. Their interest is not so much in the individual and how he functions in a relationship as in the relationship itself. They wish to explain it as a set of predictable outcomes, which are understood very much along the lines of Homans's explanation of individuals. Note, too, that their interest is mainly to explain the dyad, the two-person group, discussion of which forms the bulk of *The Social Psychology of Groups*. Thibaut and Kelley explicitly assume what Homans only implies: Exchange analysis of the dyad is

---

[25] Ibid., rev. ed., p. 41.
[26] New York: Wiley, 1959.

A's repertoire

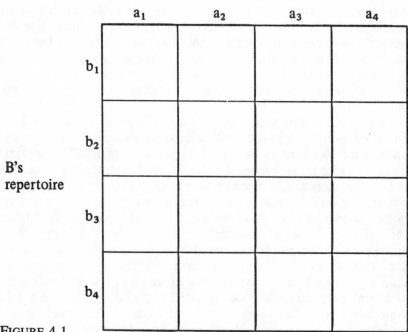

FIGURE 4.1

the proper theoretical standpoint from which to understand the larger group. They assume that if they can theoretically portray the dyad, they can subsequently extend the theory to encompass larger and more complex social relationships.[27] When making critical remarks on exchange theory, we shall return to this assumption.

Thibaut and Kelley use a "behavior matrix" as an analytical tool to clarify their idea of exchange. In the matrix, a two-dimensional space represents the possible behaviors of two persons. Along one dimension are placed descriptions of all the behaviors possible for one member of the interaction, and along the other dimension are placed those of the second person. By crosstabulating the two dimensions, several cells are constructed as shown in Figure 4.1.[28] In each cell, it is possible to imagine the desirability of the behavior of each partner by examining the outcomes represented for each. Thibaut and Kelley assume that "interaction is continued only if the experienced consequences are found to meet the standards of acceptability that both

[27] Ibid., Introduction, pp. 1–9.
[28] After Thibaut and Kelley's figures, see ibid., pp.14–18, for the general description of such matrices.

individuals develop by experience in other relationships."[29] Thibaut and Kelley expect that the cell representing maximum desirability for both persons is the one that predicts the behavior each will display, and that it predicts the relationship in which the two will engage.

In deciding the desirability of outcomes, a person necessarily has his own ideas about rewards and costs. Thibaut and Kelley divide these into *exogenous* and *endogenous* factors. Exogenous ones are those brought to the relationship by the participants in the form of values, needs, skills, or any other qualities that may transcend the particular interaction. Endogenous determinants of rewards and costs are those intrinsic to the relationship itself. These two types of factors, taken from the viewpoint of both persons, are potentially paired. A good outcome for one could match a good outcome for the other. If it does, interaction of a type allowing this to happen ensues. In this way, Thibaut and Kelley predict the *relationship* and not individual actions.[30]

Similar to Homans's theory is Thibaut and Kelley's idea that individuals evaluate their outcomes both according to the reward or cost directly involved and according to the alternatives available. Using Thibaut and Kelley's terms, these comparisons are made according to *comparison levels*. A comparison level is a hypothetical measuring rod by which a participant decides whether or not his activity is getting him a just return for effort.[31] The *comparison level for alternatives* is the external measuring rod he uses to see if a similar amount of effort spent elsewhere might gain a better reward.[32] Remember there are two balls in the air at once. Enduring interaction will be that which satisfies two persons' comparison levels for alternatives, not just one person's.

Thibaut and Kelley construct an exchange-based theory of face-to-face interpersonal behavior, but they also claim that such a theory has wider implications. Relationships developed by the maximization of outcome eventually become stable. The things we expect people to do tend to be predictable by association with the situation, and not directly from an analysis of reward and cost. When the participants achieve such a stable relationship, Thibaut and Kelley believe it becomes normal for people to be less concerned with precise calculation and comparison of reward. Habits established in this fashion take the emphasis off exchange; behavior becomes automatic. Thibaut and Kelley thus arrive at an explanation of stable exchange patterns in which the cognitive calculation of reward is of decreasing importance.

---

[29] Ibid., p. 10.
[30] Ibid., See Ch. 8, "Norms and Rules," pp. 126–48.
[31] Ibid., pp. 21–3.
[32] Ibid., See Ch. 4, "Interference and Facilitation in Interaction," pp. 51–63.

This kind of reasoning supports additional basic principles in Thibaut and Kelley's account of larger groups.

How do Thibaut and Kelley account for the third person; how does the theory of the dyad become the theory of large groups? This is important. Sociology probably needs this level of analysis more than that of the dyad alone. For several reasons following from individualistic psychology, the third person is problematic. For instance, the group might break down into smaller units, eventually reaching the dyad again. Thibaut and Kelley realize there are cases like this – isolation of members, or cases in which only two members of a group really care to continue relating.[33] But their more interesting assertions, to which we turn now, are those about the benefits of group relations for all involved.

In this category, Thibaut and Kelley include the notion that an "economy of scale" can be obtained, in which it is more profitable to produce one's favorable outcomes collectively, because for some reason it is cheaper to do so. Joint enjoyment of rewards and mutual facilitation of enjoyment are also expected. These points imply the notion that collective rewards are privately motivated, and that such rewards are easier to get collectively. (We shall return to such implications of exchange theory in the critical section of this chapter). Then too, Thibaut and Kelley suggest that sequential patterns of dyadic exchange account for the attractiveness of some groups, although a series of dyadic exchanges is not usually what is meant by group action.

An important assertion is that emergent properties of larger groups exist that do not appear with only two participants. An example of this might be found in a problem-solving team, in which each member adds his contribution, imperfect though it may be, with the result of a more impressive or better solution than could be had by one or two persons alone. Also, coalitions could be formed in which the larger group breaks up into smaller factions. The guiding principle for this breakup is the matching of favorable outcomes among subgroups. If the whole group cannot achieve a mutual matching of favorable outcomes, perhaps some members can. Failure of total mutual matching leads to pairing off of some persons, or coalitions.

Thibaut and Kelley's work has been richer in concepts than in explicit formal deductions. Their work is indeed "theoretical." They give a set of general principles that organizes the data they present. But the logical procedures for deriving conclusions from starting points are often skipped. Remember what was said about having to take theoretical ideas as we find them, and not being too quick to

[33] Ibid., p. 197.

reject something because it is incomplete. We have now seen two examples of how the work of the theoretician is indeed long and hard. Homans's propositions require considerable manipulation to achieve connective links between propositions and hypotheses. Thibaut and Kelley's work is valuable because it sets up a solid beginning in a particular mode of theory building, and it is up to the user to provide the finishing touches if he feels a need for them.

VII. *Exchange and power: Blau's use of exchange principles*

Peter Blau's book *Exchange and Power in Social Life*[34] is of special interest because his intention is to add more principles from economic theory to the social exchange viewpoint.

A. *Blau's interest in exchange*

In describing exchange theory, this chapter first emphasized individuality and the atomized view of social life that emerges when psychological elements of exchange are stressed. In the works by Homans and Thibaut and Kelley, major attention was focused on the dyad, although attempts to explain larger groups were conscientiously made. Blau concentrates on social structures that grow out of exchange, and on order, legitimation, opposition, power, and the like. Blau maintains the view, similar to that of Homans and Thibaut and Kelley, that it is appropriate to approach social structure from the individualistic viewpoint, and that, in the main, we should run into no insurmountable problems if we do. He feels we do not need any assumptions about groups themselves in order to build a theoretical account of group action. This attitude, that explanation in sociology can run smoothly upward from the smallest to the largest unit of analysis, aptly characterizes the exchange position regarding social structure.

First, consider Blau's particular view of exchange. In general, he examines the kind of mutual exchange interaction previously described, with special attention to the types of rewards and costs involved. He assumes that persons wish to maximize rewards and minimize costs, but that imbalances inevitably arise. Some exchange deals will not equally reward both parties. To the less fortunate, a cost that cannot be recouped is incurred to produce the other's pleasure. This is an *imbalance*. The unbalanced nature of most exchanges impresses Blau, and he sees this as the key issue in understanding the emergence of group structure and social power.[35] To collapse his

[34] New York: Wiley, 1964.
[35] Ibid., pp. 4–5.

theme into one statement, one might venture this: Blau is trying to work out the details of how social structures stabilize exchanges, while also depicting the ways these stabilizations engender opposing forces, eventually tending to alter stabilized exchanges.

B. Unbalanced exchanges: some consequences

Imbalance in an exchange can occur when one party is capable of rewarding more than the recipient is capable of reciprocating. Of course, there may be alternatives available and the relationship may break off; but all such relationships do not break off. In fact, Blau suggests that the usual nature of social exchange is imbalance. The lesser party in unbalanced exchanges might compensate his benefactor by a species of general reinforcement that Homans has called social approval. Blau refers to this as subordination or compliance.[36] This means that in return for getting a benefit for which one cannot pay in full measure, one tends to give up some of his will to the other and become subordinate.

Subordination in unbalanced exchanges is a kind of "credit" to the superior partner. It credits him in the sense that his position becomes well known, especially where exchanges are public. It is also credit in a more "economic" sense. His will can come to dominate, for he is allowed a kind of license to command others that ordinary persons do not have. This is likened to having command of other people's money when one receives a note of credit from a bank.

The upshot of unbalanced exchanges is not free license, of course, because complying persons always evaluate exchange according to the principles of cost and reward. They might take away their compliance. But several factors induce them to continue in subordinate positions. The great utility of having someone in command is that it promotes efficient task performance. Everyone knows that any task that is too much for one person must be divided, and this division requires a coordinator who recombines the divided parts to complete the whole. Everyone is not capable of leadership, insight, and the like. Also, everyone knows the cliché about too many chiefs and not enough Indians; coordination of effort requires that both command and compliance be features of goal-directed social systems. Finally, compliance shifts responsibility to the one in authority. For all of these reasons, people may be willing to continue in a subordinate position.

Structural analysis in sociology is the investigation of arrangements for coordinated effort toward collective goals. Blau works his way

[36] Ibid., pp. 170 ff.

toward explaining structure by way of unbalanced exchanges, plus the concept of legitimacy. Legitimate social structure has the general acceptance of participants. Where legitimacy obtains, structure may be refined and elaborated, and to the extent that it remains legitimate it will endure. To the extent that structures fail, become corrupt, exceed the control of their members, and so on, members will withdraw their opinion that structures are legitimate. Blau then sees forces arising that change the structure. Thus social structures founded on exchanges may develop, retain, or lose legitimacy, and this will either increase social stability or promote change.

But this picture is too simple. Exchanges that involve a number of people will be viewed differently by each. Legitimacy and illegitimacy of social structures are not absolute conditions, but only tendencies. There are simultaneous forces, some encouraging and entrenching social structures and others working in the opposite direction. A recurrent theme in Blau's work is that situations have particularly happy results in one way, but very unhappy results when viewed another way. In such situations, it is impossible to maximize collectively all persons' satisfaction judged by their various values and alternatives. We cannot have the cake and eat it, too. Blau suggests that when people face such situations, they sit on the fence. When one kind of result starts to outweigh the other, they alter course to minimize the unpleasantness associated with a bad series of outcomes, perhaps knowing all the time that the change will entail other unpleasantness, as well as other kinds of benefits. This lack of clear, all-or-nothing alternatives is explored but not clearly formulated by Homans and Thibaut and Kelley. Blau makes it the keynote of his view of exchange.

C. *Kinds of rewards and kinds of relationships*

There are additional parallels between Blau's work on exchange and the other exchange theories. For Homans and for Thibaut and Kelley, the concept of value implies comparisons between action at hand and other possible action. In Blau's work, this same theoretical idea turns up in the form of a typology of rewards: *intrinsic* and *extrinsic*. This typology corresponds to Thibaut and Kelley's endogenous and exogenous rewards. Associations based on "intrinsic" rewards are their own reward; there may not be much of utilitarian value to be gained in them. Where intrinsic rewards are mutual, the relationship is one of "mutual attraction," which amounts to giving a name to something considered "natural." Exchanges based on intrinsic bonds can have all the earmarks of other kinds of exchanges. They stabilize associations, give rise to norms of conduct, give satisfaction; but they are not really exchange relationships in the economic sense, where something is given and something taken, the give and take being the reason for the relationship. "Extrinsic" relationships unite exchange partners who participate in the relationship for a gain of their own choosing. "Value" enters here as a theoretical term, because it is in pursuit of some valued item that persons participate. Comparisons among alternatives become possible in principle; reciprocal extrinsic exchanges are the basic form of exchange, apart from naturally occurring intrinsic ones.

But what if reciprocation is introduced as a variable? Considering that any given exchange can be either reciprocated or not, we see that unreciprocated intrinsic relationships will lead to the grief of only one partner, as his attentions will go unrequited. This may be unhappy, but perhaps not serious. However, if an extrinsic relationship goes unreciprocated – if one expects something or is led to expect something that is not forthcoming – then we have a more potent case. If the lack of reciprocation is caused by one partner's inability to repay, then the way is open for a power dependency of the poorer on the richer. If the lack of reciprocation is on the part of the stronger, then the weaker will see his compliance as fruitless and he may withdraw it. Hence by introducing two variables (intrinsic–extrinsic; reciprocation–"unreciprocation"), we can trace the types of possible outcomes of exchange relationships.

This may all seem obvious enough, but in Blau's hands it becomes quite insightful. For instance, what appears to be an intrinsic relationship must have started as an extrinsic one. Most of the time, there is no special reason for two persons gaining reward simply by being together. Furthermore, if a relationship starts as extrinsic, there are hidden dangers in it for all parties. It is probably normal for persons getting to know one another to want to be "regular" types. Neither exposes anything that might repel the other, if they care anything about the relationship that is forming. But to be too "normal" could ruin everything, because such blandness might be insufficiently comely to attract and hold exchange partners. It is for each to select some strategy that introduces something of interest to the other without putting him off. But if such a relationship is to result in one partner's having dominance over the other, superior qualities must be exposed. Braggarts are frowned upon, but radiantly superior people are esteemed. A fine line distinguishes the two as people form exchange relationships.

In groups, similar problems beset social integration, making what might appear a simple case of mutual attraction a complex one in danger of collapse. Impressive and useful qualities are what draw people together in extrinsic reciprocal relationships. But dilemmas arise. To what extent ought the superior person be accorded esteem? Clearly if his services are not recompensed in some right relation to his worth, he will be lost. But too-willing compliance threatens the complier's status. ("No matter how valuable you are, I cannot become dirt under your feet.") Hence there will be a tendency to protect status by underpaying valued associates, and consequently a danger of losing them.

Blau has also added light to the matter of competition. Surely competition for status occurs along more than one line. Nobody has everything and everyone else nothing. Thus competition for the esteem of others has a tendency to break up the group along the different dimensions of competition. But the different ways in which one may excel tend to hold it together. If superiority is distributed among group members according to the different requirements of the group, then status competition can be smoothed over while the various tasks get done. Here Blau has again shown the utility of his structural focus on exchange. The dangers to social structure arising from competition are counterbalanced by the group's requirements, its tasks, and the various kinds of rewards its members want. He clearly shows that the structural relations among members enhance integration. It is the structure resulting from exchanges that endures despite the constant danger of collapse.

D. Microstructures and macrostructures

It is Blau's contention that the same basic processes that characterize face-to-face relations are typical of larger units. Face-to-face interactions Blau calls *microstructures*.[37] They are "structures" in the sense that regulatory rules, dominance, power, legitimate control, and task division are all supported, temporarily at least, by the rewarding nature of the interactions based on them. They are "micro" in that the interaction is face-to-face. But sooner or later size will get in the way. As the numbers to be accommodated increase, it becomes more sensible to talk about formal organizations, committees, bureaucracies, and the like. These larger collectivities are themselves composed of microstructures. Blau's view of the social organization of society is one of the interconnections among these larger *macrostructures* by a variety of means.[38] To examine his account of social solidarity in exchange terms, we do not have to introduce many new ideas. We apply the old ones, because the principles of exchange apply to macrostructures as well as microstructures.

---

[37] Ibid., pp. 253–4.
[38] Ibid. See Ch. 11, "Dynamics of Substructures," pp. 283–311, especially pp. 284 ff.

1. Values and social structure

Studying exchange has shown that persons valuing rewards for their
own reasons will congregate, by and large, in groups that can further
individuals' ends, while interpersonal dynamics assures that wildly
differing or opposed values will be modified or ejected. Also, the
common goals for which organization is undertaken will have an integrative effect. What is the consequence of this for social solidarity?
Sharing group values will have two kinds of consequences, from
Blau's viewpoint.[39] The first is that sharing becomes a mark of solidarity for those who share. And secondly, the same sharing that leads
to integration and commitment will be a mark of dissimilarity with
respect to other groups. By holding different values, groups are
marked out as distinct from each other, and this can lead to hostility
and disunity between them. More than this, values having such effects pose dilemmas for individuals. Being highly committed to the
values held in one's group is a method of gaining status in it, but such
commitment might simultaneously earn particular dislike from one
who does not share the values. Being a "good citizen" and a good
group member may conflict. This tendency is counteracted to some
extent, says Blau, by the fact that all values do not have this double
effect. For instance, commitment to financial success may have the
effect of unifying society, for it is something most agree upon. Also,
such general agreement provides a dimension of comparability, as
when financial success becomes a point of comparison between individuals. To the extent that personal competition endangers microstructures and entrenches divided macrostructures, it again presents
individuals with dilemmas of loyalty and self-interest. The fact that
financial success is a widely accepted guide to social achievement
gives some coherence to the social structure as a whole, and also
ensures that it will become divided between those who do relatively
well and those who do not. Blau is suggesting that one consequence
of having universal values is the aggravation of associated divisive
tendencies.

Again a simplified example has been invoked to make a point, and
now things must be complicated slightly to represent Blau's idea more
effectively. Social structure has opposing tendencies latent in it that
make social solidarity problematic. But over against this, we must see
a mosaic of macrostructures, all side by side at the same time. Individuals belong to many at once, and this overlap gives a continuity
through membership that usually denies divisive forces free rein.
Also, macrostructures are themselves interpenetrating; there may be

[39] Ibid., pp. 91 ff.

several with the same general goals, or with complementary ones. Movements toward ecumenism in modern religious circles can be seen as a case in point. Further, the boundaries between macrostructures may not be as clear as the theoretical description has suggested, and this fluidity (perhaps resulting from mobility of membership) will have its effect on solidarity. Because there are different kinds of macrostructures, we can expect the diversity to have a partially solidifying effect on the whole. For example, class consciousness crosscuts communities and bureaucracies, providing points of contact that could not be predicted from the knowledge of class, community, or bureaucracy alone.

E. Additional analogies to economic theory used by Blau

Obviously exchange theory borrows from economics when it employs ideas like cost, profit, and investments as theoretical terms. Blau has gone quite deeply into economic theory, seeking parallels in it to sociological explanation. His reasoning is that if we were to make preliminary assumptions about social exchange similar to those of economic theory, then, by following up these assumptions, we would be carried along toward specific theoretical conclusions about social exchanges. Following this line of reasoning, Blau's discussion of the "dynamics of change and adjustment in groups" is drawn from economic theory – specifically, from price theory. If the economists can explain the rise and fall of prices in relation to demand, supply, and economic markets, then exchange theory might attempt a similar analysis using sociological concepts. Hopefully, this exercise could yield specific predictions, obtained deductively, from general ideas.

Let us examine Blau's use of "indifference curves."[40] This will give an indication of the lengths to which the economic analogy of exchange theory may be taken, and the kind of sophistication Blau seeks. First, we must know what "marginal analysis" is. When we speak of margins, we mean additional units. If we think only of totals, problems arise: How to measure value? Because we do not have the units with which to measure value, marginal analysis does not try. Instead, it takes a comparative view. It says in effect that, rather than try to account for the value of an activity, one ought to compare the effects of having additional units of it. This approach will show how one additional unit compares with the addition of the previous unit, and how added units of others compare. Note that we do not know about a person's total satisfaction in exchange; however, we seek to make inferences about that from observing how additional units of valued action affect him.

---

[40] The following discussion follows Blau's Ch. 7, ibid., pp. 168 ff.

1. The law of diminishing marginal utility

The law of diminishing marginal utility in economics is similar to Homans's proposition 4.[41] It says that as persons receive added units of a given valued activity, each additional unit will be less valuable. This is easily seen in the case where we are down to our last dollar, or to our last unit of some social behavior. The problem is what to do with this last unit. The answer is: Do that which gains the most. To know which act will gain the most, it is important to have a comparative perspective on the several things that might be done, to compare the marginal utilities of all possibilities.

Obviously, the decision about what to do with the last unit will change according to what we have been doing recently. Alternatives will be at different levels of satiation. Less marginally useful possibilities will be rejected; the marginally more important will take precedence. There is a dynamic force at work here. Although we always expect persons to do what gains them the most with their last unit of effort, we cannot always expect this to be the same thing. The economic market analogy, based on marginal utility, is dynamic, always changing in response to its personnel. This is why Blau picks marginal analysis to try to understand the dynamics of change and adjustment in groups. He is looking for theoretical principles to elucidate the change and adjustment process and to yield predictions of group behavior, just as the economist might predict the behavior of an economic market using similar principles.

Note that by using this kind of analysis, Blau is trying to take the theoretical step between explaining the individual and explaining group structure. If he can derive out of such theory an account of stable social systems as emergent properties, while retaining the individualistic viewpoint, he will have advanced toward explaining the group by individualistic means.

2. Indifference curves

A productive use of the law of diminishing marginal utility is found in indifference curves. To use marginal analysis to understand a person faced with spending his last unit of resource, imagine the simplest case, one in which he has only two alternatives. Does he wish to give his last unit for some of this or for some of that? Does he want ten candy bars or three magazines, both of which might be bought with his last dollar? If he is indifferent, we have discovered something about him. We have discovered that, at the moment, his value

---

[41] See section V.A of this chapter for proposition 4.

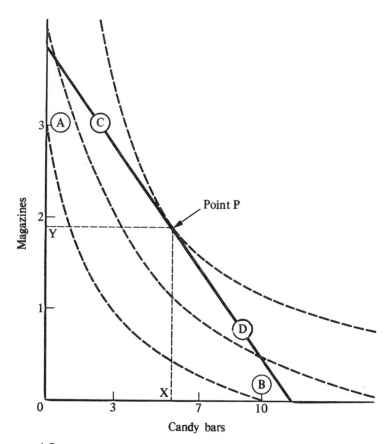

FIGURE 4.2

scheme gives ten candy bars equal value with three magazines. We have discovered something about the relative reward value of candy bars and magazines, too.

But there are other combinations. Perhaps the person would feel equally attracted to several combinations: seven candy bars and one magazine, or three candy bars and two magazines. Theoretically extending this kind of approach, we can draw up an indifference map, a set of curves on a graph indicating all the choices between two alternatives that the person is indifferent about.

In Figure 4.2, the curve AB indicates the situation just described. The additional lines represent different combinations of candy bars and magazines that may be had for different amounts of outlay. Note line CD. This Blau calls the "opportunity line"; economists call it a budget restraint line. It represents the outer limit of an individual's

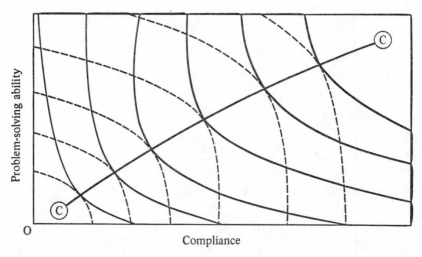

FIGURE 4.3

resources, and has been placed arbitrarily in Figure 4.2. Moving out from the origin of the graph (point 0 on both scales) indicates increased expenditure. When we reach the budget restraint line, we cannot go farther because there is nothing more to spend.

Theoretically speaking, how would a person maximize his reward with a given amount of resources? The prediction is that he would choose the combination of candy bars and magazines that gives him highest reward from both, but that is still within his means. This is indicated by the point where the "opportunity line" just touches, or is tangent to, the highest possible indifference curve (point P). It is this point on the graph that portrays the maximum satisfaction obtainable from spending the limited amount of resources indicated by the opportunity line – other points are either above the opportunity line, and unobtainable, or below it and therefore on lower indifference curves. References to the horizontal and vertical axes of the diagram from point P indicate the numbers of candy bars and magazines that represent choices maximizing utility (points X and Y).

3. Bilaterial monopoly – the two-person exchange

Follow now as Blau departs from economic theory somewhat, taking indifference curves with him. He uses them to describe the interaction between two persons in extrinsic exchange. Specifically, Blau uses indifference curves to predict exchanges, for example, between two workmates, one of superior knowledge and the other of less. Here help is exchanged for compliance. The exchange is two-sided (bilateral), and the supplies of help and compliance are entirely controlled by the persons giving them. Blau reasons that two sets of indifference curves, placed back-to-back graphically, can give a description of a bilateral exchange that ensues. In his example (see Figure 4.3), he places problem-solving ability on one axis and willing compliance on the other.

By adding two sets of curves, Blau has used the assumption explaining one indifference map for one person to explain a two-person exchange. The assumptions are that each person will try to maximize utility by getting on the highest indifference line he can. Without introducing the opportunity line again (which does play some part in the development, however), Blau concludes that the optimum conditions for exchange are the points at which the two sets of indifference curves are tangent to each other. A line can be put through these points, which he calls the "contract line" (line CC in Figure 4.3). It indicates that for any level of effort on the part of either party, there is only one point on the contract line that represents the point of adjustment to which the exchange will approximate. This point lies on the contract line. The contract line marks off quantities of "problem-solving ability" and quantities of "compliance," represented on the vertical and horizontal axes of the graph.

Blau is now attaining his objective. By economic analysis he is trying to give a general prediction about the amounts of compliance and problem-solving effort that will be spent in an exchange, considering different amounts of resources available to the two parties. His box diagram (Figure 4.3), a combination of indifference curves, summarizes information on problem-solving ability, amounts of compliance, the various combinations of these to which each is indifferent, and the theoretical points in terms of these at which the exchange will stabilize, assuming exchange partners act to maximize reward.

The scope of this description does not permit further advances into Blau's economic theory analogies. The case of indifference curves has demonstrated his approach. Notice that the analogies to economic theory are in deductive form, but not in prose. In dealing with Homans's work, we described an example of deductive theory by interpreting propositions to deduce a result. With Blau's economic theory analogies, we see deductive theory in new guise. Here it is applied in graphic form to indicate hypotheses. Blau has been criticized for his application of economic theory to social science, on theoretical and logical grounds, and for other reasons. Some of the theoretical criticisms will be discussed presently, but it should be emphasized that his work has shown how far the deductive format can carry us and how, by conscious effort to maintain a small number of basic assumptions, theoretical accounts of social behavior are built up.

VIII. Representative research arising out of exchange theory

There is a symbiotic relationship between theory and research. Rather than being in separate universes, as is sometimes thought, they complement each other. In this section, we shall discuss research that bears on the relationship between pure exchange theory and basic research. Such research shows the truth of the claim that to "prove" a theory, or at least confirm it, is a very hard job, carried out by many workers who do a variety of different tasks.

It should not be surprising that one would seek standardized measures to use with exchange theory in laboratory experiments and field observations. The basic questions are: What is exchanged, and how? Let us examine one example of a practical solution to this problem.

Longabaugh tried to work out a set of standard categories as a guide to making observations of exchanges.[42] To the question of "What is rewarding?" he can offer only an ad hoc answer. Remember, exchange theorists are loath to say anything too specific about what is generally rewarding for fear of transgressing their assumption about individual differences. But now the emphasis on individualism becomes troublesome. Longabaugh writes that rewarding things may be as narrowly defined as "my mother's smile," or as broadly as "information," and that rewards should be defined to correspond to what is "actually valued." But surely there is no systematic way of doing this! As long as values can be anything, there can be no standard categorization of value; standardized observation allowing comparison between instances of exchange will be difficult indeed. We are left with the inference that what we observe must have been rewarding. We can know nothing for certain about which aspects of situations are rewarding, and, in part for that reason, it is hard to know why they were rewarding.

But concerning the ways exchanges occur, Longabaugh proposes a set of categories based heavily on common sense. These are: seeking, offering, depriving, accepting, and not accepting. The point is that the exchange process may be regarded as a series of two-choice decisions; once one person seeks, the other has a choice of offering or retaining what is sought. Once the offer is made, the seeker has a choice of accepting or not accepting, and so on. The objective of this methodological exercise is to sensitize observers to instances of seeking, offering, depriving, accepting, and not accepting, and to develop a standardized way to note these acts. When the observation session is over, the standardized notations may be analyzed to discover pat-

---

[42] Richard Longabaugh, "A Category System for Coding Interpersonal Behavior as Social Exchange," *Sociometry*, XXVI, 3 (1963), pp. 319–44.

terns that might correlate with other measures of satisfaction, satiation, and the like.

Note that the researcher is faced with problems of empirical application that run parallel to the theoretical problems of exchange. Where the theoretical idea of "reward" is derived from general principles, so also the question of what is exchanged must be faced empirically. Similarly, when theoretical discussions turned to how an exchange would be carried out, we could expect the empirical application of exchange theory to require measurement of the process. Insofar as exchange theorists refused to say specifically what they meant by "value" and "reward," they were being true to their theoretical principles. They wished to emphasize individualism and uniqueness, and they did. But when it comes to the empirical importance of these theoretical terms, their meanings seem to vanish into thin air. If virtually anything can be of value, the researcher has no guideline to follow in making observations. In this case, a good theoretical idea turns out to be a poor empirical one.

Considerable research attention has been paid to the standard example of exchange given in theoretical work – indebtedness and the "flow" of deference and obligation from one person to another. One study proceeded on the assumption that indebtedness was an "aversive" state, and that it ought to be considered a motivator toward reduction or elimination of indebtedness.[43] In an experiment, Greenberg and Shapiro showed that feeling indebted does appear to be aversive, and that persons who do not expect to be able to repay a social debt are less likely than normal to engage in social exchanges where debts would be incurred. Similar studies have arranged things so that the subjects experience "weighted" exchanges, in which one person achieves most of a common goal for which two parties work together.[44] When self-esteem was measured independently, it was found that high achievement in the experiment led to greater self-esteem, as predicted by the general exchange approach. Additionally, obligation among friends tended to show up as deference, whereas obligation among strangers tended to appear as greater effort in later trials of the experiment.

A more general problem in sociology is understanding the attractiveness of work. Specifically, why are some satisfied with and attracted to their jobs, and why are others dissatisfied? Is this a function of the difficulty of the job itself, or how pleasant it is, or other

[43] Martin Greenberg and Solomon Shapiro, "Indebtedness: An Adverse Aspect of Asking for and Receiving Help," *Sociometry*, XXXIV, 2 (1971), pp. 290–301.
[44] Eugene Weinstein, William DeVaughan, and Mary Wiley, "Obligation and the Flow of Deference in Exchange," *Sociometry*, XXXII, 1 (1969), pp. 1–12.

facts influencing the experience of reward? Suspecting that job satisfaction is less related to the work and more related to the sociological
setting, Yuchtman studied the officers and workers in an Israeli kibbutz.[45] His finding from comparison of these two groups was that the
officers experienced more intrinsic and extrinsic rewards from their
work, but liked it less, than did the typical production workers. The
explanation for this finding is drawn from exchange theory. Yuchtman
compared the managers' experienced rewards with the apparent responsibility of the work, noting that the tasks they performed were in
an especially egalitarian setting. Apparently, even though the tasks
were rewarding to the managers both materially and psychologically,
they were not rewarding enough. The lack was explained by the egalitarian ideology. Managers appeared to feel they were not allowed due
reward, or their reward was not sufficiently different from those whose
jobs were less responsible. This is roughly the prediction that could be
drawn from exchange theory, especially from Homans's idea of distributive justice. Blau's treatment of the relationships among esteem,
unbalanced exchanges, and compliance also suggests such a finding.

Sociological field work has been done that bears in part on the
extent to which the exchange hypothesis can be widely applied. Muir
reports on research into the experience of social debt by members of
various social classes.[46] He shows that social debt is unknown to no
one, but that it is experienced in different ways. Generally, his findings are that the higher the class, the more cognitively the exchange
process is mapped by the participants; the higher the class, the more
concerned persons are with returning equal measure. Conversely, his
lower-class respondents indicated indebtedness to each other, but
were less concerned about getting or giving in proportion, and they
reported more willingness to give without expectation of reward. This
kind of work is valuable because it brings to light effects not antici-
pated by the general theoretical approach, and it challenges the theory to explain the findings. Here is an example of the way research
generated by a theory can exhibit unexpected results, which then call
for interpretation. If successfully incorporated, the results of work
like Muir's can improve exchange theory.

IX. Some critical remarks about exchange theory

It is not enough for theorists merely to outline theoretical systems.
Someone must be concerned about theories as logical systems, and

[45] Ephraim Yuchtman, "Reward Distribution and Work-Role Attractiveness in the
Kibbutz – Reflections on Equity Theory," *American Sociological Review*, XXXVII,
3 (October 1972), pp. 581–95.
[46] Donal Muir, "The Social Debt: An Investigation of Lower-Class and Middle-Class
Norms of Social Obligation," *American Sociological Review*, XXVII, 4 (August
1962), pp. 532–9.

about the ways theory contributes to empirical knowledge. Theorists who are not actually writing new theory normally do these things. We shall sketch some of the important critical work done on exchange theory, partly to understand it better, and partly as an exercise in straight thinking.

A. Is exchange theory falsifiable?

Chapter 3 emphasizes that a theory ought to be falsifiable.[47] Briefly, this means it must say things that could be proved wrong so that one could know whether the theory was "telling the truth." If there is no theoretical or practical way to check this, a theory is much less valuable as an aid to research or insight. Sadly, there are several reasons why we must conclude that exchange theory is largely unfalsifiable.

Consider reward, the cornerstone of exchange theory. From experimental psychology it enters Homans's propositions: It appears in Thibaut and Kelley's work and in Blau's. It is used by implication, in the research studies cited, for instance, in the case of the kibbutz managers' finding their jobs unsatisfying. But what, precisely, do people find rewarding?[48] Remember following Homans to the conclusion that we must not specify too narrowly what is rewarding to people, lest we violate our emphasis on individualism, human variability, and freedom to have particular values of one's own. Upon closer inspection, this decision to emphasize individual uniqueness shows some of its darker implications for exchange theory's logic. If man can value just anything, and if there must be no theoretical scheme by which we understand categories of reward, or make additional assumptions about the rewarding aspects of behavior, we can predict everything (and nothing) using reward as the key concept. For example, one critic has discovered that in some of Homans's recent writings on exchange, at some point he says it is rewarding to: husband one's resources and not husband one's resources; be an egoist and be an altruist; conform to group norms and deviate from group norms; pay a low price and pay a high price; be concerned with status and disregard status.[49] This criticism echos Longabaugh's empirical problem with value, but it has additional theoretical importance. "Reward" and "value" are indeed used as explanatory terms, but in every case they are used to explain something that has already happened, and they are used *ad hoc*. That is, we might observe a man doing something and, to explain his doing it, suggest that it might have been

[47] See Chapter 3, pp. 38–66.
[48] W. Nevill Razak raises this point, among others, in "Razak on Homans," letter to *American Sociological Review*, XXXI, 4 (August 1966), pp. 542–3.
[49] Bengt Abrahamsson, "Homans on Exchange: Hedonism Revisited," *American Journal of Sociology*, LXXVI, 2 (September 1970), p. 281.

rewarding to him or else he would not have done it. Knowing nothing about the man's values or his previous state of reward or punishment, adding the concept of reward is really to add nothing. We could say, "He did it; I saw him." What more do we know, or what more can we predict, when we add, "It must have been rewarding to him"? Whatever he might do, the explanation remains the same. There is no way to prove the theory wrong, if it is.

Additionally, reward is the basis for other central concepts in exchange theory. For example, the formula "profit equals reward minus cost" is in part derived from the concept of reward because "cost" is itself a dimension of reward (that which is forgone by voluntary choice). If we cannot specify what is rewarding, we cannot specify what is costly. If this is true, the "formula" has less explanatory power than might appear. With unspecified reward and, because of that, unspecified cost, the difference between them is not calculable in meaningful terms. It will suffer from the same deficiencies as reward and cost because it is derived from them.

B. Can the "supply" of value be quantified?

Damaging as the preceding criticism is, it does not entirely demolish exchange theory. We could still use it as a guide to observation, or a "sensitizing" theory to help us train our fire on certain kinds of acts. It appears to have been used largely this way in its research application. There are no complicated deductions in most studies. There is nothing as theoretically obtuse as this chapter's investigation of Homans's propositions or Blau's use of diminishing marginal utility. Nevertheless, such theoretical derivations remain to be evaluated, awaiting the day when they might be empirically useful.

It can be shown that borrowing from economic theory has been incorrectly done in certain cases. This could trip us up in our use of exchange principles if we are careless. The basic case of economic theory applied to sociological exchange involves trading valued items. In economic theory, value is comparative, just as it is in sociological exchange theory. The comparison is between competing items with their varying abilities to satisfy. But economic theory compares cost to the *supply* of the item in question. This is very largely what "price theory" is about–how economic markets ration goods and services by establishing their prices relative to supply and demand. Stating the case oversimply, but accurately from the theoretical standpoint, we expect the price required for an item to increase as the supply of it decreases if demand remains the same.[50]

[50] See James McGill Buchanan, *The Demand and Supply of Public Goods* (Chicago: Rand McNally, 1968).

This type of reasoning is implicit in the example of the intelligent, witty, and pleasant person. This fellow was in demand because his rewarding qualities were scarce. The other side of scarcity is the ability to pay the price for the scarce good. The example suggests that a trade between this man and his friend might ensue in which his friend paid in deference and approval for what he got in intelligent conversation. The theoretical problem here is: In what sense is the supply of wit and intelligence decreased when it is "traded" for approval and deference, and in what sense is the supply of deference and approval diminished as it is "given"?[51] It would appear that a person having these qualities has them in infinite supply, and in fact giving them away might even increase their supply, because it would give one practice. Which is the true case – are qualities diminished when they are given, or not? If there is no diminishing of commodities such as wit and approval when they are given, then there is scant economic justification for the thought that the "price" of these should respond to "demand" for them. The entire structure of the economic analogy is undermined by this simple difficulty.

Exchange theorists are aware of this problem, and try to get around it in part by speaking in terms of time when they analyze exchanges. Thus Blau asks a question about how much time the expert gives to the subordinate, how much time he diverts from his own work. By using time, something measurable and constant for everybody, it seems that the theoretical problem of quantity is solved, because time spent doing something diminishes the time available to do something else. But alas, the problem remains. From noticing that a person spends one hour "approving" of another, could we deduce that he has approved of him twice as much as if he spent only a half-hour approving? Surely, because we cannot draw up a rate for the value of "approval per minute" or some such notion based on a constant time ratio, time is only a crude improvement. It is true to say that available time diminishes as it is used, but it does not follow that the supply of whatever is given within that time diminishes in constant ratio to the amount of time spent.

Another aspect of this problem is found in Blau's work where he discusses problem-solving ability, depicting it and compliance in the box diagram (see Figure 4.3).[52] One dimension of the diagram is labeled "problem-solving ability," and when two persons are compared in the diagram, their abilities are added. But does it makes sense to

---

[51] This and related issues are raised by Anthony Heath in two articles. One is "Review Article: Exchange Theory," *British Journal of Political Science*, I, 1 (January 1971), pp. 91–119. The other is "Economic Theory and Sociology: A Critique of P. M. Blau's *Exchange and Power in Social Life*," *Sociology*, II (1968), pp. 273–91.

[52] This is Blau's name for his diagrams, which are similar to Figure 4.3 in this chapter.

add up problem-solving ability? Can we conclude that two persons could solve problems together that neither of them could solve alone? If Einstein had had a hundred assistants of moron capability on his staff, could he have come up with a theory that was one hundred "moron units" more ingenious than the one he produced alone? This sounds absurd, and it is. It is absurd because problem-solving ability is not additive; it does not diminish when it is used, and consequently theorizing about greater or lesser amounts of time spent "giving" problem-solving ability to someone else makes little sense. Apart from analyzing the problem and simply saying what one has to offer, there is no reason to suppose that doing this twice, perhaps spending twice the time, is going to produce a solution twice as good, or call forth twice the approval as a result.

C. Insensitivity of exchange theory to structural sociological explanation

It might be possible to surmount the difficulties that have already been noted. There is no reason why we could not adjust for the common mistakes of exchange theory and arrive at a logically more adequate theory, retaining the intuitively appealing "exchange" as a general idea. One way of going about this is to pay more attention to the influence of existing social structure on exchanges. Exchange theory has not done this, in part because it was born of a polemic argued between proponents of a somewhat rigid structuralism on the one hand, and exchange theorists on the other, who wished to explain structure individualistically. To some extent, Blau's work can be seen as an attempt to bridge over this polarization by deriving emergent structure from exchange. Structure then enters the picture as a more or less established fact bearing on subsequent exchanges.

An example of how exchange theorists have paid too little attention to social structure can be found by asking a simple question that momentarily returns to the matter of value. What must we conclude when we notice that value seems to be attached systematically to certain things and not to others? Is it a coincidence that most persons in a given society strive for certain ends whereas alternative goals never even occur to them? If such systematic ordering of value and reward is not to be passed over, it must be explained in sociological theory, either as basic principle or as derivation from other principles.

Recall how Homans made a stab in this direction with his discussion of the institutional and the subinstitutional.[53] He said that some persons innately have certain reactions that they influence others to

---

[53] See section V. C of this chapter for Homans's way of dealing with the institutional and the subinstitutional.

emulate. His example was the expression of grief. Some felt it, and some did not. Those who did not were encouraged by secondary rewards to display grief anyway. Homans is saying that the ultimate explanation of the expression of grief lies in basic human feelings, and that exchange comes in as the medium of secondary reinforcement.

It should be made very clear that Homans had two alternatives when he emphasized innate feelings of grief. He could have said that grief expression was "cultural." This would have located the ultimate explanation of grief expression outside the person in some independent structured cultural system. Then the argument would have been that "we feel grief on this occasion because it is part of our culture to do so." But Homans chose his other alternative. He wished to explain culture, so he could not assume it in his explanation. Instead of going "outside" the person to explain grief expression, he went deeper "inside" him, concluding that there must be innate feelings (at least among some persons), that these innate feelings were the basis on which grief was felt and expressed, and that it was on these bases that grief expression was made a norm. In choosing the second alternative, Homans decided to emphasize individuality. But in doing so, he inevitably posed the question of the extent to which all value can be explained on similar grounds. If we think it wrong to explain all valuing ultimately by innate feelings, then we simultaneously return to the question of social structure, culture, and the influence of these on value. To the extent that we accept a cultural hypothesis, we tend to reject the premises of individualized exchange theory. Of course, it is possible to "go off the deep end" with cultural explanations too, simplistically giving culture the upper hand in explaining everything. Homans has pointed out this danger. But in explaining orderly aspects of shared value, radical individualism seems to be an alley just as blind as cultural determinism. A glance at Chapter 2, section III, "The place of the individual in sociological theory," will add to an understanding of this problem.

D. Exchange theory's model of man

It has been said that exchange theory robs man of his humanity, portraying him as a calculating robot with no regard for anything but his own narrow desires and, apparently, no conscience either. Indeed, this is sometimes explicitly stated. And, to the extent that one takes theoretical exchange literally, the critical claim is just. Much is left out that reappears when we take a more humanistic view of our actor.[54]

[54] See William Skidmore, *Sociology's Models of Man* (New York: Gordon and Breach, 1974), Part I, "Exchange Theory."

But recall the complicated connections between description and explanation.[55] When we want a description, we must proceed somewhat differently from the way we do when we want an explanation. Taking exchange theory solely as a hypothesis-producing machine, it matters not at all what the propositions appear to *describe*. The important thing is that they produce accurate hypotheses. Its defenders would tell us that we have confused the objectives of explanation and description when we complain about exchange theory's model of man. Do we ask it for an explicit picture, a satisfying description of actors, or for hypotheses? Exchange theory emphasizes its duties as a hypothesizer-predictor and leaves aside its duties as a describer and curiosity satisfier.

Does exchange theory assume rationality on the part of men? If you turn back to the point in Chapter 3 where the logical analogy is discussed, you will see the skeleton of a theory that has only two operative terms: interest and rationality.[56] Interests are personal goals, and rationality is the mental facility required to reach these goals. In such theory, perfect rationality is absolutely necessary to make the system work properly as a theory.

The theorists discussed in this chapter have all faced the question of human rationality. They have all tried to sugar-coat the pill by suggesting that they are not really assuming rationality, but some kind of mental dexterity that is reasonable. This is to be expected. To assume no rationality of any kind would cause exchange theory to come crashing down; to assume rigorous rationality would be absurd. Landing in the middle only makes any assumption more vague. But we must conclude that some kind of rational man is assumed here. In this respect, exchange theory is not too removed from the eighteenth century, with its doctrines of rational self-interest, self-evident truths, invisible hands, and the like.

E. Explaining the group

We know that exchange theory borrows heavily from economic theory. One kind of economics that has always been particularly troublesome to economists is "public goods," or those things that do not belong to anyone in particular but, rather, to the community in general. These things are owned collectively, but they still cost something to provide. Examples are parks and bridges, fire and police protection, schools and roads.[57]

Note first that such things normally are provided by "government," which has the legitimate power to coerce contribution toward

---

[55] See Chapter 3.
[56] The logical analogy is discussed in Chapter 3, section IV.
[57] See Buchanan, *Demand and Supply of Public Goods*.

the common good and can punish noncontribution with legal action. This is no accident. Exchange theory teaches that persons will attempt to minimize costs and maximize gains. Logically, the most profitable combinations of reward and cost is the situation in which cost is reduced to zero. Someone else is persuaded to provide rewarding commodities free. If government did not have the power to tax, who among us would contribute voluntarily to make the state run? According to assumptions in exchange theory, we could expect little voluntary contribution to the public good, and the more "rational" citizens would not contribute at all.[58]

Consider an example an exchange theorist might have thought up. Imagine two persons are exchanging help for approval. Adam is giving help to and receiving approval from Bob. Exchange theory generally predicts that the status difference in this dyad would have Adam on top and Bob on the bottom, a situation we might expect Adam to enjoy, but that Bob would regard as the inevitable price he pays to get the help he requires.

Now bring in Charlie, who is also in need of help. We now have a "group" in the usual sense of the word: more than two persons interacting in a situation in which they all may make decisions, and from which emergent properties may arise. Such an exchange grouping bears resemblance to the "public" of public goods economics. If Bob and Charlie both want the same help from Adam, it will be in Adam's interest to give it to Bob and Charlie together, rather than to one at a time. This way, Adam can give his performance just once, saving him effort, and he can collect his approval from both. We are led by exchange theory to expect that Adam will wish to minimize his costs and that he would naturally settle on this approach.

When we consider Bob and Charlie, the picture becomes more complicated. They both know they must reward Adam in order to gain the needed help, and they both know that doing this will subordinate them to him. It must still be considered a fundamental rule of the game that both Bob and Charlie wish to cut costs. From this, the prediction based on exchange theory is that both Bob and Charlie will underpay Adam. Of course they will, because it will be in both their interests to minimize costs. Also, to the extent that status in the group is related to the deference payments, they will each wish to pay less in order to appear to need Adam less.[59]

---

[58] An aspect of this problem with exchange theory has been discussed in William Skidmore, "Social Behaviour and Competition," *Canadian Journal of Sociology and Anthropology*, VIII, 4 (November 1971), pp. 235–43.

[59] Extended discussion of this problem in the economic theory of social action is found in Mancur Olson, Jr., *The Logic of Collective Action: Public Goods and the Theory of Groups* (New York: Schocken Books, 1968), and Brian Barry, *Sociologists, Economists and Democracy* (London: Macmillan, 1970).

All this comes down to an absurdity. Exchange theory allows us to draw the following conclusion: In a group containing three or more people, in which there is a goal in common, it will be in the interests of the members not to contribute to the achievement of the goal, but to try to take advantage of others who are contributing. Of course, when everybody sees through the game, then no one will contribute. To the extent that all participants see this, the group is bound to achieve nothing: no help from Adam, no deference or approval from Bob and Charlie, and no status differential development among Adam, Bob, and Charlie.

We can think of similar examples. In the classroom for instance, the instructor may ask, "Any questions?" And even though everybody may need clarification, nobody wants to look more foolish than the rest by asking, and so no questions are asked, no clarification given. Yet we also know there are myriad voluntary associations that keep going on their own steam by willing contributions from members to the common good. How ought we evaluate these contrary observations?

The fact is, given exchange theory as it stands, both these observations could be predicted. Exchange theory can predict that groups are bound to succeed and bound to fail, that they are bound to satisfy their members and bound not to satisfy them, that persons will be attracted to groups for utilitarian reasons and that they will be repelled from them, and so on. Therefore, at the very nub of sociological explanation (the prediction of group action), exchange theory remains ambiguous, imprecise, and perhaps absurd. Here again, the prime difficulty derives from the theoretically unspecified nature of reward, and the assumption of reward maximization. This difficulty comes down to us by deductive reasoning from the basic principles. It shows the extent to which we must insist on precision at every step in a deductive theory.

X. Conclusion

The foregoing critical remarks have been rather hard on exchange theory. Literally, exchange theory fails to do anything letter-perfect and therefore, from a hard-line viewpoint, it ought to be tossed out. But this is not the way sociological science is conducted, and tossing out exchange theory is not recommended. However, recognition of its limitations definitely is recommended. The idea of exchange retains an intuitive appeal; it makes a certain kind of sense to think of social exchanges as vast trade-offs between numbers of persons each of whom has his own ends in view. Surely, this is a respectable point from which to begin. In addition, the organization of exchange theory into deductive form has obvious merit. The main benefit is the clarity this encourages. Journalistic accounts of social life, or partial stories we tell each other under the name of "theory," often do not have this clarity, which comes from an attempt at rigor.

Exchange theory certainly has its troubles with regard to empirical test and measurement. Most of its important concepts do not suggest anything like the observation necessary to confirm or falsify the processes proposed. Yet it is still possible to use exchange theory in research. But such research has been almost entirely devoted to the basic concept. Researchers have asked: Where and when are exchanges found? How do they work? Far too few empirical applications address derivative theorems. Partly because of empirical difficulties, we have not moved very far off dead center in research on exchange theory.

In case it seems curious to end the discussion of a theory by speaking of research, it should be emphasized how much research and theory are interdependent. But more than this, the intent of this chapter has been to show how much mental "research" there is in simply finding out what a theory says. Alongside efforts to find new data by empirical means, there must be theoretical research to appraise thoroughly and systematically sociology's organizing and summarizing content – its theory.

KEY CONCEPTS

exchange	intrinsic reward
value	endogenous reward
reward	indifference curves
investment	box diagram
profit	universal values
cost	rationality
comparison levels	bilateral monopoly
behavior matrix	microstructure
exogenous reward	macrostructure
extrinsic reward	propositions

TOPICS FOR DISCUSSION

1 In what ways is a nonfalsifiable theory valuable in sociology?
2 Illustrate how exchange theory might "explain" an event without being able to predict it.
3 Which theoretical analogy is most similar to sociological exchange theory?
4 What is the model of man implied by exchange theory?
5 What are some implications of the fact that "value" is largely unclassified and undefined in exchange theory?

6 What are the uses and pitfalls of borrowing economic theory for sociological use?
7 Discuss the success with which exchange theory explains social structure and culture.
8 To what extent does Homans succeed with the deductive format of explanation?
9 Try to manipulate some propositions from exchange theory to derive hypotheses not discussed in this book. Do these hypotheses sound correct to you?
10 How might you test the hypotheses discovered by doing discussion topic 9?

ESSAY QUESTIONS

What are the consequences of exchange theory's not being highly falsifiable?

Compare Blau's theory with that of Homans and come to a conclusion about which theory provides the better explanation of institutionalization.

Try to improve on present knowledge about how to classify the concept "value" so that it might become a more meaningful theoretical term.

Discuss the research findings reviewed in this chapter with a view to discovering the extent to which these research projects actually tested exchange theory.

Design an experiment in which you test whether or not a given person's status decreases if he has to ask for help from a friend. What are the implications of your findings?

Write an essay in which you combine salient points of Thibaut and Kelley's theory with those of Homans.

Construct a behavior matrix for yourself and one other person, imagining you are job partners. What attributes of the matrix are useful in predicting the relationship between you?

FOR FURTHER READING AND STUDY

Abrahamsson, Bengt. "Homans on Exchange: Hedonism Revisited," *American Journal of Sociology*, LXXVI, 2 (September 1970), pp. 273–85.

Altman, Irwin, and William Haythorn. "Interpersonal Exchange in Isolation," *Sociometry*, XXVIII, 4 (1965), pp. 411–26.

Barry, Brian. *Sociologists, Economists and Democracy*. London: Macmillan, 1970.

Blau, Peter M. *Exchange and Power in Social Life*. New York: Wiley, 1964.

Buchanan, James McGill. *The Demand and Supply of Public Goods*. Chicago: Rand McNally, 1968.

Gergen, Kenneth. *The Psychology of Behavior Exchange.* London: Addison-Wesley, 1969.

Greenberg, Martin, and Solomon Shapiro. "Indebtedness: An Adverse Aspect of Asking for and Receiving Help," *Sociometry,* XXXIV, 2 (1971), pp. 290–301.

Hasenfeld, Yeheskel. "People Processing Organizations: An Exchange Approach," *American Sociological Review,* XXXVII (June 1972), pp. 256–63.

Heath, Anthony. "Economic Theory and Sociology: A Critique of P. M. Blau's *Exchange and Power in Social Life,*" *Sociology,* II (1968), pp. 273–91.

Homans, George C. *Social Behavior: Its Elementary Forms.* New York: Harcourt Brace and World, 1961.

   The Nature of Social Science. New York: Harcourt Brace and World, 1967.

   Social Behavior: Its Elementary Forms. Rev. ed. New York: Harcourt Brace Jovanovich, 1974.

   "Social Behavior as Exchange," *American Journal of Sociology,* LXIII, 6 (May 1958), pp. 597–607.

   "Contemporary Theory in Sociology," in R. E. L. Faris (ed.), *Handbook of Modern Sociology.* Chicago: Rand McNally, 1964, pp. 951–77.

   "Replay to Razak," letter to *American Sociological Review,* XXXI (1966), pp. 543–4.

Knox, John. "The Concept of Exchange in Sociological Theory: 1884 to 1961," *Social Forces,* XXXXI, 4 (May 1963), pp. 341–6.

Longabaugh, Richard. "A Category System for Coding Interpersonal Behavior as Social Exchange," *Sociometry,* XXVI, 3 (1963), pp. 319–44.

Louch, Alfred R. *Explanation and Human Action.* Berkeley: University of California Press, 1966.

Maris, Ronald. "The Logical Adequacy of Homans' Social Theory," *American Sociological Review,* XXXV (December 1970), pp. 1069–81.

Muir, Donal. "The Social Debt: An Investigation of Lower-Class and Middle-Class Norms of Social Obligation," *American Sociological Review,* XXVII, 4 (August 1962), pp. 532–9.

Mulkay, Michael J. *Functionalism, Exchange and Theoretical Strategy.* New York: Schocken Books, 1971.

Ofshe, Lynne and Richard. *Utility and Choice in Social Interaction.* Englewood Cliffs, N.J.: Prentice-Hall, 1970.

Olson, Mancur, Jr. *The Logic of Collective Action: Public Goods and the Theory of Groups.* New York: Schocken Books, 1968.

Razak, W. Nevill. "Razak on Homans," letter to *American Sociological Review,* XXXI, 4 (August 1966), pp. 542–3.

Thibaut, John, and Harold Kelley. *The Social Psychology of Groups.* New York: Wiley, 1959.

Weinstein, Eugene, William DeVaughan, and Mary Wiley. "Obligation and the Flow of Deference in Exchange," *Sociometry,* XXXII, 1 (1969), pp. 1–12.

Yuchtman Ephraim. "Reward Distribution and Work-Role Attractiveness in the Kibbutz – Reflections on Equity Theory," *American Sociological Review,* XXXVII, 3 (October 1972), pp. 581–95.

5   Functionalism

I. Introduction

In sociology, *functionalism* has probably aroused more controversy than any other theoretical point of view. In fact, there is so much critical comment about functionalism that assuredly someone somewhere has already contradicted what others consider too well established to deserve notice. But functionalism still survives and remains recognizable.

The historical antecedents of functionalism lie in almost all the great founding intellectuals of Western thought. This sounds a bit too sweeping and inclusive, but the basic idea of functionalism is very simple: a wholeness composed of parts, which somehow form the whole and contribute to its maintenance, even though both the parts and the whole may be changing. Such a one-line description might apply to the family, the state, a living body or a species, an intellectual doctrine or a philosophy, an institution, a society. It is this whole-out-of-parts, whole-needing-parts, parts-needing-whole idea that unites sociological functionalism with so much other thought and that makes functionalism so well suited to be a pattern theory (see Chapter 2).

Basically, there are only two ways to go about analyzing something. One way is to break it up and study its elements. In sociology, this is largely what the exchange theorists had in mind. Remember that Homans titled his theoretical book, *Social Behavior: Its Elementary Forms,* to emphasize that his work was a commentary on the elemental nature of exchange propositions.

Functionalists generally take quite a different approach by desiring not to disassemble social life to lowest terms in order to understand it, but instead to grasp the fullness of the interconnected, living, mutually adjusting nature of a social system. This requires an appreciation of the unity of the parts, the ways in which parts and wholes intermingle, coalesce while retaining an identity. This general attitude toward social life is particularly suited to pattern theory, rather than propositional deductive theory, because pattern theory's main strength is in demonstrating the subtle aspects of unity that give a whole its integrity.

116

We usually trace the beginnings of modern functionalism back to Durkheim, but we could just as easily follow different paths that would lead to Darwin, Malthus, or Marx. In his *Division of Labor,* Durkheim sketched some of the consequences of divided social tasks, showing that a division of action and responsibility could only be united in a more general social context that regulated these things in the general interest. Similarly, in Durkheim's *Suicide,* the main point is that activities we normally consider highly individual are in fact largely influenced by subtle factors that are properties of whole societies.

Durkheim was much influenced by ethnography. When looking at other cultures, perhaps far away and more primitive than one's own, it is tempting to think that through a slow process of adjustment, in relative isolation, such cultures have reached a high point of functional integration. To a mind like Durkheim's the implications of such a model were infinite. For Durkheim, the essential fact uniting all social life was its cohesive collective functioning. The differences between primitive and modern societies were a matter of the mechanisms by which such functioning occurred, and the abstract or concrete nature of society's hold on the individual.

A very general idea such as functionalism as just depicted naturally covers a wide range of theorists and sociological problems. This chapter concentrates on two objectives. The first is to develop a general model of functionalism with enough sophistication to show most of the characteristic theoretical ideas the functionalists require. Second, we take up the works of Merton, Levy, and Parsons, and some important work on stratification, to show the variety of personal emphasis among functionalists and the origins of some of modern sociological functionalism's most powerful ideas.

II. Functional model

It is remarkable that functionalism, criticized so vigorously, still retains an identifiable core of unifying ideas we might call a model. The fact is that diverse functionalists have a considerable amount in common, and this common ground is very rich in theoretical resources. In this section, we reconstruct a model of functionalism that summarizes the main features of the theory. Later it will be necessary to note how some theoreticians depart from this model. But with the model in mind, understanding individual functionalists will be that much easier.

A. Function

We do not have to go very far to run into trouble. What is "function"? The best way to understand this term is to think of it as an effect.[1] Consider a gift-giving ritual. Suppose it has the effect of solidi-fying or dramatizing social solidarity. The effect of gift-giving is some concrete influence on the society resulting from the presence of the ritual. The function of any action, then, is its effect. It is only a slight mistake to say that a form of social action "leads to" an effect, but it is still a mistake. For example, to say that the function of a government policy is to create new jobs would be to use the term "function" to indicate intent. It must be emphasized that function is not necessarily intent. It could be that no one involved in performing an action has any idea of the effect it is having on society. But nevertheless the effect occurs. In the first place, then, functionalists try to identify the mutual effects of social actions. This in itself raises problems.

B. Structure

What things function? Structures function. One of the names some-times given to functionalism is "structural-functionalism"–to empha-size that the social arrangements sociologists call structures are thought to have systematic effects because of the particular way these structures are organized. It must be borne in mind that the subject matter of functionalism is not individuals per se. The statement "His function is to serve" makes no sense given the idea of function as an effect; attaching the service to the person is misleading. Functionalists talk about the function of "service." They would ask questions about the effect of service as a form of social action. For example, service was commonly required from the people of small feudal holdings by their European overlords. Such a collective fact about the relationship between lord and common people would be called a structure.

Patterned relationships between personal roles are structures. But this is, indeed, only part of the story. In addition to these, much more complicated multirole relations are often of interest to sociologists. For instance, an institution is usually thought of by functionalists as a vast set of interconnected roles organized together because each role contributes something toward an overall goal. An example is educa-tion as an institution, in which all who participate have some effect on the institution, and in which the various sectors of the institution affect each other. The institution, in turn, has an effect on society – the institution functions.

1. Levels of structure

Note that abstracting institutions for analysis calls attention to the various *levels* of functional analysis. The "lowest" level concerns the

---

[1] See Ernest Nagel, "A Formalization of Functionalism," in Nagel, *Logic Without Metaphysics* (New York: Free Press, 1956), pp. 247–83.

individual role: What are the functions of the roles individuals play? On a "higher" level, what is the function of an institution in society? The first question asks: What is the effect of a role on its structured social environment? The second question asks: What is the effect of an institution on *its* structured institutional environment? Although it is possible to have a functionalist answer both questions, the entities that function are quite different. In the first case, it is the role (strictly speaking, not the actor, but the role), and in the second, it is the institution. Obviously, an institution might be thought of as being composed of personal role activities, but it is the collective effect of all these personal actions taken together that is of interest at the "institutional" level of analysis. At such a level, the behaviors of individuals are usually neglected, while the "behavior" of the whole institution is scrutinized.

On the scale of levels of structure, the "highest" is the total society, in which structures doing the functioning are commonly institutionalized procedures, rituals, and the like. The lowest is the single individual role. Intermediate levels of structural analysis are possible, and often useful. The thing to keep in mind is that no matter what the level of analysis, functionalists ask similar questions about structure and the effects of structure.

2. Systems

The concept of *system* suggests relatedness. When several functioning units affect each other, it can be said that they form a system, which itself might show its own characteristics. To understand a structure's functions, we must know its specific kinds of effects, and the exact extent of these effects. We need to know in what ways the effects of a social structure will be felt; we need to know what things to consider in the search for a given structure's function. The concept of system speaks to these problems.

The concept of system is admittedly abstract. This is part of its great usefulness. A whole society is often thought of by functionalists as a social system; but intermediate and small-scale social arrangements that behave more or less as units unto themselves can also be thought of as systems. The point is that the concept of system is intended to describe the abstract and general activities that are characteristic of social systems, and to show the extent of these activities.

(a) Environment of a structure. The realm of interconnectedness, so to speak, surrounding a given structure is the *environment* of that structure. Sets of related structures may be marked off for analysis, more or less arbitrarily, and discussed as though they were a system;

whatever surrounding structures are left out of this process form the environment. We can do this knowing that there are relationships between system and environment. The idea of system designates the territory in which we expect to observe the effect of some structure or other. If the system is properly described, with particular attention to its structures, we can speak more clearly about the distinction between structure and its effects.

An example will help to clarify this. A well-known paper by Merton describes the phenomenon of bossism found in an earlier era of American big-city political life.[2] In brief, Merton says that political bosses (persons who by legitimate and illegitimate means perpetuate themselves in formal positions of power) often engaged in vote buying and other less obvious forms of trading favors for political support. These favors were most effective when offered to persons in the greatest need, because such people were perhaps most easily won over. Also, ethnicity played some part, because many of those whose political support was bought were recent immigrants, perhaps ignorant of the duties of democratic citizens. Of course, the favors given in return for votes were real enough. Bosses put food on the table and boots under it.

Merton pursues the implications of this. He says a certain kind of structured relationship came to exist, in which what we might call "institutionalized bossism" had the effect of providing welfare relief for people who had tenuous means of support. Such favors strengthened the boss's hold on life in the cities. Structured bossism had several systematic effects: keeping families together, promoting loyalty, breaking down immigrants' isolation from their new country, and introducing people to ranges of social acquaintance they might otherwise have missed. Conversely, this structure kept the bosses in power. Bossism's good health could be explained by the systematic effects of giving favors and receiving votes.

Bossism formed part of the social *environment* in which poor and immigrant people lived. Part of the general social system in which they lived their lives was bossism. It was *environmental* to them. Bossism existed as one structural feature of the social scene. Its environment was, of course, the complete range of institutions composing American society.

(b) System boundaries. A critical stage in the description of the functionalist model has been reached. We have just made a case for considering the systematic effects of structures on neighboring structures. Exactly where to stop looking for these systematic effects must

---

[2] Robert K. Merton, *Social Theory and Social Structure* (New York: Free Press, 1957), pp. 72–6.

be specified clearly, and to do this functionalists have introduced the idea of boundary. Boundaries are partly convenient fictions. If we say that the boundary around a structure is a certain place because it is impossible to observe beyond that place, we define the system of relevance for that structure partly by conveniently forgetting whatever is outside the boundary. However, there might be a theoretical reason to identify the extent to which a structure has functional relevance. This theoretical boundary within which mutually influencing structures are contained is the *system boundary*.

Anthropologists who employ functionalist theory have often benefited from a certain vagueness about the concept of boundaries around social systems. In the bush, or on an island, when it is fairly obvious where the physical territory of a given people ends, the boundary around the social system in consideration is little problem. In such empirical cases, one can conveniently think of the system as a functioning unit without having to consider thoroughly the theoretical extent of it. There is nothing so obvious about the extent of modern societies. If we wish to draw a boundary around "Canadian society," for example, what do we do with the North? Do we include the Eskimo or not? Culturally speaking, it might make more sense to draw the boundary to include the United States and exclude the Eskimo. Obviously, physical or political boundaries are not what is meant by social system boundaries. In fact, a variety of indicators demarcate a boundary around a social system. Some of these are language, custom, ceremonial or ritualistic rites indicating membership, and the like.

But what about the boundary problem within a society? Here the empirical problem the anthropologists ignored becomes an analytical question. We make the boundary where we want it, for purposes of logical necessity – to which we turn now.

(1) The logical status of the bounded social system. Explanation is what we seek. Functional explanation is the elaboration of a structure's effects on the environment in which that structure is embedded. A complete explanation of a given structure must therefore include all the effects on all parts of the environment. All the ground inside the boundary must be covered, and it must be shown that the designated effects do not come from a structure other than the one under analysis. When these rather rigid criteria are met, it can be said that a functionalist account of a structure in a bounded social system has been given. If the boundary is ambiguous, or if it is penetrated by intruding factors, the functionalist program of explanation is upset. Therefore, a rigid boundary (analytically speaking) is necessary; the logic of functionalism requires that it be present.

C. Integration

Functionalists view social structures as being environments for other social structures, and the whole to which they are all related consists of all of them together. Furthermore, this whole is generally thought to have a quality called *integration*. An integrated whole is one in which all the structural units, the parts, fit together with at least some minimal amount of mutual compatibility. This comes about through the effects of one structure on another. Structures that endure in social systems have effects which, in general, help other structures to perform and to contribute to the maintenance of the whole. The extent to which there is mutual compatibility among structures in a social system is considered to be the state of the system's integration. The concept of integration normally does not imply a state of perfection. Rather, it implies a state toward which social systems tend. In a mechanistic sense, this is predicted by extending the concept of function as an effect. It is expected that social structures existing together will shape their mutual environment so that compatibility comes to exist among the structures in the normal course of events.

1. Social evolution

The idea of *social evolution* in its more strictly biological form is out of fashion in sociology now. But, as noted in Chapter 3, it is still around in other guises. Some functionalists say social systems have tendencies by which, over time, integration grows. This means that in the time between when we start observing a society and when we stop, some kind of orderly social change occurs. Such change is functionally important, for it enhances integration. It might be rapid or imperceptibly slow. But the idea of a functionally integrated whole does suggest evolutionary adjustment toward such a whole.

The important point about the evolutionary metaphor applied to societies is that the society as a whole is thought to be reaching some state on its own, which must be understood in holistic terms and not necessarily with reference to conscious intentions. Integration refers to a condition of the system, not to persons "in" the system. To better appreciate this, we require additional detail on the functionalist model.

(a) Manifest and latent functions. Of course, social structures are built and maintained by persons. To say otherwise is to reify social structures, making them the masters of men. But the structures men create may have effects that are unintended or unnoticed by persons involved in their creation. Furthermore, persons can be mistaken

about the effects of their actions. Where they intended one outcome, another may actually appear. Merton developed the concept *manifest function* to denote the observed or expected consequences of social action. *Latent function* indicates the unanticipated or unseen consequences of social usage. Note that both kinds of functions are real, in that they are both effects.[3]

Consider latent functions. A theoretical difficulty arises with the separation of manifest and latent functions. Latent functioning implies that social evolution and integration are to some extent at least unplanned, uncontrolled, and unexpected. This is so because whenever integration arises from latent functions, it is produced as an unrecognized or unplanned effect. Evolution and integration, in other words, occur irrespective of the motivations of people who create social structures. Something about the system itself, unknown or misunderstood by the participants, causes systems to evolve the forms they do.

An example from Durkheim at this point should clarify latent function. In the *Division of Labor,* Durkheim is interested in explaining the effects, and the cause, of the division of labor into increasingly specialized tasks.[4] The cause of the division of labor he identifies as increased population density and the accompanying "moral density." He says that when these densities increase, a crisis arises in which men find themselves in unbridled competition, a threat to everyone and therefore to the social order. The point about a threat's rising from unrestricted competition is an old one, addressed notably by Thomas Hobbes and other contract theorists. But the Hobbesian solution to this problem was the appeal to reason, an individual characteristic, and to reasoned personal motivation. Hobbes saw the solution to uncontrolled antagonism in a rational sovereign who was given the power to regulate society; he thought people were sensible enough to accept regulation, because not to do so would cause the situation to revert to its original destructiveness.

In contrast to Hobbes, Durkheim adopted an alternative point of view that employs functional thinking. He thought it was more realistic to expect people to adopt solutions that were less abstract and required less vision and political understanding. He saw that one way of accommodating to increased population density was to take economic advantage of the division of labor. Rather than try to remain self-sufficient in the face of increasing economic demand and competition, men would adopt the idea of divided labor, in which specialization made it possible for people to concentrate on specific tasks and

---

[3] Ibid., pp. 60–6.
[4] See Emile Durkheim, *The Division of Labor in Society,* tr. George Simpson (New York: Free Press, 1964).

to do them more efficiently. The ultimate result of this specialization was unexpected by the persons taking part in it. Specialization created the need to organize the combination and exchange of specialties, and this organization reduced the threat to the social system implied by the unorganized chaos of large population and high moral density. A new kind of social integration emerged, born of population increase and the accompanying threat to society. Men, in accommodating to the threat, created a system of mutual dependencies which called for a new social integration. But new integration was not their aim. Survival was the aim. Durkheim saw the implications of separating the intentions of individuals from the consequences of their acts. Their intentions may be egotistic, concerned with themselves. But Durkheim thought he saw a socially useful consequence of this that no one intended should occur, because no one thought of it. This unintended consequence was the development of a new kind of social integration to combat the chaos of individual, densely packed, egotism. Now the plaguing theoretical question here is simply this: If the cause of this new social integration was not to be found in human conscious intention to bring it about, then exactly what *was* the cause? Durkheim's analysis is that in some way the system[5] of social relations acted on its own to protect itself, and that the participants were accomplices, even though they did not know it.

2. Functional requisites

Durkheim's discussion of the division of labor in society, together with the concept of integration, leads in an interesting theoretical direction. Do social systems require at least a minimum level of social integration to function as wholes? Must this level be constantly maintained? If we define a social system by its integration, thinking that every system must have at least a minimum level of integration, then the answers to these questions must be yes.

What crucial functions must be performed for a social system to be integrated sufficiently? In other words, what are the *functional requisites,* the functions absolutely necessary for a social system's survival? Could this question be decided by examining several societies to see what common features they exhibit? This is too simple. There are no examples of societies that are *not* minimally integrated. We could never find a test case. There are only examples of existing social systems, ones that by definition have the necessary integration. Hence we have to decide how to think about the question of necessary functions. Let us explore the possible approaches:

---

[5] But Durkheim did not use "system" terminology.

1 We could say that the question of necessary functions cannot be answered; therefore, we ought to forget it. In fact, after giving the problem a passing nod of recognition, this is often what happens in functionalist literature.
2 Another way of facing the question is to compare a wide variety of societies to see what institutional arrangements they have in common in order to get an empirical approximation to the answer. This has been tried; but it has yielded a bewildering array of answers. Comparative studies have not provided a satisfactory solution.
3 Also, a plain ad hoc tactic could be used, in which necessary functions are delineated for a particular social system. In fact, some argue that this is the only acceptable method. Here no attempt is made to generalize from one system to another.
4 Finally, functional requisites could be deduced from the abstract concept of social system. This approach searches theoretically for differing requirements placed on the social system by its environment. This is the method used by Parsons; details of his scheme will be reserved until later in this chapter.[6]

(a) System needs and personal needs. The question of functional requisites implies the idea of *needs*. Thinking about functional social systems has led us to envision a system that must fulfill certain requirements as a minimal basis for survival. But in what sense could an abstract social system have concrete requirements? The idea of a social sytem's having needs of its own has sometimes bothered functionalists and has fostered differing accounts of needs.

One approach is to derive the needs of social systems from the needs of persons. Representative here is the theorizing of Bronislaw Malinowski, who built a theory of culture and social organization from an analysis of what he called "human nature."[7] The basic reasoning is this: If men have continuing needs as a consequence of their physical and psychic composition, then these basic needs will call for social arrangements that consistently fill them. These arrangements will become the bases from which social systems develop. It may appear that social systems are organized according to their own principles, but for Malinowski at least, this is never really true. Instead, he would say that beneath any form of human social system, there exists a basic personal need.

Does Malinowksi solve the problem? Remember that the question of

---

[6] See D. F. Aberle et al., "The Functional Prerequisites of a Society," *Ethics,* LX (January 1950), pp. 100–11.
[7] See Bronislaw Malinowksi, *A Scientific Theory of Culture* (New York: Oxford University Press, 1960).

social system needs developed from the discussion of functional requisites – what must social systems accomplish to survive? Also remember that functional requisites derived from the observation that social systems evolve independently of personal motivated actions. Malinowski has tried to reestablish the linkage between men's motivated conduct and their social systems. His theory of needs suggests that it is because of motivated individual action that social systems are built.

We now have two choices. We can accept Malinowski's hypothesis about needs. If we do, but also believe Durkheim (that social systems seem to act on their own), we must conclude that persons are motivated by their needs but that such needs are largely unrecognized. This puts us in the position of saying that unconscious desires for social integration must exist. If we reject Malinowski's personal needs hypothesis, we are left with the needs of social systems somehow existing on their own, not coupled to the needs or actions of persons. In functionalist theory there is no agreement on this at present.

D. Equilibrium

Functional theory employs the idea that needs are associated with the system itself. Bypassing the debate about the source of these needs, we retain the idea of a system that undergoes evolutionary changes toward the end of need satisfaction. Thus the idea of system needs links up with the concept of social evolution.

The end toward which a system is thought to evolve is *equilibrium*. This concept is basically mechanistic, rather like the idea of a ruler balanced on the tip of your finger. Once it is in place, its tendency is to remain there. It remains because the immediate environment of the ruler (your finger) and the ruler itself work together toward the "end" of the ruler's balancing.

Social equilibrium is thought to be something like that. We could see this in Durkheim's discussion of the division of labor. Because of population increase, some internal changes had the effect of enabling the social system to cope with the increase. Theoretically speaking, we could say that the population increase was an aspect of the environment. An environmental crisis set off mechanisms in a social system that protected the integrity of the system. Moreover, the change to more highly differentiated labor had profound consequences for other institutions, not just those directly associated with work. Settlement patterns changed, family organization and life-styles were altered, and relations between the sexes became more sharply defined in terms of tasks and less by ascribed status. These readjustments were made necessary by a shift in the ways of coping with the environment: the division of labor.

Again we arrive at a point on which all functionalists do not agree. It could be argued that the successive changes and adjustments to social institutions lead toward some final state of social relations. We have named this process *social evolution*. Thought of in this way, the final state itself exerts some kind of pull on the system, draws it ever nearer to the end configuration. But if the end state is de-emphasized while the idea of a shifting equilibrium is retained, social evolution loses its directedness. The picture then is not one of straight-line progress to an end, but rather one of adjustment, wandering, and alternation.

For functionalists not particularly concerned with social evolution, the focus is shifted to the interplay of internal functions. Without emphasis on the end state or environment, the idea of equilibrium usually takes one of two forms. One emphasizes the adjustment process itself. The other emphasizes the states of the system at any one time, tracing out the lines of functional relatedness without paying serious attention to the shifting nature of the social bonds involved.

1. Equilibrium, social evolution, and social change

Critics have said that functionalism is unable to explain social change. This charge will be considered more fully later. However, at this point it should be noted that the general model of functionalism outlined previously can accommodate at least one kind of change. It can handle the change that results from the system's adjustments to cope with its environment. About this kind of change there should be little argument. It is almost the first principle of evolutionary thinking that changes occur as responses to environment.[8]

One additional refinement of the functionalist model is required now to suggest how complicated its account of change and equilibrium can get. Remember the concept of levels of systems. One social system may contain several lower-level systems, perhaps called institutions. Similarly, these are composed of even lower levels. The level of social organization we consider depends upon interest and convenience; various aspects of social life may be regarded as "in" or "out" of the system when we discuss a given set of functional relations.

All those aspects of a system outside its borders are, by definition, parts of the environment of the system we are explaining with functional analysis. We explain the change in one level of system by reference to more inclusive levels. But what if the whole of the social system is what we are interested in knowing about? What do we do? If we shift up to the highest level of abstraction, considering the

[8] See Chapter 3, section 4.

whole society the functioning system, we have no environment from which to draw explanations. This problem has led some mild critics of functionalism to observe that the model draws attention away from social change, even though functionalism can, theoretically, "explain" it.

E. Values

Sometimes functionalists are said to have a "value" perspective on social theory. Of course, functionalists are not the only theorists to use the idea of values. But functionalists, like other theorists, have their special meaning for values. Values usually appear in functionalist literature as *value systems,* shared by participants in structured social action and giving coherence, form, and shape to their action. This does not say that people have to think alike to accomplish social coordination. It does say that people must share in an organized stable pattern of values so that one person can have reasonable expectations about the other person's behavior.

Notice that the discussion is now about value patterns. The exchange theorist might still agree at this point on values, although he would chafe a bit about the systems of values' becoming too rigid. However, the exchange theorist and the functionalist would definitely part company when the functionalist talks about the values appropriate to a given social position. The functionalist says there are action types that are inherently necessary to the performance of a structured role. Similarly, inherent in the position opposite these performances is a set of structured expectations appropriate to receiving the action and properly reacting to it. Notice that it is expectations that are structured. The structure does not dictate what to do, per se, as in "Open the door, take five steps to the chair, sit down, question the patient, examine the patient, write a prescription," and so on. The value pattern gives, in general terms, appropriate ways of acting in specific situations. For example, in the doctor's office, it is appropriate to remove one's clothes on command, but on the street this is hardly a normal action.

Values, which attach to structured patterns of action, are the bases on which everyday judgments of appropriateness and reasonableness, of right and wrong, good and bad, are made. The functionalist says that values cannot be individual or unique. They must bridge the distance between the private world of the individual and the external, social, and public aspects of his actions. The individual will know what activities are expected by referring to the values appropriate to his role. He will refer to a value system. Value systems show the same coherence, unity, and appropriateness of implied action as the role systems to which they are attached.

1. Socialization and motivation

From the discussion of values, we can understand the importance of *socialization* for most functionalists.[9] In broad terms, socialization refers to the inculcation of values and skills so that persons occupying roles have sufficient knowledge of what to expect and how to act, plus the desire to expect and act in these ways. If these objectives of socialization are achieved, then it is reasonable to view action-in-role as being motivated activity of valuing persons, whose acts are consistent with other persons' valuing motivated behavior. This consistency has not been imposed (although, in one sense, anything taught has been "imposed"). Rather, actions are self-generated, once people have acquired and become committed to the basic value patterns systematically attached to the social fabric.

This position on values and action assumes that persons can be brought to embrace almost any value system. Indeed, there is some evidence for this in the wide variety of value systems found in different societies. But is there a limit? We have not successfully implanted wholesale altruism; for all the preaching, the Golden Rule seems far from being established. Even if there is a limit beyond which it is not possible to teach people values, and no matter what that limit might be, the functionalist view remains broadly based on socialization. Subtly, socialization implants the basic motives from which persons will construct their actions. Activity then becomes the resultant of role prescription, value attitudes, and maturation.

F. What kind of an explanation does functionalism give?

We now have an outline of functional explanation used by sociologists. There are some additional points to raise before passing on to a discussion of some functionalist literature. These points are not part of the functional model. They are, rather, comments on it – things to keep in mind when thinking of and criticizing functionalism.

1. Pattern theory, categorical thinking, and reality

What we have is a set of theoretical categories. Structure and function are the main ones. They are, as it were, class names for the things discussed by functionalists. Is something a structure? How does that structure produce an effect on other structures, or the system made up of all the structures? Functionalism provides a class of questions to ask when researching some concrete aspect of society.

[9] See Talcott Parsons and Robert F. Bales, *Family Socialization and Interaction Process* (New York: Free Press, 1955).

In a similar way, the concept of "system" is a general name for the interrelated structures we often look for. If we see the world in system terms, it makes sense to ask a functional question. It makes sense because the idea of system is bound up with the idea of parts and wholes – the parts fitting together to enhance survival value, integration, stability, or some other property of the system. The development of the concepts of manifest and latent functions can be seen as a variation on this theme, further specification of the main categories of which functional theory is made.

Functionalism may be regarded as offering an abstract conceptual pattern of theoretical categories that can be made to explain concrete action. The idea of system is entirely abstract; the boundary around a system is arbitrary for theoretical purposes. It does not matter, with respect to the theory, where we draw the boundary, or what we call the system. These abstractions are portable and can be moved about as the occasion requires. The important thing is that functionalism, taken as a coherent set of ideas, be at least partially descriptive. The categories must be understood to be "about" the world.

In describing the functional model, we did not trouble ourselves with questions of whether or not we were describing anything real. But if we are to use this model to analyze real social action, then we must keep one thing clearly in mind: The model is not intended to be a literal description of anything. It is intended to be a meaningful mental apparatus by which we can make sense of what we do observe in society. The model and the society are not the same thing.

But the model is derived from serious attempts to understand human social organization, and it is useful in further attempts. There is a sense in which the model of society is also descriptive of it. To the extent that observations suggest that the model is useful in understanding a society, the conditions and processes hypothesized in the model may have their counterpart in the real world. That means, in other words, that the model is analogous to reality and can make plain aspects of social organization obscured to raw observation. Theories are made up for a purpose. They should not be taken literally. Functionalism does enough things badly to prevent its literal use as a description, but it certainly provides useful concepts and categories into which we can fit our thoughts to make sense of them.

2. Functionalism as ideology

Functionalism could be used as an ideology, just as other sociological theory could. Theory becomes dogma whenever a person adopts a theory in order to turn its abstract theoretical ideas into assertions. A theory using the concepts "function" and "structure" could be said to emphasize these ideas. The term "structure" can easily slip over the bounds of its definition to take on additional meanings, such as "constriction," "limitation," or "regimentation." And if structure is thought to be more concretely descriptive than it is, then a picture of a limited, bounded, narrow field of action emerges in which people are imprisoned in structures. Because these possible implications are obnoxious to our moral or political sentiments, structure might come into bad repute as a concept.

If "function" is understood to mean effects, all is well. But somehow function can subtly turn into "purpose." Durkheim separated the causes of the division of labor from its functions, as we have seen. But he also indicated that the effect of the division of labor was the reintegration of society. Yet for those involved, the "purpose" of the division of labor was not the promotion of integration. Purpose implies motive rather than effect. One common confusion about this is to suppose that functionalism implies someone somewhere knows how to manipulate social structures, and that structures are being run to someone's particular benefit. Where is the person who does not sometimes think himself caught up in a system cunningly contrived by others? And here is how functionalist thinking can be turned to polemical use. Making the mistakes of imputing conscious purpose to social structures and supposing that individuals have too much power and diabolical wisdom, or that they know too much about the future, can turn functionalism into an indictment of any society. Because society can be thought of as a system, it can also be criticized as too much of a system, too well run, perhaps by the wrong people.

The idea of interrelated functions leading to social integration does not necessarily imply approval or disapproval of those functions or that integration. Moral judgments are not appropriate to serious analysis using the functional model. The model's only legitimate use is explanation. If a functionalist personally approves of the structures and functions he seeks to understand, his responsibility is still to report the ways in which functionalist theory explains these structures and functions. If he does not approve of them, he is no less obliged to employ functionalism dispassionately, constructing an explanation of the system under examination.

III. Robert Merton and functionalism

In this section some of the important features of Robert Merton's work as a functionalist will be reconstructed. From its title, "Social Structure and Anomie," it might seem that Merton was interested mainly in individual behavior. And, of course, to some extent, he was. But his overall goal was to suggest a typology of ways of behaving. The typology and the discussion of social deviance following it are derived from a functional model of society.[10] It is this general scheme to which we now turn.

A. Structures

As we would expect of functionalist literature, Merton begins with a description of his idea of social structures and what they do. He also considers it important to refute explanations of deviance resting particularly on individualistic or psychological hypotheses. His purpose is to show that social structure makes available to people a variety of ways of acting ("modes of adaptation"), and that it is this structural condition that is the root cause of social deviance. He is not interested in deviants or crime as such. He is interested in the social structural sources of the tendency to act in unorthodox ways. In fact, deviance, under the circumstances he describes, is really normal behavior.[11] Persons who deviate are not especially odd or psychologically deficient. They are doing what could be expected of them, given the circumstances. Merton regards this "doing what could be expected" as the crux of his explanation. He is showing how normal and predictable it is for certain types of action to arise in certain social conditions. That's good sociology.

Merton understands social structure basically as it was described in the general introduction to this chapter. It is social regulation of acceptable means by which to achieve goals. The regulations (the norms, the mores) are constraints that persons face when they contemplate action. Not that these regulations are necessarily considered impediments. Usually, persons accept rules as giving guidance, comfort, predictability, and some coherence in situations that would otherwise be chaotic. Structures provide standardized ways of acting to achieve ends, ways that give form and shape to action without directing it in every detail. To Merton, the salient feature of structures is that they have effects on the social system of which they are a part. Because he is a functionalist, we expect Merton to describe the structures in which he is interested, and tell how these structures have these effects. He does just this.

1. Goals and means to success

Of specific interest to Merton are, first, institutionalized, structured guidelines for action.[12] In addition, he notes, there are institutional-

---

[10] R. Merton, *Social Theory and Social Structures*, pp. 131–60.
[11] Ibid., p. 131.
[12] Ibid., pp. 132–9.

ized guidelines for deciding what to try to achieve. It is natural for a functionalist to pay equal attention to both of these. The argument is that what people do is only half the story; the other half is finding out why they do it. There are institutional conventions regulating both.

Merton is particularly intent on documenting the "success goal" in America. His original paper was published in 1938, during an era when personal striving appeared to be of crucial importance to survival. His purpose in documenting this theme is to show that institutionalized definitions of what to value and seek are as important as institutionalized regulatory norms about how to pursue these goals. Merton's view is that a particularly strong emphasis on material success was institutionalized in America.

Merton's second major point is to show the social regulation of the means by which persons achieve success. There are, of course, legal rules detailing what one must and must not do. But there are also rules of ethics and etiquette in business and the professions, rules one understands implicitly about how to treat his neighbor, his lodge brother, or his community colleague. These regulations form the rules of the game of success. Of course, such rules do not tell exactly how to play; there is room for considerable individuality. Merton theorizes that when extreme individuality becomes paramount, and winning success the only consideration, then a subtle but important change takes place. The informal rules lose their power to regulate, and the whole idea of rules is devalued and debased. Institutionalized sanctions as a means to social order become inoperative, and all persons are thrown onto their own ingenuity and resources. This results in what some sociologists call the destruction of "integration."[13]

B. Integration

In focusing on institutionalized goals, means to achievement and specification of the terms in which success ought to be measured, Merton sets up what might be called a system. *Integration* is a name for the state of the relationships between parts of the system. Merton places his boundary for analysis around only some features of American society. The integration of interest to him is the relationship between the institutionalized goals on the one hand, and the institutionalized means on the other. The mutually influential tendencies of institutionalized goals and means create the functional relationship between these structures. It is in this sense that Merton is not directly interested in deviance, but rather in explaining the system. He wishes

---

[13] In doing this, Merton groups extreme individuality and social disintegration together and opposes them to well-regulated social integration.

to inspect the systematic effects of overemphasis on structured success goals.

Merton describes a poorly integrated social system, in which the malintegration is the overemphasis on the socially defined goal of success and a corresponding underemphasis on means to reach it. The malintegration persists because most people discover that such success is not available to them, at least not within the confines of social regulation. Finding this, people turn to deviant ways to succeed. This has the functional result of further debasing social regulation. Structural imbalance causes rules to decrease in importance, while the goal of success by almost any means remains. Logically, the extreme case of this situation would be no rules, no integration, and a free-for-all of individuality.

C. The typology of modes of individual adaptation

Of course, Merton is not talking about a free-for-all. He is still talking about a social system, which varies in its degree of integration. The system he sees is not moribund, but it is strained by the overemphasis on goals and the underemphasis on means. He views equilibrium as the balance that might obtain between emphases on these two structured parts of the social system. It is at the point where integration breaks down that the *modes of individual adaptation* enter the picture.

Mainly, the idea is that collective acceptance of both the goals and the means to achievement constitutes a balanced harmony between these two structured aspects of life, and this mode is labeled "conformity."[14] But rejecting either the goal, or the means, or both, leads to one of four modes (typical ways) for individuals to cope with malintegration:

innovation	–the goal is accepted but the means are not
ritualism	–the means are accepted but the goal is not
retreatism	–neither are accepted
rebellion	–the goals and means are altered, and a new type of integration between new goals and new means may be set up

In making up this typology, Merton's intent is to show that one may expect systematic effects on social behavior to result from the malintegration of society resulting from a rejection of the success goal, or the typical means of achieving success.

D. Function and dysfunction

Another contribution to the language and literature of functionalism was made by Merton in "Manifest and Latent Functions," which con-

[14] *Social Theory and Social Structure,* pp. 140–57.

tains a full interpretation of functionalism as well as two concepts in its title.[15] Merton consistently maintains interest in states of social integration. The concepts *function* and *dysfunction* assist us in thinking about the effects of structural features of society on its integration.

By itself, "function" means something quite simple – an effect. But historically functionalists have given most attention to those effects that result in the maintenance or enhancement of integration. These positive effects may be referred to as "functions." This is especially so if an evolutionary view is taken, in which it is presumed that badly integrated structures will naturally pass away. But Merton, in "Social Structure and Anomie," gave an instance of the need for another concept, "dysfunction."[16] This expresses the idea that a structure may have ill effects on the system, effects leading not to better, but to poorer integration.

This might seem obvious to us. We have become accustomed to thinking about social structures as arenas for competing forces. But to persons who envisioned societies as bounded, mutually supportive bundles of institutions, the concept of dysfunction opened up functionalism. It gave the functionalists a way to talk about social systems without the inherent error of assuming that every structure contributed to functional integration. Merton maintains that we can still talk about equilibrium, about functional integration, and about social systems, without implying harmony in an ossified skeleton of social convention.

IV. M. J. Levy and structural-functional requisite analysis

No analysis of structural or functional *requisites* is given in Merton's work. Merton did suggest, indirectly, that a social system too poorly integrated was in danger. He implied that some minimum level of integration of the system was necessary for social system survival. Levy makes the elaboration of such requisites and related structures the main focus of his theoretical work.[17]

A. Levy's empirical emphasis

Levy's specification of what these requisites are, however, should not be taken as final. He cautions that a complete list of the requisites for any society is found only with reference to the specific setting (environment) of that society. This position emphasizes Levy's empirical intent. He would consider it a mistake to draw up

---

[15] Ibid., pp. 19–84.
[16] Ibid., pp. 5, 53.
[17] Marion J. Levy, *The Structure of Society* (Princeton, N.J.: Princeton University Press, 1952).

an entirely theoretical list of functional or structural requisites. It would be another mistake, in his view, to derive these from some abstract definition of society not based on actual circumstances. Levy takes this approach in order to maintain the close connection between sociological theory and actual societies. He would think the term "system" too abstract, although he applies a great deal of system thinking in explaining societies.

B. What functions are required?

Functionalism implies that requisites of social systems are undeniable requirements. To go on existing, social systems appear to make demands – to have "needs." Concerning these needs, the functionalist question is: What effect of social structure does the system require? Levy has actually turned this question around, but he means the same thing. His question is: What are the things that would directly entail the termination of a society if they (or any one of them) were not there?

By a "society," Levy means "a group of human beings sharing a self-sufficient system of action which is capable of existence longer than the life-span of an individual, and which is recruited at least in part by the sexual reproduction of the members."[18] From this, it is obvious that several kinds of things commonly called societies do not really qualify. The Society of Practicing Gurus is not the kind of group Levy is talking about. But the United Kingdom or the Hutterites would come under his definition. Also, note that Levy is talking about a system of action and not directly about the people who do the acting.

Levy suggests that four things could lead to the termination of societies:[19]

> biological extinction or dispersion of the members
> apathy of the members
> war of all against all
> absorption of the society into another society

Biological extinction seems like a commonsense idea – no people, no system of action. On these grounds, Levy combines in one requisite the regulation of sexual activity and the regulation of the relationships between the society and its environment. It is imperative for survival that a society provide personnel and keep them physically capable of action. Hence we expect institutions to be devoted directly to personnel definition and recruitment, and to relations between society and the physical environment.

---

[18] This definition is derived from Levy's more elaborate one; ibid., pp. 111 ff., "The Concept of Society."
[19] Ibid., pp. 137–40.

The concept of apathy implies the danger to societies should members fail to maintain their social system through lack of effort. It is possible for persons to lose sufficient motivation to do the right thing, or enough of it, to keep essential services in action. This includes cultural and mental sustenance as well as more practical material motivations. Some of the functional requisites are justified in terms of the need to control apathy.

The war of all against all is somewhat more complicated. This notion implies that, lacking constraints, there is a natural tendency for individuals to be self-seeking and unlikely to form collectively beneficial social conventions. This danger exists in any society. Even if it were obvious to an outside observer that cooperation was required, involved individuals might still decide that yet further competition would win them big gains. Extremes of this would lead to the destruction of society as such. Levy puts it thus: If instrumental efficiency were the only consideration in social action, we could expect no society at all to result.[20]

Finally, the concept of absorption of a society by another does not necessarily mean political takeover or physical movements of persons or loss of territory. It means, rather, that a loss of identity is possible through which the uniquenes of the system disappears into a more general society by absorption.

C. Functional requisites

These four points are Levy's rationale for the following list of functional requisites, which he offers as the main organizing principles for a functionalist-inspired account of any society.[21] A society must have:

1 provision for relationship to the environment and for sexual recruitment
2 role differentiation and role assignment
3 communication
4 shared cognitive orientation
5 shared articulated set of goals
6 the normative regulation of means
7 the regulation of affective expression
8 socialization
9 the effective control of disruptive forms of behavior
10 adequate institutionalization

[20] It should be noted that this is a point of view divergent from that taken by exchange theorists, who would be more likely to argue that an unfettered individual is the best guarantee of well-ordered society.
[21] *The Structure of Society*, pp. 151–97.

A typical chapter from Levy's book on functional theory describes the action specific to a given institution or social convention by making reference to these functional requisites. Not all the requisites would be appropriate to a given structure, but Levy's general intention is to show that the structural features of societies can be accounted for in terms of the ways in which they fulfill the needs outlined above.

D. Functional requisites and role differentiation

As an example, Levy's chapter on role differentiation will be summarized briefly.[22] This is the distribution of positions in a social system according to the specific tasks associated with each, and the various duties and obligations accompanying them.

How might we expect role differentiation to take place? What would be the salient categories in which to find social roles differentiated? Levy's answer is that societies are differentiated in general according to the following empirical criteria:

    age
    generation
    sex
    economic allocation
    political power
    religion
    cognition (thoughtways)
    nonhuman environment
    solidarity

Each of these categories of differentiation and role allocation is given a theoretical justification by reference to a functional requisite. Levy works out reasons for the various aspects of differentiation on the basis that they satisfy one of the requisites. In other words, the methods of differentiating roles can be explained by the needs, or requirements, of the system (except for the final two types of differentiation in the list, which are handled somewhat differently). These parallel justifications, in order of the categories of differentiation, deserve our attention now.

Age differentiation is divided into absolute and relative age, and the former category is further divided into the familiar categories of infancy, childhood, adulthood, and old age. The progression from young to old emphasizes that at each particular stage the individual's physiological relationship to the environment changes, and his ability

---

[22] This description follows Levy's Chapter 7, pp. 299–348.

to perform tasks also changes. It is necessary for society to define the performances expected of persons at each stage of life, and as a consequence of this, an arrangement of social differentiation we call age structure results.

The *generational* structure of role differentiation is somewhat similar, but it is relevant to another aspect of the requisite: the requirement to provide new persons via sexual recruitment. This requirement highlights the fact that all societies regulate sexual activity and specify family and parenthood obligations. Societies make plain the role differentiation occurring between generations – the generational structure. Additionally, role differentiation on the basis of *sex* is derived from the first functional requirement.

Role differentiation based on *economic allocation* is derived from the requisite of relating adequately to the environment, and also from the idea of the war of all against all. Levy notes that no one can be self-sufficient. Hence it is inevitable that economic goals, the means by which they are reached, and the distribution of economic resources would be institutionalized.

Differentiation based on *political power* is derived from the requisite of controlling disruptive action. In general, Levy theorizes, society is organized so that functioning structures will not be significantly hindered, because what they do is vital to the society's survival. Overly disruptive action is, therefore, a strike against the very existence of society, and there must be an institutional basis for controlling it, that is, political power. Thus it is to be expected that social roles will differ with respect to power in such a way that disruptive action will be minimized and controlled.

Differentiation on the basis of *religion* derives from the requisite of shared cognitive orientations and the regulation of affective expression. It appears that Levy views religion as a regulator of goals, because religious activity is not considered a means to an end, but an end in itself. Hence role differentiation regulating religious practice and evaluation contributes to fulfilling a continuing need.

Socialization is the requisite on which differentiation by *cognition* is based. But it goes further than this. Persons in control of key ideas, or expert knowledge, hold a particularly crucial position respecting the survival of the whole society. Hence a system of institutionalized differentiation develops devoted to the regulation of this kind of power.[23]

Levy extends the functionalist work done by Merton. He uses Mer-

---

[23] In conclusion Levy notes three kinds of additional differentiation, but these are not directly based on the requisite analysis of the previous kinds of differentiation.

ton's manifest and latent functions, and the ideas of function and dysfunction. Although he uses these ideas much the same way Merton did, Levy is far more global in his theoretical goals. Merton did not actually try to account for all, or even most, structural features of societies, preferring instead to concentrate on a smaller number. Levy, by contrast, set himself the task of deriving a functional explanation of a total society from theoretical thinking about functional requisites. If societies had to perform crucial tasks to survive, then each structural development in any society could be explained by reference to the contribution it made to collective survival. Hence Levy's functionalist writing, as the example of role differentiation shows, is devoted to showing that regulated social action contributes something of survival value to societies. The continuing emphasis on the survival value, or signal importance, of institutionalized social action is itself a sign of functionalism's family resemblance to evolutionary theory.

V. Functionalism's treatment of stratification as motivation

Note that in describing Merton's and Levy's functional sociological theory, little has been said about the individual. As one critic put it, functionalism seems to contain a great deal about "systems of action" but not very much about "action." Even Merton's typology of modes of individual adaptation to goals and means is not directly about action; it is a list of possibilities derived from a structural argument. This is not to find fault with the approach taken by functionalism – describing systems of action. There is nothing especially wrong with this. But inherent in this approach to theoretical explanation is the possibility that individual motivation will be overlooked or underemphasized. Levy noted the need to recognize motivation in his theory. He calls it the problem of apathy. Because social systems are formed around certain continuous threats to order, the institutional structures designed to address these functional problems must operate effectively. Failure would lead to the termination of the society. Hence it is an imperative not only that persons understand the rules of social life, but that they actually play by them. Why persons play by the rules is what functionalist theories address under the heading *motivation*. Motivation is linked to the inevitability of the functional requisites. There are certain things that must be done to retain society. It is this necessity that puts the "action" in the "system of action." Incidentally, it also lays functionalism open to the criticism that it is really a grand comment on what must remain a psychological theory.

A. Stratification

Motivation has been accounted for in part by *stratification*. K. Davis and W. Moore, in a classic paper on this topic,[24] attempt a functionalist treatment which has the following as its main objectives:

  to show that a set of stratified positions exists;

  to show that this stratified set of positions is needed;

  to show that the action required by these positions implies motivated persons to perform it;

  to show that a scheme of differential rewards provides the motivation required.

The functionalist theory of stratification is not really concerned with the essential contributions of stratified positions, but rather with the means of getting tasks performed. Davis and Moore would not deny that garbage collectors are important, but they would argue in principle that it is easy to get people who are qualified to collect garbage.[25] Therefore, the position of garbage collector will not normally be accorded high status or highly rewarded. Alternatively, highly skilled jobs, or positions for which special scarce qualities of some kind are required, will usually be more difficult to fill. These will require larger legitimate rewards to be attached to them as motivators. Competition to achieve these rewards will ensure that the more demanding positions find persons to fill them. It is not that certain positions carry greater rewards that make them higher in rank, but just the reverse: Some positions are necessary, yet difficult to fill; these must carry sufficient rewards to induce persons to fill them.

We can now see how Davis and Moore have tied together the ideas of social system, position, and individual action in their discussion of stratification. The general theme is that individuals must be motivated to act in roles relevant to the functional necessities, and that this placement process must be sensitive to the relative supply and demand of talent, skill, willingness, and so forth. Davis and Moore

---

[24] "Some Principles of Stratification," *American Sociological Review*, X, 2 (1945), pp. 242–9. This paper and some of the ensuing debate is reprinted in Rinehard Bendix and Seymour M. Lipset, eds., *Class, Status and Power: A Reader in Social Stratification*, rev. ed. (New York: Free Press, 1966), pp. 47–72.

[25] There has been continuing confusion about the functionalists' theory of stratified positions. Critics have noted that *all* positions in an integrated social system are crucial, because the removal of any of them would be a disruption to the differentiated system of interdependent roles that is a society. This is true. In fact, the more differentiated and interdependent a system becomes, the truer this is. Big-city garbage collectors demonstrate this when they strike; instantly it is clear that their "lowly" occupation is indeed crucial. But Davis and Moore do not debate this point. Their intent is to show that a scarcity of talent and interest accompany positions of high rank, not that only positions of high rank are important.

regard stratified positions as having evolved naturally over time, according to the particular needs of social systems. Of course, there is no one stratification order, but as many as there are societies. The point about evolution emphasizes the dependence of the stratification hierarchy on the social system itself. And because stratification has evolved naturally, it cannot be explained wholly by reference to rationally arranged schemes of power dependencies, or oppressive measures taken by elites. The explanation of stratification must lie in society's need to motivate individuals to perform tasks dictated by the functional requisites of that society.

Davis and Moore analyze stratification in some institutional areas.[26] Like Levy, they try to show that a social system is most highly regulated in those institutions that are most directly related to the survival of that social system. They point out, for example, that religious institutions are highly stratified and that priests have historically been accorded high rank because priests stood in a particularly significant relationship to the deity.

Davis and Moore note that it is in the realm of legitimate monopolies over force and the setting of goals for society that another highly stratified order exists – government. Additionally, even though technologists have lately been accorded high rank, they are usually not ranked with the leaders of religion, government, or business. Davis and Moore attribute this to the fact that the technologist is engaged in finding efficient means to ends that are specified elsewhere. It is the definition of approprite ends, and not the means to them, that is the greater functional problem for societies; this relationship between goals and means explains the relative ranking of technologists. It agrees also with Merton's diagnosis of American society.

B. Stratification and values

In the general discussion of values as found in functional theory, we saw that *values* are the appropriate goals and evaluations of actions that go with a given social situation. Perhaps this implied that functionalists feel shared values cause persons to be content with their lot in life. But appropriateness must be kept separate from the idea of better and worse situations. Functionalists do not mean that societies necessarily will be manned by happy, contented people, living in harmony because of shared values. Merton, and Davis and Moore do not reach this conclusion. Their functionalist views do not suggest natural harmony. The picture one gets from them is that values do indeed coalesce into systems, with overriding goals perhaps as the

---

[26] This discussion is similar to Levy's chapter on differentiation summarized previously.

keystones of these systems (as when Merton discusses the success goal). These goals and values attach themselves to the roles organized to pursue them. But, as shown especially by Davis and Moore, there is within this structure considerable flexibility and competition. In fact, there would be no striving to fill positions of high responsibility and rank if there were not competition, the individual desire to achieve, and a willingness to take risks. Functionalist thinking on stratification is quite explicit on this. The temptation to regard orderly role systems and their attached values as harmoniously functioning units must be resisted.

Functionalism remains, however, somewhat ambiguous about value, socialization, and individuality. On the one hand, if the processes of socialization are emphasized, a rather passive picture of social action as role-acting emerges. This does not fit well with Davis and Moore's view of stratification, or with Merton's hypothesis that people will become uncomfortable if their rewards in life do not come up to their expectations. On the other hand, if the competitive aspects of social life are emphasized, as in the functionalist view of stratification, then the image of value systems spelling out appropriate actions appears inadequate. This point will be discussed again later in this chapter.

VI. Talcott Parsons

Talcott Parsons has contributed a great deal to sociological theory. Even his critics agree on that; and his critics are legion. Parsons has made what is perhaps the most debated statement about social systems in all of modern functionalism. A discussion of Parsons's work[27]

[27] Some of Parsons's theoretical works used in preparation of this chapter are: *Essays in Sociological Theory* (New York: Free Press, 1949); "Pareto's Central Analytical Scheme," in J. H. Meisel, ed., *Pareto and Mosco* (Englewood Cliffs, N.J.: Prentice-Hall, 1965), pp. 71–88; "The Pattern Variables Revisited: A Response to Robert Dubin," in Talcot Parsons, ed., *Sociological Theory and Modern Society* (New York: Free Press, 1967), pp. 192–219; "The Place of Ultimate Values in Sociological Theory," *International Journal of Ethics*, XLV (1934–5), pp. 282–316; "The Point of View of the Author," in Max Black, ed., *The Social Theories of Talcott Parsons* (Englewood Cliffs, N.J.: Prentice-Hall, 1961), pp. 311–63; "The Present Position and Prospects of Systematic Theory in Sociology," in Parsons, *Essays in Sociological Theory*, rev. ed. (New York: Free Press, 1954), pp. 212–37; *Social Structure and Personality* (New York: Free Press, 1964); *The Social System* (New York: Free Press, 1951); *Societies: Evolutionary and Comparative Perspectives* (Englewood Cliffs, N.J.: Prentice-Hall, 1966); "Some Comments on the State of the General Theory of Action," in M. L. Barron, ed., *Contemporary Sociology* (New York: Dodd, Mead, 1964), pp. 572–89; *Structure and Process in Modern Societies* (New York: Free Press, 1965); *The Structure of Social Action* (New York: Free Press, 1949); "The System of Modern Societies" (mimeographed, n.d., n.p.); Parsons and Robert F. Bales, "The Dimensions of Action-Space," in T. Parsons, and others, *Working Papers in the Theory of Action* (New York: Free Press, 1953) *(continued)*

should begin by recognizing it as a synthesis.[28] Parsons did not develop his ideas from one theoretical framework. Although it is legitimate to label his work almost wholly functionalist, he was not always to be found within this tradition, nor was he trying to be identified with any tradition at all. His earlier training was in the arts and in economics. His use of Weber's theory shows an interest in economic history. And Parsons has also dabbled in psychology.

Yet Parsonsian theory, emerging over the past forty years, has not been simply eclectic. One by one, his works have appeared, each a substantial contribution, while a scheme of unification for them all was developing concurrently. It is usually this unifying scheme that is called the "Parsonsian system"; and it is mainly this conceptual scheme, this pattern theory, that will be discussed here.

A. The objective

The objective of all theory is to explain. Parsons's overall objective is identical to that of all other social theorists. He is trying to explain the "problem of order,"[29] that is, why there is social order. Parsons felt that his early works in this direction were empirical. But he had a curious way of using this term. His "empirical" method was to research previously published works to see how these accounted for order. Parsons felt that many of these writers were on the right track. Although all of them had missed at least some of the truth, there was much of value in competing theories. Parsons's "synthesis" was to unite portions of other theoreticians' works that were convergent (i.e., similar, although stated in different terms) so that a more complete theory of social order would result. For this program to be carried out, he needed three ingredients; (1) the works of these men, which might be called the content of Parsons's theory; (2) a language; and (3) a conceptual scheme in which to unite them. Parsons may be regarded as pursuing his career as a theorist by continually elaborating his conceptual scheme, enhancing its contents, and extending both to a wide variety of topics in sociology. Parsons has never been much of a data gatherer. Rather, his strength is as a conceptualizer, an interpreter of events, an organizer of ideas. This emphasis fol-

pp. 63–110; Parsons and Bales, *Family, Socialization and Interaction Process;* "Phase Movement in Relation to Motivation, Symbol Formation, and Role Structure," in *Working Papers,* pp. 163–269; Parsons and E. A. Shils, eds., *Toward a General Theory of Action* (New York: Harper, 1951); Parsons and Neil J. Smelser, *Economy and Society: A Study in the Integration of Economic and Social Theory* (London: Routledge and Kegan Paul, 1957).

[28] *The Structure of Social Action* details Parsons's understandings of some previous sociological and economic theory and concludes by noting that several central ideas found in these works converge on common themes.

[29] See *The Social System,* pp. 30–3, for one of several discussions of this point.

lowed from his original intent to unify various views on social order, and contribute his own.

B. Early ingredients of the Parsonsian system

1. Voluntarism

Parsons knew what mistakes he wished to avoid. In the first place, theory should be *voluntaristic*. Theory should not picture individuals as mindless automatons but should state that persons, by their own cognitive and emotional efforts, come to conclusions about how to act. Parsons wished to avoid the absurdities associated with too strong an emphasis on "group will," "collective determination," and the like. He rejected ideas of societies in which there was no room for individuality.

Yet Parsons wished to avoid the opposite extreme. Suggesting that social life was composed wholly of privately contrived and individually evaluated actions would lead to a picture of chaos rather than order. Surely empirical evidence indicated that persons do not make their decisions independently of the values and decisions of others. Parsons's objective was to arrive at a starting point for theory that would avoid both extreme individualism and extreme determinism.[30]

2. Rationality

Other pitfalls had to be avoided. One of these was *rationality*. Parsons thought it would be absurd to suggest that persons behave rationally, if by that one meant that persons always knew all their alternatives and always understood precisely what the outcome of each alternative would be and always made a choice of action consistent with the most efficient alternative. Clearly, rationality of that kind was out. But what else is there? Parsons did not reject the whole idea of persons' behaving with ends in view or doing what they thought would result in a predictable outcome. The means–ends scheme was retained, but without the rigorous implications of rationality.[31]

3. Value-attitudes

Rejecting a thoroughgoing rationality left a grand problem: What *are* the mechanisms that grossly regulate choices and order alternatives? The answer came in the form of "institutionalism" in economics.[32]

Parsons's training in economics informed him that attempts to ap-

---

[30] *The Structure of Social Action*, Part II.

[31] A cogent critique of the means–ends scheme implied by this is found in R. Bierstedt, "The Means–Ends Schema in Sociological Theory," *American Sociological Review*, III, 5 (October 1938), pp. 665–71.

[32] *The Structure of Social Action*, p. 702.

ply classical economic theory failed in many cases because the assumption of a randomness of desires was not justified. Wants do not spring up in random isolation, as though in a vacuum. Obviously some group influence as a whole constrains individual wants into more coherent patterns; these patterns could be called culturally determined *value-attitudes*. Parsons saw that the institutional economists were assuming voluntaristic and somewhat rational behavior on the part of individuals, but they also equipped these individuals with communally validated and restricted sets of alternatives. Thus they added a qualifying condition to classical economics. It is the restriction of alternatives that Parsons accepted. He added the basic idea of "value-attitudes" to his scheme.

Some further notes remain as enlargements on the point of value-attitudes. It is one thing to suggest that the community restricts or defines what its members will consider valuable. Where these restrictions originate and what sort of restrictions they are is another question. Should they be considered cognitive restrictions, intellectualized and accepted knowingly by all the community? There is good reason to believe not. For one thing, collective restrictions of that kind would be easily circumvented, and they would probably be arrived at by more clearly defined procedures than are evident in human society. Also, there is much evidence that persons are deeply attached emotionally to their judgments and values, and usually these opinions cannot be accounted for completely intellectually. It was Parsons's tentative conclusion, then, that value-attitudes ought to be thought of as expressions of sentiment that went deep into the collective life of the community. They were not always easily available to intellect and reason alone.[33]

Furthermore, communally derived value-attitudes were a property of the collective life and not directly attributable to individuals. There was something about the generation of these attitudes and ways of evaluating that could not be removed from their social context. This collective property made them appear to each member of the community as something outside himself. Each person realized that value-attitudes were not due to his own thinking; rather, they were in his experience as an external property of his world – mental images in which he participted, yet images that were external.[34]

4. Preliminary synthesis

Parsons's synthesis of various viewpoints about social action now begins to appear. He hoped to account for action that was not con-

---

[33] *The Social System*, p. 44, and *The Structure of Social Action*, Part II.

[34] Parsons discusses Durkheim in this context. See particularly his "The Present Position and Prospects of Theory in Sociology," in T. Parsons, *Essays in Sociological Theory*, Ch. 8.

trolled and determined, but that was volunteered by individuals. Such action occurred in a community that had an abstract power to define, in a general way, the appropriateness of actions and the ways they were to be evaluated. But the ultimate ends of action were not determined rationally. Still, persons did not act superstitiously or impulsively. Emotional and nonlogical choosing of alternatives and defining of ends and means were to be expected. It was also accurate, Parsons said, to regard the influence of communally derived value-attitudes as a property of the community. In that sense the "spirit" of the community, or what we might call its culture, had a unity and coherence of its own that impressed itself on individuals as being exterior to their private consciousness.

C. Systems and environments

We can now apply some of the general scheme of functionalism to Parsons's ideas. In voluntaristic social activities that form into coherent patterns as a result of the communal power to define and limit action in an integrative process, Parsons had the makings of a "system" view of social action. It was clear that acts themselves were not random. They were regulated, normative. Furthermore, they were regulated in a systematic way; similar behavior in similar situations tended to receive similar responses. This Parsons knew from everyday sociological data. In itself, this is only a trivial idea. But Parsons applied the concept system to this fact.

When Parsons viewed action as a system, it followed that there might be certain uniformities about the action system itself. These uniformities of the action system would be inherently abstract, because they would not be constraints on social action, but on types of action and types of situations. The action system did not limit or constrain action per se, but types of action. For example, we should expect that there would be uniform ways to behave when buying something from a stranger in a shop. These uniformities would be systematically different from action appropriate to intimate social relations among members of a family. The system of action prescribed uniformities of orientation, evaluation, and thought appropriate to situations, leading people to perform typical actions in a typical spirit, but these actions were in no concrete way predetermined because they were systematic.[35]

Functionalism argues that a system makes certain demands on its components' behaviors in order that the system may survive. This is the idea of system requisites.[36] To derive these features of human

[35] See *The Social System*, Ch. 2.
[36] Ibid., pp. 26–38.

148   *Functionalism*

social action systems as Parsons did, we must think commonsensically about what human social action really is. A social act entails a series of choices on the part of the actor. Actions are directed toward social objects, which may be other people or groups of people. Hence among the first choices is how the actor will regard the object. The general problem of how to regard objects Parsons calls the question of the actor's "system of *orientations.*" Is the object wanted, or not? What is the significance of the object to the actor? and so on. Parsons has outlined the orientation of the actor with reference to both motivation and value.[37]

These orientation choices appear to Parsons to be standardized. There are basically two kinds, and each of the two is subdivided into two parts. First, in making decisions about social objects, the actor faces dilemmas about his own attitudes toward the objects. Secondly, he must decide what motivational orientation to take up toward them.[38]

Considering the actor's attitude toward an object first, there are two choices to make:

1 Shall the actor be gratified by the object and expressive toward it, or withhold this?
2 Does the actor orient to the object no matter what the gratificational interest, or in relation only to some specific gratificational objective?

Concerning the choices of *motivation* toward objects, actors face another set of dilemmas. These dilemmas are concerned with how the objects are related to the actor, or to each other.

1 An object may be important because it is of particular relevance to the actor himself. It may be of no value to anyone else. Alternatively, it may be valued for its general properties, independent of the actor.
2 The object may be important because of what the object is inherently, or because of what it does. The first is an intrinsic quality; the second concerns the performance it makes.

1. The pattern variables

Parsons calls these pairs of dilemmas of choice the *pattern variables.*[39] To give them their Parsonsian names now, in order of their introduction, they are:

[37] *Toward a General Theory of Action,* Introduction; *The Social System,* pp. 3–24.
[38] *Toward a General Theory of Action,* pp. 76–84.
[39] Considerable critical comment has been made about the pattern variables. See Max Black, "Some Questions About Parsons' Theories," in Black, *The Social Theories of Talcott Parsons,* pp. 268–88; Robert Dubin, "Parsons' Actor: Continuities in Sociological Theory," in Parsons, *Sociological Theory and Modern Society,* pp. 521–36; Parsons, "The Pattern Variables Revisited," pp. 192–219.

affectivity *vs.* affective neutrality	the dilemma of whether to feel gratification or to withhold gratification
specificity *vs.* diffuseness	the dilemma of whether to orient to the whole object or to some part of it
universalism *vs.* particularism	the dilemma of whether to act toward the object in the light of its particular relation to the actor, or because of its general attributes
quality *vs.* performance	the dilemma of whether to be concerned about an object because of what it is, or what it does

It is risky to introduce examples too soon, but consider the way Parsons might characterize a genuine love relationship between a man and a woman. Such a relationship proceeds in terms of *affectivity* and *diffuseness* (one is gratified, and by the whole partner) and via *particularism* and *quality* (special aspects of the object's relation to the actor alone define the relationship, and the gratification coming from the relationship is due to what the object is and not what the object does). The pattern variables are directly related to Parsons's theory of the social systems in which they occur, as we shall see in the next section.[40]

2. System problems

We must now reconstruct Parsons's view of the invariant problems social systems must solve in order to survive. The appropriate attitudes and motivations to adopt in solving these problems can then be described by use of the pattern variables. In this way, Parsons can link together abstract aspects of the social system with the components of individual voluntary action.

Consider a scaled-down example of a social system: two persons in a railway station. The mutually oriented actions of these persons constitute this action system, and all the others and the building itself make up the environment. Now if this system wishes to accomplish something, it must expend energy.[41] Of course, the energy is derived from the participants, but the goal toward which the energy is directed is another question; it is defined by aspects of the social relations between the participants and by the environment, as well as by the individual desires of the persons. If our two persons in the railway station wish to talk, the mutual goal of communications entails con-

[40] See *The Social System,* pp. 58–67, "The Pattern Alternatives (Variables) of Value-Orientation as Definitions of Relational Role-Expectation Patterns."
[41] Parsons, *Societies,* pp. 28–9.

sidering how loud the noise is, who might overhear, where to sit down, and so forth. Thus performing this simple act entails some complicated decisions, all of which involve the systemic and environmental aspects of the relationship. This example suggests two general system problems: *adaptation* (existing and acting in a given environment) and *goal attainment* (deriving a goal toward which to expend energy in order to adapt the action system to its environment). When a system solves a problem of adaptation by expending energy toward a goal, the system will inevitably experience internal consequences. The expended energy will be gone, and something new may have been incorporated into the system in solving the problem. In general, the social system will be different in some way after solving the adaptation problem. Such differences pose a problem of readjustment, which Parsons has called *integration*. Finally, if the reintegrated system is to continue in action, it must have some ability to maintain itself. This Parsons calls the problem of *pattern maintenance*. Parsons means that in the absence of activities designed to maintain patterns of action, the social system would lose its coherence. He also suggests that pattern maintenance is a state of readiness to address new adaptive problems as they rise.[42]

We have now seen that social systems face the abstract problems of adaptation, goal attainment, integration, and pattern maintenance, no matter what the specific system, how large or small, significant or insignificant. Parsons has presented a separate argument to the effect that all systems (more accurately, all abstract systems) face similar problems. Anything considered a system faces these. Cultural systems and personality systems, as well as social relations, are analyzed by Parsons using this scheme.[43]

Now we may return to the pattern variables to discover how the dilemmas of choice are linked to the general system problems. The guiding principle is still rather simple, although many new terms will be used. The pattern variables are general statements about universal aspects of human social action. They are preliminary and indispensable to enacting social conduct toward objects. How do the universal system problems of adaptation, goal attainment, integration, and pattern maintenance link up with voluntaristic action as described by the pattern variables? Parsons must (1) give an explanation of the social system in terms of personal action and (2) give an explanation of personal action in terms of system action.

[42] This summary of the adaptation, goal attainment, integration, and pattern maintenance scheme is based on "Phase Movement in Relation to Motivation, Symbol Formation, and Role Structure," in Parsons, Bales, and Shils, *Working Papers*. The scheme is found in almost all Parsons's theoretical works.

[43] See *Toward a General Theory of Action*, p. 62, where Parsons and Shils discuss how they apply the general scheme to various "levels" of analysis.

We begin at the beginning by explaining adaptation. Adaptation is the accommodation of the social system to its environment.[44] War is the supreme example of a crisis of adaptation where two societies threaten each other's survival. There can be no mistake about a war – an active enemy cannot be anything but a hostile aspect of the environment.

Consider warlike behavior in terms of the pattern variables. First let us take universalism versus particularism. In warfare, the orientation of actors to objects is one of *universalism,* that is, cognizance of the object (the enemy) as a member of a class of things (called enemies). Paying too much attention to one *particular* enemy soldier as an individual might lead to thinking too much about his humanity, in which case it might be psychically impossible to kill him. But he might not make the same mistake about us.

However, adaptation in war is not the same thing as wanton murder. The second pattern variable, specificity versus diffuseness, suggests that interest in the enemy is *specific;* only insofar as he is engaged in hostile action against you do you oppose him. Decisions about how to orient to him are not made according to his whole being, but rest on how his acts as an enemy are relevant to your goals.

The next pattern variable is quality versus performance. In adaptive crises such as war, troublesome objects (enemies) are dealt with because of what they are doing, not because of what they are. This orientation to the object Parsons has named *performance.* Finally, note that it is inappropriate to attach affective or emotional sentiments to the object of adaptation. Everyone knows that soldiers do not usually think of their enemies as "people" while they are killing them. The affective bond is withheld or never developed. The orientation is one of *affective neutrality.*

Let us review this quickly in somewhat less concrete fashion. When social systems face adaptive problems, the most effective solutions to these problems will be gained by social action characterized by affective neutrality, specificity, universalism, and performance. The four pattern variable choices appropriate for adaptation form a general pattern of orientation. Persons involved in action will behave according to this pattern for best results in adaptive dilemmas. There is no specification of concrete acts here. The pattern is an abstract description of modes of orientation and evaluation. Adopting these modes will place a social system in the best position to accomplish adaptation to its environment. An adaptive role, therefore, were it to be institutionalized, would be nothing more than these general requirements for adaptive behavior applied to some specific situation.

---

[44] Sometimes Parsons uses the term "mastery" of the environment, by which he means to emphasize the active nature of social systems.

adaptation	goal attainment
pattern maintenance	integration

FIGURE 5.1

The other system problems are linked to the pattern variables in much the same way as adaptation. According to Parsons, for each problem of goal attainment, integration, and pattern maintenance, there is a unique combination of the pattern variables that satisfies the needs of the system in each of these phases. The four system problems form what is probably the most famous of all Parsons's ideas—his fourfold conceptual scheme, found in Figure 5.1. This fourfold idea carries us further. Taken together, the four system problems themselves form a system. Any surviving social system is consistently and continuously solving the four basic problems.[45] Recall the discussion of levels of analysis associated with functionalism. Because the fourfold scheme is completely abstract, Parsons can move it about. He can move it up in level of generality, or down, to account for the actions of whole societies, institutions, or even persons. Or he can define one of the four problems itself as being a system, and it will then display the fourfold scheme.

In Figure 5.2, the goal attainment subsystem has been taken as the subject for analysis. It has been broken down into the same four constituent abstract elements as the larger system of which goal attainment was a part. The other three systems now become environmental to the goal attainment subsystem. Parsons is saying that the fourfold scheme is a description of the way any system works, and because systems may be as large as societies or as small as interpersonal groups, the fourfold scheme may be used to make the same kind of general analysis of any social relations.

[45] "Solving" is not exactly the correct usage here. Parsons means that societies successfully cope with these problems. They do not solve them in a final sense. See Parsons and Smelser, *Economy and Society*, pp. 46-7.

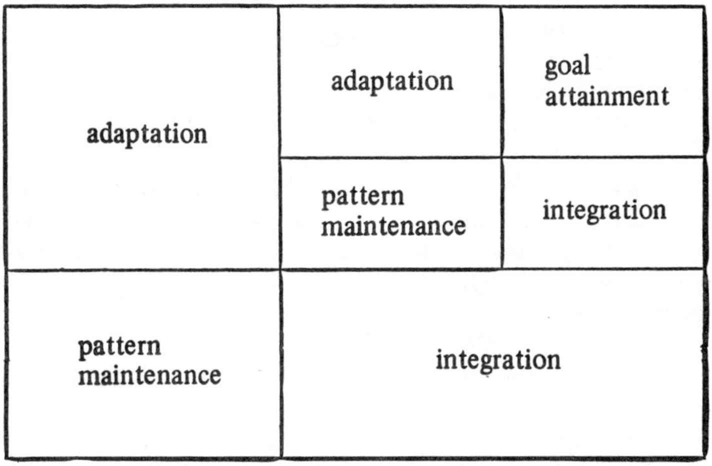

adaptation	adaptation	goal attainment
	pattern maintenance	integration
pattern maintenance	integration	

FIGURE 5.2

D. What kinds of systems are there?

Parsons regards his basic idea as completely abstract; by this he means that it is not intended primarily as a description of anything, but a way of conceptualizing system interdependencies and environments. It turns out that Parsons has applied the idea to several levels of analysis. Terminology becomes a problem here, because although Parsons uses the system idea very widely, he often means "society" when he uses the phrase "the social system," as for example in the title of his book.

The Social System describes Parsons's ways of thinking about societies. But Parsons could have written other system books as well. For example, there is the realm of ideas and values. In fact, says Parsons, social systems rely on *cultural* systems (systems of values, moral precepts, and symbols organized on exactly the same abstract principles as the social system). The fourfold paradigm, abstract and portable, can be applied to the cultural system, too.[46] Cultural systems have a unity, a coherence, and an internal logic quite like the action systems they accompany. Furthermore, the two systems are interdependent and influence each other.

Moving to another level of analysis, it is possible to think of the human *personality* as a system organized according to the fourfold

[46] Parsons, *Knowledge and Society* (Washington, D.C.: Voice of America, 1968).

scheme. It, too, is separate from and environmental to the social system and the cultural system.[47] At yet a lower level of abstraction, it is possible to consider the *physical organism,* apart from personality, as being the system from which all the rest of social and cultural behavior takes its energy.[48]

Taken together, the physical organism, the personality system, the social system, and the cultural system form a grand, mutually influencing array – they form a system.[49] Systems are the environments of systems, and as such they provide the potential for solving each other's problems. They could also be the sources of those problems. The whole picture (which might be called a "vision" on Parsons's part) works as an integrated unit, yet each part is internally coherent and analytically separable.

Let us expand somewhat on the application of this abstract fourfold concept to the theory of society. Applying the grand fourfold scheme to all the other systems, Parsons identifies the *social* system with the abstract idea of *integration.* Integration means relating the parts of the whole together. Interdependent social action does this, and society is interdependent social action.[50]

Associated with *pattern maintenance* is the *cultural* system – an orderly part of the social system's environment composed fundamentally of the legitimizing principles on which normative acts are based. It is one thing to say, "We act in a certain way"; and it is another thing to say, "We act this way for a specific reason." Ultimately, the only justifications for action in a society are the deeply felt and strongly held values and principles that are more or less common to members. These are systematically articulated in religious beliefs, descriptions of the nature of the world, art as emotional expression and embodiment of individuality, and the like. These aspects of culture all in one way or another express a meaning connected with social life. The cultural system provides highly abstract answers to the question "Why is life like this?" Cultural patterns endure relatively long. They lend coherence to diverse activity; hence they are pattern maintaining.

Associated with goal *attainment* in the general paradigm is the personality system. Personality is the learned mental organization of the

[47] See Parsons and Bales, *Family, Socialization and Interaction Process.*
[48] See *Societies,* pp. 28–9.
[49] Ibid., p. 29.
[50] The integration subsystem of the grand scheme is given another name in Parsons's later writing, the "societal community." By this term Parsons indicates the sum total of integrative acts that takes place among participants in the community. These normatively regulated acts spell out membership criteria as well. Those who act as though they belong, and are acted toward in a corresponding spirit, are by such action defining the societal community.

individual. Persons do not entirely act on their own toward privately contrived goals. Rather, the goals and the means that occur to them are massively influenced by the social relations in which people participate. Therefore, Parsons's concept of the personality system is one of a socialized, coherent, mental organization dependent on both the social system and the cultural system. The social system requires cooperation from each individual. Hence built into personality must be the desire to be rewarded by the things other people have to give, and the willingness to reward in acceptable ways. These desires, motives, and viewpoints (personality system) so necessary for integrated social action (social system) are, in turn, expressed and legitimized by the cultural system.

Associated with the remaining part of the general system, *adaptation,* is the purely physical aspect of the person and the organic and physical environment he lives in. Basically, Parsons's idea is that societies have to come to terms with their natural environments as a matter of survival, and the methods by which they come to terms are crucial. Collective social adaptation can only be realized by the coordinated application of individual energy to collective problems, that is, mobilization of the *physical organism.*

So far Parsons has made a simple set of associations between the parts of the general system, stated in abstract terms, and the more concrete systems: culture, society, personality, physical organism. The accompanying table summarizes these associations. As a way of making the general system idea clearer and to show its classificatory powers, examine next a Parsonian classification of social *institutions.* Social systems must institutionalize solutions to the four problems of general systems. If these solutions are not formulated, the system ceases to exist. Parsons shows that there are institutions of the social system associated with each of the four general system problems. He demonstrates that institutions perform the general functions of adaptation, goal attainment, integration, and pattern maintenance.

Classifying institutions by general system concepts, it is probably easiest to start with *adaptation.* When Parsons considers adaptation,

Functions in general system terms	Concrete systems
Pattern maintenance	Cultural system
Integration	Social system
Goal attainment	Personality system
Adaptation	Physical organism

he asks about the methods by which social systems accommodate their environments. It is natural, therefore, to find Parsons associating the *economy* as an institution with the adaptation function.[51] The economy produces the wherewithal societies need to accomplish survival. The health of the economic institution indicates the society's state of preparedness to cope with its environment. If orderly (institutionalized) economic activity ceased, adaptation would be impossible. It is no surprise, Parsons would say, that we have an array of laws, agreements, trusts, basic understandings, and ethics that governs economies. It is precisely because of the centrality of adaptation that it must be regulated; institutionalized norms grow up to do just that.

Now let us pass on to *goal attainment,* but keep the adaptation function well in mind, because the two go together. Economies as productive engines do not, in the last analysis, determine what is done with the wherewithal they produce. There are separate institutionalized and often formalized procedures for setting goals. This is the polity, or the *political* institution. In all countries, firms making up the industries that form the economy are regulated and controlled by laws that are not of their own making. Even though they may influence government, they are not the government. Social will is expressed through some regulating body of law and ongoing governing system. This and custom determine what general directions will be taken by a society, what its priorities are, and who shall be the beneficiaries of economic activity, in what proportions.[52]

Integrative institutions are those that standardize social relations of significance. In particular, legal norms that spell out certain duties individuals have to each other are examples of institutions devoted to system integration. The institution we might call *the law* fulfills principally an integrative function insofar as it standardizes expectations, gives decisions on justice, and defines particular duties and rights of citizens.

Pattern maintenance is associated with institutions that pertain especially to the conservation and articulation of what we might call

[51] *Economy and Society* details especially the economic institution's role in this scheme of classified institutions. For a good secondary treatment of Parsons's scheme of institutional relations with particular emphasis on politics, see William Mitchell, *Sociological Analysis and Politics* (Englewood Cliffs, N.J.: Prentice-Hall, 1967).

[52] See Parsons's "The Motivation of Economic Activities," in Parsons, Bales, and Shils, *Essays in Sociological Theory* (New York: Free Press, 1949), pp. 50–68. Recall here that Davis and Moore see the rewards attached to various social positions as inducements to cause persons to take up various occupations. This is just what Parsons would have predicted. Collective decisions attach fruits of economic endeavor to stratified positions. This is necessary because of the relative importance of these positions and the scarcity of the means to fill them. The processes of collective decision making and direction finding are the special province of *political* institutions, not economies.

"basic truth." *Religious* institutions are an example. Religious institutions make legitimate pronouncements on matters of high moral principle or ultimate reality, and interpret these into moral statements. This may be done in a roundabout fashion, but ultimately behavior is legitimized by reference to a cultural value. Parsons would say our pattern-maintaining institutions define for us the enduring "rightness" of certain activities. This rightness forms the moral basis of socialization and education, and is the backdrop for the evaluation and control of social practices. The value of life, the Golden Rule, or the significance of social responsibility, cannot ultimately be upheld on grounds of rationality or efficiency. They are moral precepts that emerge from religious or sentimental feelings that are institutionalized as cultural values.

Now we may see how a social norm that regulates concrete behavior unites the elements of the general system. Norms are followed by socialized persons because norms are satisfying and because proper conduct is rewarded by others. Socialized persons accept norms and are happy to perform them because norms are actual behavioral expressions of cultural beliefs. In that sense, acting according to a legitimate norm helps to confirm the legitimacy of the cultural system. Also, when one receives rewards for performance of a role, those doing the rewarding are seen to have right motives and desires and an adequate and properly organized personality system. Similarly, the personality that accepts legitimately offered rewards is confirmed and entrenched in the acceptance. Thus the social system, the "scene" where the action takes place, unites the personality system and the cultural system into a total action system that contains them all.

E. Cybernetic relations among the four parts of the general system

Parsons needed a coherent way to summarize his thoughts about the relationships among the four parts of the general systems. These parts do not stand alone; there is no cultural system in the absence of social system, personality system, physical organism; no social system in the absence of cultural system, personality system, physical organism and so forth. What is required is a means to express their interdependent yet separate nature. Parsons has chosen to do this by borrowing ideas from cybernetics, a science originally developed by mathematicians and engineers to express relations of input and output between related entities, and to express the ways these mutual influences affect the total system in which they are found.

Consider two central ideas: information and energy. Information, in a pure state, is powerless. Pure ideas do not act, cannot act. Similarly, pure energy has no direction. If we think of energy in action, we

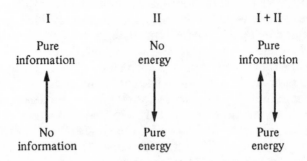

FIGURE 5.3

always think of its doing some particular thing, and never of its doing everything at once. Usually, ordinary concepts of energy and information actually mix the two. Information and energy need each other, so to speak, for either to be conceivable in a concrete way.[53]

Cybernetic thinking spreads the concepts of information and energy on two continua. The energy continuum goes between the pole of pure, undirected energy at one end to a lack of energy at the other; similarly, the information continuum goes from pure information on one extreme to no information on the other (see Figure 5.3). When these two continua are combined, it turns out that the gradations go in opposite directions. If the two are side by side, the end of the energy continuum representing pure energy is next to the "no information" end of the information continuum. The "no energy" end of the energy continuum is next to the "pure information" end of the information continuum. Of course, the extremes of these continua are purely theoretical, but Figure 5.3 suggests an interesting schematic plan. Parsons uses it to display the components of the general system. It would be natural to think of social action as the utilization of energy. This follows from Parsons's concept of social action, too—it is a motivated expenditure of energy toward some goal. The energy available, the types, kinds, and the cost of it, are "conditioning factors," which influence decisions about what actions to take. Similarly, as action is formulated, it is shaped, controlled, directed, and channeled. Information is combined with energy to do this. Information enters the act in the shape of "controlling factors" that give direction. Note that no action is possible without both information and energy. Note also that, depending on the point at which the action takes place along the continua, either relatively larger or smaller amounts of information and energy are needed to comprise the act, and that these

[53] The following discussion is based on Parsons, *Societies*, Ch. 2.

Parts of the general system model	Analytically separated systems	Cybernetic hierarchy
		<u>Information</u> (controlling factors)
Pattern maintenance	Cultural system	Cultural system
		$I\downarrow$ $\uparrow E$
Integration	Social system	Social system
		$I\downarrow$ $\uparrow E$
Goal attainment	Personality system	Personality system
		$I\downarrow$ $\uparrow E$
Adaptation	Physical organism	Physical organism
		<u>Energy</u> (conditioning and facilitating factors)

I = controlling factors derived from pure information.

E = conditioning and facilitating factors derived from pure energy.

FIGURE 5.4

amounts are inversely related. Earlier we saw Parsons relate his four-fold table of abstract system functions to personality, cultural and social systems, and to the physical organism. He now links these up according to the "conditioning" and "controlling" continua suggested by the cybernetic relationship between information and energy. The main point is to show the nature of the ways the four functions mix to form a coherent whole, to show what each gives to each.

If we refer to Figure 5.4 we note that on the left, in ascending order, are the names of the parts of the general system model. Opposite these, horizontally, are the physical organism, the personality system, the social system, and the cultural system. To the right, these are repeated showing the cybernetic relationships in which they stand to each other in terms of inputs and outputs of information and energy.

Moving up the cybernetic hierarchy from the physical organism, we note, as expected, that the physical organism contributes conditions and facilities for action, and that it receives normative controls as its input from the personality system. Notice that these controls come not directly from the cultural system, but arrive via the systems of social relations and personality. Thus, although controls applied to a physical organism and the personality system have a basis in culture, they are not directly related to culture. Rather, they have this relation articulated to them through action taking place in the intervening social system.

The social system is the system of mutually oriented interdependent social activities. Interdependent social action, in Parsons's language, is enacted in the *double contingency bond*,[54] which comes down to this: What I do is dependent on two things. One is what I want to do; the other is what you want me to do. What you do is regulated the same way. Now for us to get together, I must want to do what you want me to do, and you must want to do what I want you to do. If this condition obtains, then each of us will be rewarded in our actions from two sources. We will have our self-respect and our internal satisfaction from doing what we wanted, and we will have external gratification from the other person. Social interaction has repercussions both inwardly and outwardly. In the inward direction, it finds its gratification in individual personality processes. These, in turn, appear in the personality through social learning and familiarity with cultural themes. Parsons often discusses these processes under the heading of "need dispositions" when he means culturally influenced individual motivation. In the outward direction, social interaction is rewarded by other people.

The double contingency bond unites the systems below and above the social system into concrete behavior, and, by doing so, it contributes to the integration of these systems with the social system itself. From the personality system the social system receives conditions and facilities, and from the cultural system it receives normative controls. To the personality system normative controls are sent and to the cultural system conditions and facilities are sent. Through union of information and energy in the social system, normative voluntaristic action can take place; and as it occurs, it affects the systems environmental to it. Parsons suggests that over time the four systems mutually adjust to be more consistent with each other, so that energy and information united in action embody legitimate cultural values and personal needs. Thus Parsons says it is natural to expect to find persons wanting to do what they are required to do. Orderly activity of the social system is no longer problematic. The question of how order comes about is answered.

[54] *The Social System*, pp. 36 ff.

F. *Social evolution*

In the 1950s and 1960s, Parsons's theories were often criticized for giving too static a picture of social systems. It was said that his theoretical scheme, with its emphasis on well-ordered personalities, having clearly defined expectations, and acting in an integrated social system, implied too much integration and stability. Partly in response to such criticisms, Parsons sometimes applied his ideas more directly to the question of social change. Given functionalism's tradition and Parsons's systems thinking, it is not surprising that an evolutionary theory emerged.

Parsons's 1953 publication, *Working Papers in the Theory of Action* (coauthored by Bales and Shils) is of particular interest, especially Chapter 5, "Phase Movement in Relation to Motivation, Symbol Formation and Role Structure."[55] This outlines once again the fourfold paradigm and links it to the pattern variables. But here more clearly than elsewhere, Parsons et al. explain that the relationship between the four system problems involves a process of "moving equilibrium." Abstractly speaking, the four system problems together can be seen as a unit that appears fixed in space and time, but in practice it is not so. Parsons uses the idea of *phase movement* to express continuing changes in the relative importance of the four system problems in any total system, and the shifting nature of the relationships among them.

Analytically, one instance of social change may be called a phase movement. A phase starts with adaptation. The system as a whole must continually adapt, and an instance of this might be called an "adaptation problem." Appropriate to adaptation problems are immediate and maximum "instrumental adaptive activities" (or, in plain terms, maximum effort toward solving the problem at hand). However, as the environmental problem is mastered, it becomes increasingly appropriate for the newly adapted system to have a different relationship with its environment. A phase is reached in which environment is newly accommodated to the now altered system. This calls for a shift in attitude to the environment; there is a new relationship between the environment and the system, neither of which is exactly the same as it was before.

Following this is a further change. After new goals are attained, circumstances are somewhat altered. For one thing, energy has been used up. The system might be "tired." Similarly, it is not exactly the same system any more, and the environment-to-system relationship is changed. The system now has a different set of problems. A new

[55] Pp. 163–269.

integration is required, a reordering of things. Finally, following reintegration of the system, a phase of solidification and entrenchment is
required, one that will stabilize and maintain patterns of action until
the system encounters another adaptation problem. Then the cycle
will repeat. Note that this analysis is simply the application of adaptation, goal attainment, integration, and pattern maintenance categories
of action in sequence.

Of course, the environment might not wait for a full fourfold cycle
to be completed before it presents further adaptation problems. The
relationships among the four system units might be continually in flux
and several phase movements could be in progress at once. The point
Parsons would want us to see is this: The system, as an abstract
entity, remains the same. The four functions to be performed do not
change. However, the actions implied by the phase movement, the
particulars of each phase, and the solutions reached in each are
unique. There is a continuing pattern of theoretical order, but the
concrete system is changing. This approximates Parsons's view of
what has come to be called *social evolution*. There is a moving equilibrium among adaptation, goal attainment, integration, and pattern
maintenance. The emphasis on movement suggests that this is em-
phatically not a static idea.

Parsons later specifies that continually more differentiated and
specified social relations are evolved by the moving equilibrium. As
problems are faced, techniques and forces to deal with them are contrived that then go into the repertoire of skills and roles a society has
for doing its work. This amounts to greater specialization of function,
which calls for different, perhaps more complicated, coordination of
these differentiated activities – a more "organically" related set of
mutual dependencies arises.

Parsons approaches close to organic analogies in this treatment of
social evolution and in his specification of "evolutionary universals."[56] In principle, we might think social evolution would take so
many forms that after some time in the life cycles of societies, it
would be difficult to make comparisons among them. But Parsons
sees things differently. His idea is that some forms of social organization are "sufficiently important to future evolution that, rather than
emerging only once, [they are] likely to be 'hit upon' by various
systems operating under different conditions."[57] In other words,
there are forms of social organization that Parsons predicts will eventually evolve in all societies. All a society requires to set this process
going are: a language, some kind of kinship organization, a religion,
and rudimentary technology.

[56] See Chapter 3 for a discussion of the organic analogy in sociological theory.
[57] Parsons, *Sociological Theory and Modern Society*, p. 491.

Parsons says the first structure likely to evolve is social stratification, a vertical dimension of social differentiation often loosely called "social class."[58] He notes that in primitive societies, ones without social class as he means it, ascription of social status often depends upon biological relationships. Where status is distributed on this basis, there is no freedom for the system to select talent and to allocate social positions apart from persons. A person enjoys a status because of who he is rather than what he does. Under such a system, if traditional lineages are quite ancient, and everyone is related to everyone else, there is an inherent inability of the system as a whole to develop a hierarchy of positions, each with duties and rights. Parsons thinks that as time goes on, concern about personal advantage comes to outweigh kinship status, and there develops a tendency for families to be ranked. When this takes place, evolution toward an impersonal stratified system of ranks has begun. The end result will be an entirely impersonal emphasis upon rank as an indicator of preference and not family or lineage. Closely associated with stratification as an evolutionary universal is the emergence of legitimate institutionalized definitions of the society as a whole, to which all can refer. As stratification develops, impersonal divisive tendencies are introduced that threaten cohesive life in society. But parallel with stratification, universalistic definitions and pride in "we" feeling evolve. Evolution of a new "we-ness" gives a broader normative base. When a people is proud of its heritage, the tendency is for this pride to be turned into increasingly explicit normative rules expressing belonging and citizenship. As these rules take form, universal normative grounds for social unification take the place of particular concrete obligations. With broadened, more secure collective identity, there is more adaptive freedom and more room for innovation, more adaptive potential.

Following these developments, Parsons sees an additional stage, that of evolving bureaucratic organization. Today, "bureaucratic" is sometimes a term of abuse. But what Parsons means is not the alleged evils deriving from bureaucracy, but the adaptive advantage bureaucratic organization gives a society. Implicit in the bureaucrat's habit of acting impersonally is the idea that authority resides not in the person but in the office. In principle, two advantages flow from this. One is that the office (or, more broadly, the status) is viewed as acting in the name of the whole social unit. Legitimate bureaucratic organization is a routine expression of the cultural themes uniting men. Hence there is always a degree of acceptance of the bureaucrat's role as "right." Institutionalization gives this rightness a more solid foundation. In addition to conferring established legitimate au-

---

[58] The following discussion is based on Parsons's chapter on evolution, ibid.

thority to act in the name of the group, the evolution of impersonal status allows the system to apportion activities more consistently and rationally. A bureaucratic office implies duties and rights with respect to a closely circumscribed area of competence and power. Without bureaucratic specialization, authorities might carry altogether irrelevant status or importance. The freedom to allocate persons and act toward them according to their legitimate positions gives the system the competitive advantage of better utilization of talent, and more flexible responsiveness to environmental exigencies.

Evolving alongside bureaucratic organization are money economies and markets. The adaptive advantage of these is increased economic flexibility. A society must be readily able to transport its available resources to the industries and organizations most in need of support. This is best done when a common system of evaluation of goods and service is available, as in a money economy. Similarly, money markets liberate persons from entanglements that might otherwise hold them back. Ability and willingness to buy or sell goods and services are more inclusive criteria for economic action than are ascriptive or restrictive ones.

In addition to the sequentially developed practices of stratification, cultural legitimation, bureaucracy, and a money economy, Parsons sees generalized universalistic norms evolving, and democratic associations arising. Universalistic norms are those that apply to a position and are viewed as binding on persons taking that role.[59] The role remains open for all who might occupy it, irrespective of extraneous distinctions, prejudices, or irrelevant selection criteria. Democratic association is the extension of this tendency into collective action. Universalistic norms applied to politics yield essentially democratic governments. Such norms, used to select the powerful and to monitor their performance, maximize political responsiveness and adaptive potential.

Parsons views these developments as universal in social evolution and sees them as cumulative. The first ones are required for the emergence of the others. But this is not to say that complete perfection of any is required for onward movement in social evolution. Indeed, after a given level of development has been reached, it appears to Parsons that several social forms evolve together, and vestiges of previous practices may remain within systems that operate in a predominantly different spirit.

If we revert to Parsons's general scheme again and ask about the origins of present-day social change, one or two points may be added to this picture. So far, social change originating outside the social system has been discussed. Social evolution is adaptive change in

---

[59] Universalistic norms are perhaps best understood as an outgrowth of bureaucratic tendencies.

response to environmental conditions. That is why Parsons thought the first institutions to evolve would be those making the greatest contribution to adaptation. It is in this sense that evolutionary change is originated outside the system. In the absence of the need to adapt, social evolution would not have begun. But once it starts, internal adjustments are required to accommodate a society to its own changing nature, and a parallel set of internal changes begins. These do not originate directly in adaptive problems, but come as a consequence of society's adaptation. Internal changes of this sort we see about us in highly developed societies today. Parsons calls these *strains,* to differentiate them from the *stress* of externally generated evolutionary change.

VII. Research and functionalism

There is so much research literature that could be called "functionalist" that even to list the subjects of it would be beyond the scope of this book. Nevertheless, some broad outlines about functionalist research can be described.

A. Levels of research

The discussion has so far concentrated on functionalist theory applied to total societies, or at least to large subgroups. Davis and Moore, for example, work with the whole society; stratification is accounted for by reference to society's natural requirements. Levy and Parsons theorize at the same level. Hence one would expect considerable research on total societies, and it is extant. Especially regarding comparative social systems, comparative institutions, and social change, functionalism has provided the conceptual categories by means of which one can arrange data about particular social systems. An example of this kind of work will be described presently.

But functionalism has been employed at lower levels of analysis. Factories, organization of both formal and informal groups, schools, and hospitals are just some of the places where functionalism has become basic theory for research. Sometimes the objectives of functionalist social research change slightly when it is applied at different levels. Working from basic functionalist theory of stratification, subtle variations on the theme have often been introduced. For example, in a paper by E. Burnstein, R. Moulton, and P. Liberty called "Prestige Versus Excellence as Determinants of Role Attractiveness,"[60] functionalist theory is altered in a revealing way. In general,

---

[60] In *American Sociological Review*, XXVIII, 2 (April 1963), pp. 212–19.

the Davis–Moore argument says that positions of higher importance in a society have greater rewards attached to ensure recruitment of talented personnel. Burnstein et al. interviewed a variety of persons whom they could classify as having either "high" or "low" motivation to achieve. They questioned them on their feelings toward the jobs they held or aspired to, with special emphasis on jobs that demanded excellence and talent and jobs that conferred high prestige. The Davis–Moore argument suggests that a given job would be rated high on both, or low on both, but that in all events the demand for excellence would accompany posts of high prestige.

Burnstein et al. found, however, that these were not necessarily the feelings of their respondents. When the gross distinctions of high and low prestige were refined, their subjects told them in effect that one could be more or less concerned about the excellence demanded, independently of the prestige; and similarly, one could be concerned about prestige, independently of the excellence demanded. Furthermore, the determinant of whether one was sensitive to the prestige or the excellence demand in a given job was one's "achievement motivation." Those high on motivation to achieve were typically more motivated by the excellence demanded, and rather less by the prestige of the job. Conversely, those low on achievement motivation tried, in effect, to get the greatest prestige value for a given level of excellence demanded – they were sensitive to prestige before excellence.

This finding is theoretically significant; it shows that the Davis–Moore theory is oversimplified because it apparently neglects psychological or personal factors. Burnstein et al. effectively insert a psychological factor into the hypothesized correlation between excellence demand and prestige. They wished to see if, when the psychological factor was varied, any significant variation occurred in the ability of society to motivate by offering prestige. Such was found to be true. Davis and Moore might say that this variation was minor, on the scale of things, and that although variations of this kind occur, their general theory would still apply if stratification were considered in its full range. And at least in part, the Burnstein et al. data support this. Burnstein et al. did find that prestige was a powerful motivator of persons having low or only ordinary achievement motivation. Burnstein et al. found confirmatory evidence for the Davis–Moore theory and contributed a theoretical refinement to it.

B. Research on functional alternatives

Sometimes it is deduced from functional theory that the competitive advantage of a certain practice renders that practice essential to society. In saying this, the theoretical emphasis is shifted from the function to the concrete substance of the practice. Occasionally, the functional theory of stratification has been used this way – taken to mean that inequality of prestige and status is necessary to achieve basic recruitment. Indeed, in the discussion of Parsons's "evolutionary universals," we seemed to note this. However, it must be kept in mind that Parsons was saying that *some* system of universalistic recruitment must evolve, not one particular system – he implied there could be functional alternatives.

However, there is no evidence in the world that could prove that a system of stratification would be necessary for social survival if there were alternative means of solving the recruitment problem. The ubiquity of stratification systems is often cited as proof that a stratification system is the only way to accomplish recruitment. But this has not prevented sociologists from giving examples of functional alternatives – means by which to solve the problems of recruitment and a motivation that do not involve ordinary stratification.

The idea of functional alternatives implies reservations about functionalism's use as an empirically grounded theory. If functionalists can supply convincing explanations for social systems as they find them, or make comparative use of their data, well and good. But if functionalists say that whatever "is" must be a functional solution to some basic requirement, then they are not really illuminating basic requirements at all; rather, they are turning functionalism into a tautology.

Schwartz has given an example of research into functional alternatives.[61] He compared two agricultural communities in Israel. One, organized on a collective basis, distributed goods and services according to need; each person worked at assigned tasks. The other community was arranged so that land was divided among families. Each family was responsible for production, but it could proceed in any fashion it liked. Using Davis and Moore's stratification theory as a guide, Schwartz expected the first community to have a high proportion of routinized jobs and little opportunity to practice social differentiation by means of unequal rewards. In the second, he expected a highly developed reward system among members of the families. His findings did not exactly conform to predictions.

In fact, he found sociological adaptations in both communities that allowed each to work with neither too little nor too much individual initiative. In the first community, these adaptations involved mechanization, job rotation, and outside work that decreased the subordination of the individual to the community, while maintaining the overall communistic social organization. In the second community, where Schwartz expected exaggerated social differentiation according to

[61] R. Schwartz, "Functional Alternatives to Inequality," *American Sociological Review*, XX, 4 (August 1955), pp. 424–30.

family rank and skill, he found instead cooperative enterprise among families and "corrective" measures, such as training and education, to equalize the members. Additionally, there was migration in and out of both communities; personnel tended to change to fit the conditions.

Schwartz's data do not basically contradict the Davis–Moore theory of stratification. Schwartz shows that within the context of functionalist thinking, there are many alternative explanations for observed stratification practices in a given community. Although functionalist theory is basically retained, predicted details are either reinterpreted or explained in some novel way. Work on functional alternatives has usually expanded the scope of functionalism rather than narrowed it. As previously suggested, a possible danger is that functionalism may be made so broad as to "explain" everything, and therefore explain nothing.

C. Research on types of communities and societies

Pattern theory is principally *typological* theory. This way of thinking derives from German sociology in which ideal types are drawn up as conceptual models with which to compare actual situations. Of classical importance here is the *Gemeinschaft–Gesellschaft* typology employed in some form or other by Tönnies, Durkheim, Redfield, Becker, and others. Today, typological thinking survives in Parsons's theories. One can view the pattern variables, for instance, as a modern refinement of the *Gemeinschaft–Gesellschaft* typology.

For these two classical types, the usual English translations are *community* and *society*. In the community (*Gemeinschaft*) type, relations based on kinship, location, loyalty, friendship, and tradition are emphasized. In the society (*Gesellschaft*) type, relations based on law, contract, public opinion, exchange, and rationality are the key features. For Parsons and his pattern variables, the trouble with this typology was that many different ingredients were combined into only two concepts. Fine distinctions could not be expressed. Was it not possible to have some elements of each type? The pattern variables, as Table 5.1 shows, break down the old community–society typology into what Parsons regards as its main operative features.

The pattern variables become a research tool in the analysis of types of social organization for McKinney and Loomis.[62] For example, they compared two agricultural villages in Costa Rica for size, type of routine, geographical layout, and accessibility. In some of these they found differences that indicated one village was less

[62] John McKinney and Charles Loomis, "Systematic Differences Between Latin American Communities of Family Farms and Large Estates," *American Journal of Sociology*, LXI (March 1956), pp. 404–12."

TABLE 5.1

Community (Gemeinschaft)		Society (Gesellschaft)
affectivity	versus	affective neutrality
particularism	versus	universalism
quality	versus	performance
diffuseness	versus	specificity

"primitive" than the other. After this they identified persons in each community who had particularly powerful positions. In one village, these persons were the administrator and his subordinate; in the other these were persons of similar status.

McKinney and Loomis's idea was to examine the ways in which these authoritative persons used their position, by describing their roles according to the pattern variables. Did anyone behave according to the *Gemeinschaft* qualities of reliance on kinship and personal loyalty, tradition, and emotional action? How about the more rationalistic, legally based, and publicly oriented *Gesellschaft?* Their data supported the expected polarity. In the community that was more inaccessible, that had residents of longer tenure, where the farm practices were less determined by routine and schedule, and where family units were of more central importance in social organization, the measurements taken with the pattern variables gave *Gemeinschaft*-like indications. However, in the village that was less *Gemeinschaft*-like, the pattern variables did not quite turn out *Gesellschaft*-like. The responses from this second village more approximated the center of the continuum between *Gemeinschaft* and *Gesellschaft*. In a way this is understandable, because both the villages were quite remote and rural, by North American standards; but the idea of a middle ground between these two social types raises theoretical problems that McKinney and Loomis do not address. We will return to this point when criticizing functional theory.

D. Research on social evolution

Buck and Jacobson tested Parsons's theory of evolutionary universals in a creative and stimulating way.[63] Again we find that research with

---

[63] Gary Buck and Alvin Jacobson, "Social Evolution and Structural-Functional Analysis: An Empirical Test," *American Sociological Review,* XXXIII, 3 (June 1968), pp. 343–55.

a given theoretical background results in the refinement of theory. Buck and Jacobson develop Parsons's theory of social evolution by showing variations in the evolutionary sequence foreseen by Parsons. Buck and Jacobson agree with Parsons that most existing societies have experienced at least some social evolution. But when the idea of "levels" of evolutionary progress is added to the theory, it is not unreasonable to expect existing societies to be at different levels and developing at different rates. (A level is the same relative degree of development on each of the evolutionary universals postulated in Parsons's theory.[64]) Buck and Jacobson's objective was to test Parsons's theory of evolutionary universals along with their extension of it – the concept of levels of development. Additionally, they developed methodological techniques for doing so.

A selection of fifty countries was made, probably according to the theoretically possible range of evolutionary development. It was not thought necessary to select countries at random for analysis. Rather, the idea was to develop the measurement methods and apply them to a sample yielding information on both the level of development and on the usability of the scales.[65]

With ten different measurements (derived from the ten indications of evolutionary development given by Parsons), it immediately became possible to test the idea of levels of development. Data were displayed on (1) communications, (2) kinship organization, (3) religion, (4) technology, (5) stratification, (6) cultural legitimation, (7) bureaucratic organizations, (8) money and markets, (9) generalized universalistic norms, and (10) democratic associations. If these data showed relatively consistent levels of development for a given country, then the idea that social evolution occurred in a nonrandom way according to some general principles would be supported.

Basically, the ten indicators gave consistent levels of development for each country in the sample. Furthermore, it became possible to show that the sample of countries studied followed a pattern of "upward progression" through the levels. For example, New Zealand,

[64] The evolutionary universals were: stratification, cultural legitimation, a money economy, universalistic norms, and democratic associations.

[65] It is not necessary here to delve into the exact measurements used to check each of the characteristics of development mentioned by Parsons. Some of the information came from United Nations publications, part from other research. For example, anthropological evidence was employed in measurement of kinship systems, whereas technological development was measured as the per capita production of electric power, the percentage of the gross national product originating in agriculture, and the percentage of the labor force employed in industrial as opposed to agricultural or forestry work. The "democratic nature" of the societies was measured by the constitutional status of the government in power, the presence or absence of a party system of elections, the representative nature of the regime, and the current status of legislatures.

Britain, Australia, the United States, and Sweden appeared near the top of the list. Canada, Iceland, and West Germany grouped nicely in a position just beneath the top. Near the bottom were Nigeria, Uganda, and Tanzania. The empirical pattern encountered by the researchers was, roughly, the pattern theoretically predicted; this is what we expect from pattern theory.

Of particular interest is the sequence of evolution found by Buck and Jacobson. In itself, the listing of countries at various levels of development only suggests the conclusion that these countries arrived at their levels by passing through evolutionary stages. It does not indicate whether they passed through them in the sequence Parsons postulated. Of course, it is impossible to gather data directly on a developed society's sequence of passage through levels of development. But Buck and Jacobson were able to find variations in the data that give insight into this question. They note that in the lowest level (Level I), there was "underdevelopment" and "overdevelopment" on different universals. Some universals were less well developed than others; this is what they expected. But which ones? Theory alone predicts the sequence to be stratification, cultural legitimation, bureaucratic forms, money and markets, and so on, ending with democratic associations.

However, within Level I, Buck and Jacobson found a somewhat different series. Most developed in Level I was bureaucratic organization; least was money and markets. Their explanation is that underdeveloped countries often import developed institutions more or less intact, and that colonial experience might overdevelop bureaucracy. But note here that the sequence is roughly in the order Parsons predicted: Money and markets fall toward the end of the predicted series, and bureaucracy falls toward the beginning. In Level II, Buck and Jacobson discovered that the overdevelopment of bureaucracy disappeared. Some of its development that had led to Level II was actually impeding further social evolution. Also established technology and kinship organization were not leading to social change in Level II; they were holding it back. In Level IV, there was a shift in relative development of the universals so that money and markets, technology and communications were leading the developments, while other previously developed institutional practices were impeding social change.

In general, this research shows that it is possible to establish facts about the relative social development of various countries, and that this information generally suggests the sequence of evolution hypothesized by Parsons. Buck and Jacobson have improved things somewhat, however, by showing that, within levels of social evolution, Parsons's series is not always found. Hence, although the general theory has produced some good basic confirmatory evidence, it has also led to refinements that ought to be incorporated into the general theory to make it more accurate.

VIII. Critical remarks about functional theory

It is a credit to the field of sociology that functional theory, almost "orthodox" throughout the 1950s and 1960s, was also subjected to serious critical examination during that time. Functionalism has somewhat declined in popularity in recent years, partly because of damaging criticisms, and partly because of the fad-following that plagues the social sciences. Yet large numbers of workers use some form of functional theory as their basic thinking. They may not all call themselves "Parsonsian" or "Mertonian," but there is still evidence, as Davis has argued, that functionalism is the basic theory of sociology.[66]

As one would expect, the logic, substance, and method of functionalism all have been criticized. These categories of criticism provide convenient organizing criteria for a review of critical remarks. But first we must consider criticism that alleges that functionalism is not really a theory.

A. Is functionalism a theory or a model?

It could be said that functionalism cannot properly be called a theory at all; rather, it is a set of methodological canons. Largely, this criticism addresses the highly abstract nature of functional theory, and the fact that its main principles are not really researchable. For example, the concept of "system" especially in the work of Parsons, is a purposely abstract concept, applied to institutions, to personality, to the relationship between the two. Because it is pliable in this way, there is virtually nothing that could be empirically proved about its applicability to a given situation.

Similarly, it is in the nature of functional theory to postulate things that cannot be proved wrong. Serious instances of this are the ideas of functional requisites, social evolution, and the fourfold scheme of Parsons. It is held that a social system, if it is to survive, must solve typical problems of social organization and institutionalized practice. This argument leads to the search for functional requisites. But we have no societies that are not, by definition, "surviving." Hence it would seem that whatever these societies do are the necessary things. This line or argument, taken to its conclusion, suggests the charge that functional theory does not give an explanation of society at all.

---

[66] Kingsley Davis, "The Myth of Functional Analysis as a Special Method in Sociology and Anthropology," *American Sociological Review*, XXIV, 6 (December 1959), pp. 757–71.

Rather, it gives an abstract model implying that *if* a society were engaged in a survival struggle, then the society would be solving certain functional problems. A model explains by analogy (see Chapter 1, section II); hence functional theory could be said to lack empirical grounding and only to suggest analogies, not hypothesize relationships. The idea of functional alternatives leads to reinforcement of this criticism. If there are an infinity of concrete ways to solve functional problems, then it will surely be difficult to discover the root reasons for a given institutional practice in a given society.

If the substance of functional theory is so hard to document and rigorously research, then we are left with the dictum that "social structures have systematic effects on neighboring social structures, and possibly on individuals." This is not very enlightening; if such criticism is taken literally, functionalism becomes only an arbitrary dictum to "seek effects."

B. Criticisms of functionalism as a theory

Obviously it is not unanimously agreed that functional theory exists. But among those who consider functionalism a theory, several types of critical material have been advanced. Some theoretical and logical criticisms of functionalism will be considered first; criticism of functionalism as a method follows after.

1. Logical and theoretical criticisms

(a) The problem of tautology. Tautology means circularity.[67] Circular thinking is a matter of creating a closed system by defining one thing in terms of another, so that both seem to be separate entities, yet are actually the same thing or are analytically inseparable. Abstractly, if we define *A* as *X* and define *X* as *A,* then *X* and *A* share all attributes in common. If they have any distinguishing features, the definition of neither is sensitive to the distinguishing marks.

Functionalism is charged with making this kind of mistake in logic. The most notable and central point at which this happens is in the definition of a society. For example, Levy's definition of a society includes:
1 a plurality of actors oriented to the system, who
2 are self-sufficient for the action of the collectivity, and
3 the whole system is capable of existing longer than the individual members who make it up.

[67] See Ernest Nagel, "A Formalization of Functionalism," in *Logic Without Metaphysics;* Carl Hempil, "The Logic of Functional Analysis," in Llewellyn Gross, ed., *Symposium on Sociological Theory* (Evanston, Ill.: Row, Peterson, 1959), pp. 271–307.

Because we cannot look at a society from time to time and readily recognize that it is always *the same* society, we can only assert its continued existence in self-sufficient form. The definition of a society becomes an assertion about the empirical nature of social systems. Giving concrete meanings to one's abstractions by definition and then "discovering" these empirically only shows that the characteristics were true by definition. Such an exercise suffers from logical circularity.

(b) The question of teleology. A teleological explanation is one that explains the parts of a system (be it social science, biology, or mechanics) by making reference to the purpose of the parts with regard to their future states within the whole. It seems that functionalism does this despite conscious attempts to avoid it. An example is found in the functionalist theory of stratification, in which the general argument is that stratification has beneficial effects on society, and is retained because of these effects. To make such an argument, logic requires that all the effects of stratification be known and that the precise nature of the system in which these effects occur be made clear. With the human body, for example, if the heart stops, we have enough knowledge about the body to say that it dies because the contribution of the heart is lacking. In social sciences, there is a greater difficulty in demarcating the precise extent and effects on structures. It is, therefore, hard to tell what the teleological explanation of a social structure should be. Furthermore, the exact nature of a structure's contribution must be known and it must be known that the structure does not have deleterious effects. It is by no means agreed that stratification has the effects claimed by Davis and Moore, and that it does not have destructive effects instead. Yet this theory of stratification continues its teleological explanation as though logical criteria for a teleological explanation had been met.

But perhaps teleological explanations are desirable in sociology. We noted that functionalists try to avoid imputing motive or purpose to abstractions like "social structure." Still, it may be argued that it is in the nature of man to have purpose, and therefore an explanation of social institutions in terms of intentions is proper. This argument has some power when applied to manifest functions that are intended. But functionalism shows its greatest strength in explaining manifest functions that are *not* intended, or in explaning latent functions. When the concept of social evolution is added, the inherent teleology of functionalism becomes more apparent than ever. Durkheim suggested in *The Division of Labor* that the eventual consequence of a threat to social solidarity was an alternative solidarity. This suggests that, unknown to the participants, society was "protecting" its solidarity. It had its own purpose in mind, as it were. This makes society into an entity having powers of choice. Surely this is absurd. Persons have minds, but do societies? Durkheim's thesis challenges us to find an alternative explanation if we do not accept the idea that social development involves a self-correcting society. Do we actually want teleological explanations or not?

It has been noted also that functionalism seems to reverse the chronology of cause and effect.[68] Because we observe no cause, but only impute it, we are uncertain that the cause of a thing lies in its history and not in its future. Yet from "commonsense" observation it would seem silly to say that the cause of an institution's form of organization lies in the future effects that institution will have. Particularly for sociologists concerned about methodological positivism and the establishment of cause and effect, the reverse chronology seemingly implied by functionalism frustrates rather than facilitates inquiry.

(c) Reductionism and functionalism. Toward the end of the 1950s, theorists especially impressed with exchange models of society made a damaging criticism of functionalism and started a debate that continues to this day. They claimed that functionalism is trivial because everything functionalists try to establish can in turn be reduced to propositions about individual behavior. Hence the only real theory in sociology is psychological theory, because it is psychology that establishes motives. Because they were reducing functionalism to psychology, these critics were called *reductionists.*[69]

Among the objectives of functionalists is to separate the theory of society from the theory of man. This entails explaining societal forms and institutions by reference to ideas about the societies themselves, and not by reference to the motivations of the people who populate them. The justification for doing this is that people may have various and unique motives, but they act collectively, and there is something about their collective actions that is not reducible to individual motives.

Immediately, motivation became a problem for functionalism. If institutional structure, at its own level of abstraction, explained social order, functionalists had to account for why persons act normatively with respect to institutions. Wrong has complained that this led to an "oversocialized" concept of man as essentially an empty bucket into which society could pour all of its requirements for social action.[70]

---

[68] William Catton, Jr., "Flaws in the Structure and Functioning of Functional Analysis," *Pacific Sociological Review*, X, 1 (Spring 1961), pp. 3–12.

[69] For example, see George Homans's "Contemporary Theory in Sociology," in R. E. L. Faris, ed., *Handbook of Modern Sociology* (Chicago: Rand McNally, 1964), pp. 951–77.

[70] Dennis Wrong, "The Oversocialized Concept of Man," *American Sociological Review*, XXVI, 2 (April 1961), pp. 183–93.

Not only was man theoretically oversocialized, but society was theoretically overinstitutionalized. We got a brighter picture of man from functional theory when we saw him competing for prestige and material benefit in Davis and Moore's theory of stratification. But did this very theory of stratification not imply a psychologically self-interested motive? If so, it was only a short step to the conclusion that stratification should be explained in individual competitive terms without functional requirements, social evolution, institutional systems, and so forth. So went the argument.

But the reductionist critics of functionalism had an equally devastating problem on their hands. Where did the individual desires and motives come from that were supposed to be the reducing agents that dissolved functionalism? Either they came from instincts, "deep" inside the person, or they were fashioned in experience. Homans largely took the second alternative. But this is just what functionalism was trying to say – that common unified collective experience fashioned motives, that motives were to be explained by institutional structures.

So, is it that functionalism is reduced to psychology, or is psychology to be "expanded" to functionalism? Sociology cannot easily do without the concept of motivation, unless it simply becomes a study of comparative institutions. Similarly, psychologistic theories in sociology cannot easily put aside structural thinking. Here the matter should probably rest.

(d) Problems related to the concept of system. System is typically found in functionalism as a "closed" concept. A system is usually a bounded, sealed entity. There is good reason that this should be true. The logical necessity of a boldly demarcated system has already been explained.[71] However, this very feature of systems has come under fire from critics who would have functionalism an "open" system. Openness of the system, the argument runs, would be beneficial because greater flexibility could be explained in terms of it. There would be less fuss in taking in new ideas; the theoretical pattern would be more sensitive to "reality." All this sounds good. But making the system open in this way invites indeterminacy and vagueness. What emerges from this argument is a paradox. The paradox is that the logical and the empirical requirements of functionalism run at cross-purposes. To be made more empirically sensitive, the system should be thought of as open. To be made logically defensible, the system should be made more securely and definitely closed.[72]

[71] See this chapter section II, B.
[72] See Walter Buckley's critique of the functionalist use of "system" in his *Sociology and Modern Systems Theory* (Englewood Cliffs, N.J.: Prentice-Hall, 1967).

(e) Research using pattern variables criticized. The pattern variables as methodological guides in the work of McKinney and Loomis are ambiguous. McKinney and Loomis attempted to scale informants' responses to questions based on the pattern variables. Parsons means the pattern variables to be polarities. He does not think that there is a middle ground between affectivity and affective neutrality, for example. One is either being gratified by an object and releasing motivational energy toward it, or one is not. Yet McKinney and Loomis used the concepts as continua, along which they found responses distributed.

One question arising from this is to what extent, if at all, could it be said that McKinney and Loomis "tested" the pattern variables as a theoretical idea? Holding to Parsons's conception of the pattern variables, the answer is that McKinney and Loomis mistook Parsons's intent, and hence no test of hypotheses was made. But there is an additional point that shows something about Parsonsian pattern theory. McKinney and Loomis's findings show that even if the pattern variables are fundamentally misconstrued from a logical point of view, they give illuminating knowledge of the ways in which their two villages differ. The theoretical scheme does receive some support from their findings.

The question of how to interpret the pattern variables in research arises because the concepts turn up in so many places in Parsons's theory. As personal dilemmas of choice, it is hard to see how they could be anything but sets of mutually exclusive choices. But Parsons's theory does not stay at the level of personal action choices. It builds up from there to become even more inclusive, embracing whole societies laced together by their adaptation, goal attainment, integration, and pattern maintenance functions. Now we saw that there are typical pattern variable choices appropriate to each functional area. To the extent that society is in flux, that persons are caught between competing loyalties and the like, it does seem that the pattern variables might become continua, when viewed from the perspective of whole societies and social change. But thinking of the pattern variables in this way does considerable violence to the basic logic of the social act as worked out by Parsons as the basis of all social relations. Such fundamental ambiguity of basic concepts almost always leads to ambiguous empirical work, as in the case of McKinney and Loomis.

C. Criticisms of the substance of functional theory

In addition to the critical fire leveled at functionalism by logical and methodological opponents, critics have pointed to errors of either omission or commission. Some critics are concerned less with the logic of the theory than with its descriptive accuracy. Appreciate that these are different questions. A "true" picture, empirically justifiable, need not be logically construed; a logical construct is not necessarily accurate.

1. The oversocialized concept of man

Wrong suggests that the functionalist view of motivation neglects individuality and implies the overinstitutionalized society. But this criticism is somewhat polemical, because nowhere does functionalism seriously argue that it accounts for all behavior. In principle, there could be all sorts of behavior falling outside of socially organized boundaries, about which sociological theorists could have little to say. Such action could hardly be called "overinstitutionalized," nor those doing it "oversocialized."

Nevertheless, the polemic exposes theoretical failure. For instance, the sociology of risk, decision under uncertainty, decision making among unstructured alternatives, uniqueness, and, generally, the less regulated aspects of everyday life are not well accounted for by functionalism. Socialization and social control are commonly explained in functionalism as the effect of institutionalized sanctions. In empirical applications where these sanctions are confused or nonexistent, there is a real theoretical problem. Recall Merton's work on types of individual adaptation to overstressed success goals. Merton logically outlined the pathways an individual might follow if he did not choose conformity. But Merton was conspicuously silent about using sociological theory to predict *which* pathways would be followed, and by whom. In shifting focus from social structure to the individual, Merton automatically gave up the chance to do much more than outline possible individual choices. Although the tendency of functionalism is toward the oversocialized concept of man, its actual content is a long way from it.

2. Power, force, and voluntarism

Partly deriving from the "oversocialized" criticism, and partly as a complaint about functionalism's emphasis on the interdependence of institutions, is the criticism that *power* and *force* in human affairs are not well portrayed.[73] Power is the capability of one person or group

---

[73] See Ralf Dahrendorf, *Class and Class Conflict in Industrial Society* (New York: Free Press, 1956); C. Wright Mills, *The Sociological Imagination* (New York: Grove Press, 1959); John Rex, *Key Problems of Sociological Theory* (London: Routledge and Kegan Paul, 1961).

to cause another to do its bidding. But functionalists view the role relationship as a situation in which expectations and rights accompanying a social position are normally legitimate. One makes demands and the demands are met, not because of force, but from both parties' sense of the appropriateness of the demand. These legitimate demands are said to have *authority*. Authority ultimately comes from the cultural system to which the social system is connected; it is the sharing of belief in similar cultural values that assures legitimate authority. This is the foundation of Parsons's concept of the double contingency bond, institutionalized norms, and pattern-maintaining social systems.

The concept of the double contingency bond and the idea of legitimate authority are directly traceable, especially in Parsons's work, to a desire to create a theory that emphasizes *voluntarism*.[74] This refers to the cognitive, evaluative, and emotional basis of personal decisions to act. Personal decisions are confined by training and selective rewarding, as well as by value-attitudes. Hence every act is not a predetermined step, unrelated to the individual's will, but a step into which a predictable and controlled will enters. In this sense, for all the talk of collective action, systematic patterning, and the like, the Parsonsian system is individualistic.

When the individual is construed in this way, it is difficult to explain action apart from the legitimate authority of role systems, or action that forces others to behave against their will. How can such situations be theoretically explained by functionalism? To treat such problems may require a new set of starting points, a new definition of action, and perhaps a new sociological theory. Functionalism simply does away with the question of power by subsuming it under authority. By arguing that even in the most constrained of situations there is always some alternative (one could always take the poison rather than submit), functionalism evades the question of force and power, but not convincingly.

3. Change and conflict

Here are areas in which functionalism stands up somewhat better to its critics. It is sometimes said that functionalism is unable to explain *change,* but this criticism is perhaps confused with the assertion that certain functionalists are not concerned with change as a theoretical problem. Functionalism embraces the concept of social evolution very closely. Even if functionalist works do not emphasize them,

[74] This chapter, section VI, B.

functional theory may be applied to questions of social change and historical dynamics.[75]

But functionalism's account of social evolution perhaps implies slowness and a lack of control over social change by participants in it. Yet there is no reason, in principle, why social evolution could not take place rapidly and as a result of planning. Also, planned events often do not turn out as the planners intended. Even if social change is rapid and planned, social systems might actually react to change in ways resembling more the evolutionary picture than the planner's vision.

More serious is the charge that functionalism is incapable of explaining changes that are consequences of the use of power or open *conflict*. The criticism here arises because the theoretical idea of power is not well suited to functional theory. It might be possible to argue that a system responds to power-originated change by bringing its evolutionary adaptive machinery into play. But this does not account for the changing agent, and leaves functional theory essentially lacking.

4. Criticisms of the theory of stratification

The Davis–Moore paper on stratification reaped a bumper crop of criticism.[76] In general, critics noted that the functionalist picture of stratification is insensitive to the inheritance of status, to nepotism and special advantage.[77] Because they emphasized the incentives and abilities required to fill positions, and the individual's route through the social system, the authors were accused of neglecting important structural facts about society. Similarly, critics said the theory neglected the possibility that stratification would limit opportunities to discover talent by not encouraging it. This criticism rests more on observed differences of motivation among persons in different classes than on theoretical ideas. But from the basic charge that stratification decreases talent available, rather than increases it, several other criticisms followed. One was that societies are handicapped by stratification because full use of talent is not being made. Another was that unfavorable self-images are systematically created among less suc-

---

[75] Lewis A. Coser has considered conflict as in some ways "functional." See *The Functions of Social Conflict* (New York: Free Press, 1956).

[76] The paper was answered by Tumin, whose paper was criticized by Moore and Davis. Tumin reappeared with further criticism. Others entered the debate, including Buckley, who in turn was answered by Davis. Several papers generally related to the functionalist theory of stratification appeared that did not criticize the Davis–Moore paper directly, but certainly examined some of it in a critical light.

[77] Dennis Wrong, "The Functional Theory of Stratification: Some Neglected Considerations," *American Sociological Review*, XXIV, 6 (December 1959), pp. 772–8.

cessful persons that impede their progress more than external disadvantages do. Related to criticism about self-image was the charge that stratification decreases loyalty to the social system as a whole, encourages hostility, and so forth. It was also suggested that stratification gives a manipulative opportunity to the higher classes to retain their positions in spite of the free competition hypothesized by the model. All in all, these arguments were intended to suggest that, theoretically, stratification should be considered a hindrance rather than a benefit to society, and therefore the theoretical justification of stratification as a required social structure could not apply. Note that such criticism does not contradict the point that societies need means to recruit and motivate persons; it only argues against stratification's efficiently performing this function. Thus such critics do not really attack functionalism as such, but only one of its hypotheses.

In somewhat different fashion, it has been argued that if stratification were what Davis and Moore say it is, disruptive consequences would follow.[78] There would be constant and fierce competition for places at the top, and the rotation of persons in and out of positions would be deleterious in the extreme. From this it has been concluded that the Davis–Moore theory is not accurate because what it predicts is not happening. There is no rapid and continuous rotation of personnel as talent emerges, people do not consistently compete for high positions, and so forth.

Later developments suggested that the Davis–Moore theory has some use, but that it tells only some of the story. For instance, Lenski thought the functionalist theory of stratification gave the true picture only among "non-elite" groups. Elites have their positions for reasons unexplained by functional theory.[79]

5. Is functionalism conservative?

Related to the debate over stratification is the charge that functional theory "justifies" the status quo. Davis and Moore resist this charge, and have pointed out that they are trying to understand societies "as they find them," not give justifications for the institutions they discover. In the sense in which they seem to explain their defense, there can be no doubt that they are right. Sociologists of every political persuasion have noted that the institutions of advanced Western countries depend heavily upon competitive forces that catch up individuals and sometimes treat them with brutality. Sociological indictments of the business and commercial ethic in the United States usually castigate the emphasis on "getting ahead," professional suc-

[78] Ibid.
[79] Gerhard Lenski, *Power and Privilege* (New York: McGraw-Hill, 1966).

cess, and the like. In a way, those who criticize such institutional systems on humanitarian or political grounds are in fact offering evidence for the Davis–Moore theory and functionalism. They are complaining that stratification does, indeed, induce striving. They also are complaining that various institutions are geared together, forming a comparatively integrated whole.

But the more crucial theoretical point in this debate is raised by those who wish to talk about power and force. Some argue that stratification systems exist essentially because they are made to exist by powerful interests. Tumin says the stratification system does have functions, but that Davis and Moore have not pointed to them all.[80] In fact, Tumin and other critics imply that stratification has nothing to do with the functional interdependence of institutions, talent recruitment, and the like. Rather, it is an order imposed by those already in possession of wealth, position, and prestige.

Those who call functionalism conservative are usually those who are impressed by the theory of power in human affairs. Their main criticism is that by drawing attention away from power and focusing instead on authority, functionalism sweeps a significant question under the rug. Functionalism characteristically addresses social reform in ways that do not imply rapid upheaval, complete social redirection, or radical shifts. But it is clearly wrong to conclude that functionalism cannot illuminate problems of social change, social dislocation, and the like, especially if such problems result from institutional flux, technical change, and so forth.

Theories are neither conservative nor radical, but men are. The spirit in which a theory is approached can make it appear to justify some political viewpoint. As long as theories are kept properly in their place as conceptual technologies by which persons explain their experience, emotional debate about their political nature can be minimized, and useful criticism enhanced.

IX. Conclusion

We have found that the critics of functionalism have exposed some serious weaknesses in the theory. Theories in sociology are normally not very rigorous. But just as with exchange theory, the conclusion is not that we should abandon functionalism, but that we use it cautiously. Knowing the weak spots, we can give them attention, and we can benefit from such knowledge in interpreting findings. Similarly, when evaluating research, it is often useful to be aware of the theoretical strengths and weaknesses from which these findings are drawn.

[80] Melvin J. Tumin, "Some Principles of Stratification: A Critical Analysis," *American Sociological Review*, XVIII, 4 (August 1953), pp. 387–93.

And there is much in functionalism that is not weak. As long as it is the aim of sociologists to explain social order apart from individual motives, functionalist conclusions are bound to crop up, one way or another. When we ask a question about the relationships among institutions, functionalist answers will be tempting. Especially as it is applied by Parsons, the system concept can be a valuable tool to sociologists, and not only to functionalists.

Functionalism is a theory that generates reasonably coherent patterns. These "explain" by appealing to the sense of insight one gets when a reconstructed picture fits the facts. This fitting is a matter of conceptualizing observations into abstractions that have coherence of their own. It is a kind of translation from the language of what is seen into the abstract language of how such things coexist and influence each other. Of course, functionalism could be stated in propositional and deductive form, but its great strength is that it is not in that form. Propositional form is eminently useful for the generation of logically true hypotheses, but it tends to break up patterns. Pattern theories, on the other hand, have less rigorous clarity, but maximize the sense of connectedness inherent in social relations.

KEY CONCEPTS

function	structure	boundary
equilibrium	functional requisite	functional
system	pattern maintenance	alternative
system problem	pattern variables	goal attainment
social evolution	environment	structural levels
voluntarism	teleology	values
affectivity	affective neutrality	adaptation
diffuseness	quality	specificity
universalism	particularism	performance
system needs	social system	integration
theoretical pattern		power
socialization of		
motivation		
war of all		
against all		
cybernetic relations		
of systems		

TOPICS FOR DISCUSSION

1 In what sense is sociological functionalism a scientific theory?
2 What are some of the theoretically important facts about Parsons's pattern variable scheme?

3 Describe a "system" by reference to its boundary and its environment.

4 A system can have environments both "inside" and "outside" itself. Explain.

5 Social evolution is said to be a continuous development of social systems toward more adaptive forms of organization. Suggest concrete examples.

6 The functionalist theory of stratification is based on the economic ideas of supply and demand. Discuss. Does this suggest that social stratification approximates a "free market"?

7 Discuss the success of functionalism in explaining social organization by describing it as an abstract theoretical pattern.

8 Discuss functionalism's evolutionary perspective on social change. Is evolution a bad concept to use if change is rapid? Why or why not?

9 In what sense might functionalism engage in teleological explanation?

10 To what extent do you think Parsons succeeded in retaining voluntarism in his theoretical scheme?

ESSAY QUESTIONS

Compare Parsons's ideas of the double contingency bond with exchange theory. How does the double contingency bond differ from or approximate the meaning of exchange?

Discuss the research projects reviewed in this chapter, and come to a conclusion about whether or not they actually confirm functionalist ideas.

Do Parsons's idea of social evolution and Davis and Moore's idea of stratification complement each other? Write an essay in which you explore the extent to which these two ideas are similar in theoretical inspiration.

Using the pattern variables, characterize the orientation a professor should take toward a student when marking an examination paper.

How does Parsons's idea of cybernetic relations between cultural and social systems help prevent his theory from becoming culturally deterministic?

Apply some of Levy's ideas to modern role differentiation by age. Do recent changes in political or social behavior of youth confirm or contradict Levy's theory?

Examine the relationship between the educational institution and the economic, using functionalist ideas to describe the "inputs" and "outputs" from each to each.

Functionalism cannot explain social change. Discuss arguments for
and against this assertion.

Is there any *theoretical* reason why functionalism must be considered
conservative or radical?

FOR FURTHER READING AND STUDY

Bendix, Rinehard, and Seymour M. Lipset (eds.). *Class, Status and Power:
    A Reader in Social Stratification.* Rev. ed. New York: Free Press, 1966.
Black, Max (ed.). *The Social Theories of Talcott Parsons.* Englewood Cliffs,
    N.J.: Prentice-Hall, 1961.
Davis, Kingsley. "The Myth of Functional Analysis as a Special Method in
    Sociology and Anthropology," *American Sociological Review*, XXIV, 6
    (December 1959), pp. 757–71.
Demerath, Neil S., and Richard A. Peterson (eds.). *System, Change and
    Conflict.* New York: Free Press, 1967.
Fallding, Harold. "Functional Analysis in Sociology," *American Sociologi-
    cal Review*, XXVIII, 1 (February 1963), pp. 5–13.
Levy, Marion J. *The Structure of Society.* Princeton, N.J.: Princeton Univer-
    sity Press, 1952.
McKinney, John C. *Constructive Typology and Social Theory.* New York:
    Appleton-Century-Crofts, 1966.
Merton, Robert K. *Social Theory and Social Structure.* New York: Free
    Press, 1949.
Mitchell, William. *Sociological Analysis and Politics: The Theories of Talcott
    Parsons.* Englewood Cliffs, N.J.: Prentice-Hall, 1967.
Moore, Barrington. *Political Power and Social Theory.* New York: Harper,
    1958.
Ogles, Richard. "Programmatic Theory and the Critics of Talcott Parsons,"
    Pacific Sociological Review, IX, 2 (Fall 1961), pp. 53–6.
Parsons, Talcott. *The Social System.* New York: Free Press, 1951.
    Societies: Evolutionary and Comparative Perspectives. Englewood Cliffs,
    N.J.: Prentice-Hall, 1966.
    (ed.). *Theories of Society.* New York: Free Press, 1961.
Parsons, Talcott, R. F. Bales, and E. A. Shils. *Working Papers in the Theory
    of Action.* New York: Free Press, 1953.

6 Symbolic interactionism

I. Introduction

The subject of this chapter is the sociological perspective called *symbolic interactionism*. First the distinguishing marks of a "perspective," as opposed to deductive and pattern theories, will be described. We have seen that the theory of sociology is usually built upon a philosophical base of some kind and that the philosophy colors the resultant theory. This is as true for symbolic interaction as for other viewpoints, and it is crucial to recognize in this case. We shall concentrate on the elements of philosophical pragmatism most closely related to the symbolic interaction perspective.

In fact, it was a philosopher, George Herbert Mead, who inspired the symbolic interactionist school of theory and whose influence in it is still very young. To obtain an understanding of Mead's sociology, it will be necessary to introduce some of his philosophical ideas and some of the background that influenced his work.

II. The perspective

A perspective is not quite the same as a theory. A theory often has more ambitious aims, considers logical and conceptual rigor more crucial to success, and has explanation or prediction as its goal. These are the objectives of most sociological theorists; and even among symbolic interactionists these words are used. But often for interactionists, explanation does not mean rigorous deduction from logically prior premises. A symbolic interactionist may indeed be able to predict, but this is usually more a matter of his native wit and insight into human affairs than the manipulation of variables and constants to arrive at logically true hypotheses.

A perspective, however, may be just as coherent as any other theoretical stance. To say that symbolic interactionists pay less attention, on the average, to the standard aims of science is not to bring a pejorative case against them. Rather, it is to point out that essentially different objectives motivate interactionists. These aims are, in general, to apply a set of basic ideas to specific cases of human action

186

with the intent to "understand" the action somewhat as the participant himself understands it. Although the participant would probably use different language to describe his behavior and feelings, the general intent is to discover the actor's predicament and situation as he sees it. This is the prime purpose of sociology from the symbolic interactionist's point of view.

But symbolic interactionism does not stop at this. In addition to the sympathetic insight that is sought, the interactionist has at his disposal what the man in the street does not usually have: an additional overview of the situation, knowledge of institutional forces or constraints, a broader vision with which to make comparisons, and so forth. Putting together his view of the world with that of the actors he is studying, the interactionist's program can result in a description of life-as-lived, as a developing process influenced by individuality and institutions, morality and mores. This description is often nearly equal parts art and science, or sometimes mostly art. It is really creative imagination that makes for good symbolic interactionist work, and in it the language of the arts is often used to describe human relations. Especially drama, with its stage-front and backstage action, its roles enacted by creative players who both say the lines and enliven them, its scenes, often to be "managed" by the actors as they carry the play, and its presentations, fanciful yet real in the emotions and predicaments of the actors – drama has lent its language to symbolic interactionism. There is much in common between the kinds of knowledge one receives from the drama and from symbolic interactionist work. To experience a play is to observe action progressing, multiplying, and connecting to other action in a flowing procession of detail. This is very different from the quality of knowledge one gets from close reading of functionalist or exchange literature, where the action is made to derive from abstract first principles.

The basic components of the symbolic interactionist perspective are not testable ideas, as is supposed to be the case with scientific theory. Rather, the perspective is taken as a given, somewhat in the way the intent of drama is taken as a given by the playgoer. With symbolic interaction, the observed activity is fitted to the perspective, not the other way around. Nearly everything has an interpretation within symbolic interactionism's framework; but this is not taken as a sign of logical weakness, as it would be, for example, in deductive theory. Rather, interactionists assume that their main organizing concepts are correct as basic descriptions of reality, and that the practice of their craft requires that this inherent truth be brought to empirical examples. Thus "testing" symbolic interactionism is not really the objective of research, and even though interactionism has spawned empirical work, it is usually not the investigator's purpose to test specific hypotheses.

It is possible to have a fair variety of sociology going under the name of symbolic interactionism. One of the strengths of this school is that it does not restrict sociologists too much. It gives them a kind of commandment to "go forth and do sociology," but it also throws them on their own devices much more than do other theories. There is an amazing array of subject matter treated under this heading, as a look into almost any symbolic interactionist "reader" will show. The variety is given some coherence by the fact that most interactionists are followers of Mead, C. H. Cooley, William Thomas, or, to a lesser extent, John Dewey and William James. Additionally, symbolic interactionism is not terribly far removed in time from these "founding fathers." Mead died in his working prime in 1931. One of his most famous students, Herbert Blumer, has seen to it that Mead's work is carried on and is still actively doing just this. Today, we are only a few generations removed from the founders of the field, and this fact, along with the proselytizing of Blumer and others, has kept the interactionist perspective from becoming too diffuse.

Nevertheless, additional influences since Mead's death have entered the picture. Often it is difficult, in fact, almost impossible, to determine whether someone's work is really symbolic interactionist or not. For instance, Erving Goffman, whose formal academic training is in the arts and anthropology, has contributed significantly to the field. His subject matter has an everyday quality about it typical of interactionist work; he has adopted the language of symbolic interactionism and added to it, attending particularly to aspects of self and identity, central interactionist themes. But it would be hard to make the case that Goffman bases his work on Meadian theory in any philosophical sense.

Some sociologists who take Mead as their mentor have attempted to make their work methodologically scientific and rigorous. Kuhn's name is linked with this move. He and his students developed tests of self-concept, self-presentation, and the like, as a variation on the basic themes of interactionism.[1] However, Kuhn has found it convenient to omit much of what other interactionists would call basic material from Mead. Thus it is not altogether clear whether or not Kuhn's "self theory" is indeed symbolic interactionism.

In itself, the problem of precisely who is an interactionist need not worry us. The problem is to make a judicious choice from among the many recognized contributors to the wide and diverse field so that the resultant description retains coherence, yet includes sufficient unifying detail. To achieve this, we shall first examine the problems ad-

---

[1]   See Manford Kuhn, "Major Trends in Symbolic Interactionism in the Past Twenty-five Years," *Sociological Quarterly*, V, 1 (Winter 1964), pp. 61–84.

dressed by the founders of the field. This is the philosophical base mentioned earlier. Secondly, we shall describe Mead's ideas, especially as expressed in *Mind, Self and Society*,[2] *The Philosophy of the Act*,[3] and numerous papers. In addition to this, we shall outline the follow-up work of Blumer and Kuhn, because these two are leaders of their respective schools. Some critical remarks have been made that have resulted in defenses by interactionists. As we shall see, some of these defenses have added materially to the perspective. Additionally, we shall review some research literature taking symbolic interactionism as a foundation.

III. Pragmatic philosophy and symbolic interactionism

Pragmatic philosophy arose in the United States in the last third of the nineteenth century. Some say it was a uniquely American philosophy because it took a disapproving view of pure abstraction for its own sake and because it put considerable emphasis on action, as opposed to thinking, logic, and the mind. This is supposed to be an American philosophy because America was a place where there was considerable action, movement, building, and change, and where traditional philosophical concerns received little attention. But pragmatism, to its philosophical adherents, did not mean simply "If it works, it's good," as is sometimes said. This may have been the crude rendition of the pragmatic rule by the farmer or the businessman. But, philosophically at least, pragmatism was a movement that took some traditional concerns of philosophy as a point of departure from which to defend a somewhat novel way of looking at these problems.

A. The mind–body problem

The mind–body problem goes back eons into philosophical history. The problem is this: Each of us has consciousness of his own "mind"; hence it seems reasonable to suppose that "mindedness" is a natural condition of people. However, there is no known physical entity or process in the body that corresponds to mind. Of course, there is the brain, from current evidence a kind of computer. But mind is the quality that seems responsible for fantasy, imagination, sympathy, emotion, and feeling, as well as mental creativity such as creative writing, musical composition, human relations, and so on. Furthermore, moral and ethical understanding appears to be a property of mind that has the power to control the physical body. In fact, if one takes mind as a starting point, explaining behavior results in a

[2] Ed. Charles Morris (Chicago: University of Chicago Press, 1934).
[3] Ed. Charles Morris (Chicago: University of Chicago Press, 1938).

strange anomaly: the mind, which is unaccounted for, seems to be in control.

In general, there were two types of philosophical thought on the mind–body question, excluding the viewpoint that became pragmatic philosophy. One says that there is no sense questioning the existence of mind, because it seemed certainly to be there somewhere. It was mind that controlled persons in their actions, and some thought a kind of aggregate mind could exist, uniting the activities of groups or nations. Group will, national spirit, and a variety of other expressions of this sort formed one way of handling the mind–body problem. From this viewpoint, action is preceded by thought, or "mental activity." Insight, mental penetration into action, is required before the action can be carried out. Logically, some controlling power lays a plan for action prior to it, and directs it in its course. The more behavior comes under the power of mind, philosophically speaking, the more the body becomes subservient to it. Scientifically, to strict behaviorists, this is an outrage, because such a "spook" in the machine of the body could not exist. In fact, it can be argued that the word "mind" is a symbol with no referent, because the entity to which it refers is indescribable. This being so, no philosophical discourse can be carried on about the mind; the definition of the subject cannot precede its discussion.

It is worth emphasizing that action, social action as well as every other kind, which takes mind as its determining factor, puts the action itself in a derivative, secondary position. The act comes after the thought. Thus the activities of people are in a way determined by qualities of mind, and have no actual life of their own. Used in this deterministic and logically prior sense, mind demotes action. Additionally, it seems to demote the individual, because action appears to be under the control of an entity into which the actor has little insight and over which he has little control.

The alternative way of disposing of the mind–body problem is to say that mind does not exist, or that it is an illusion of the nervous system. The mechanical body is all that exists. In this view, experience enters the nervous system through sensation and is coupled with actions being performed. There being no mind, action is, in principle, completely explicable from this mechanistic viewpoint. It can be argued that if we only knew enough detail about the physical brain and the pleasure and pain experiences of Beethoven, we could explain his writing of symphonies, sonatas, and his opera.

The "no-mind" group certainly had a case to begin with, because the superficial fact that mind could not be empirically accounted for was well known. But to assume the extreme position that the physical body is in complete control over human creativity seems to result in an absurdity. Similarly, the "mind over matter" position yields the empirical absurdity that "mind" cannot be found.

B. Rejection of metaphysics

The pragmatists came upon the scene with this philosophical battle raging, and they simply swept it aside. Much of what underlies symbolic interaction theory today is contained in their critique of the way the mind–body problem was framed as a philosophical question. Fundamentally, the pragmatists said that it is unwise to make the distinction between mind and body. The mind–body problem is more a matter of the human tendency to separate things artificially for analysis than it is an empirical or philosophical question. Instead, what we call mind arises in the action of the body and its senses. There can be no separation of the two, because to divide them is to cut off the sustenance of both. In fact, even to talk about a philosophical distinction between mind and body is nonsense, because to make that distinction is to give names to two things that are really one thing. To make philosophical distinctions between things that do not have separate existence is to build conceptual castles in the air. A difference that makes no difference is no difference. Thus the pragmatists took a swipe at both traditional philosophical speculation and the way the social sciences tended to frame their questions. They said that both the mind and the no-mind positions led to absurdly placing action in a secondary, derived position, giving it an "explanation" by relying on a fictional abstract distinction. Their alternative is to take human action as the basis. Do not attempt to derive it, or to explain it away; instead, begin from it.

The pragmatists handle another old problem in a similar way – the traditional question of the primacy of either the individual or the society. Should we see persons as the primary unit, societies being built up out of them as a building is made up of bricks; or should we first take society, and deduce individual action out of it? Pragmatic philosophy said there could be no meaningful distinction between society and the individual. Individuals are obviously created and formed in and by society, but just the same, creative, human, individual action makes society what it is. To say anything else is either to reify society into something it is not, or to give individuals a primary control over society, which individuals clearly do not have. When the individual and society are taken together as one, the question of human social action is altered: How do we explain motivated acts as facets of individuality carried out in a constraining, yet flexible social context? This position does not make persons merely role-players, unconsciously saying the lines society has written on their scripts.

Nor does it overemphasize the primacy of individual desires, values, or motives (see Chapter 2, section III).

C. Symbols and communication

1. Importance of communication

Pragmatism leads away from traditional distinctions between the individual and the group. So far, we have seen the pragmatists assert that the person and his group are inexplicable when unnaturally divided for analysis. What facets of life do we examine to follow up this assertion? Certain answers to this question are untenable. Rejected are answers that would follow one or another of the discarded abstractions: the individual–society and mind–body distinctions. Hence seeking instincts, deep-seated unconscious drives, stimulus–response conjunctions, and so forth, will not do. Nor will realist philosophy, such as group mind, collective coherence, will to power, or the like. In fact, what we have left to go on is what people experience, and the only way to know this is to hear what they say about their experience. *Communication,* more than just a method of reporting, is thrust into the foreground of the whole theory. The point is that individual lines of action are worked out among persons when they communicate their desires and intentions among themselves. Persons act on the basis of these communicated meanings. It is not that people *react* to the behavior of others, but that they act on the basis of communicated intentions. They conduct themselves partly by communicating their own intentions to themselves, and partly by observing the adjustments made by others to the intentions they have communicated.

The observer of all this is in a place analogous to that of the participants. In order to understand the action, the observer must gain from it the meanings being communicated among the participants. This is taken as a confirmation of the principle that symbolic communication is the basis of all social action, and the methodological foundation for finding out about it. All persons are in analogous positions, in that their actions are adjustive processes in situations in which they interpret action symbolically. Communications are at the very center of action, and must form the basis of a true perspective on social events.

Communications assist persons to define their situations. Of course any actual situation has an existential reality – it exists, apart from what anyone knows or does not know about it. But things unknown or forgotten by participants are not part of their definition of the situation. The salient features of situations are those used by the persons involved to give situations meaning. The definition of a situation, as distinct from the existential situation (the two may or may not be similar), is the crucial factor in the ways persons construct their behavior. It is in a situated context that meanings arise and stabilize. Thus a situation, as it comes to be defined among group members, surrounds each member with a meaningful context of action. Meanings for acts are derived from action, and action is invested with meaning.

2. Art as an example of this view of symbolic communication

Much of what has been said by symbolic interactionists about communication has grown out of the pragmatists' philosophy of art.[4] Art is accounted for as an aspect of communication. Artistry is the construction of works that have exactly the same symbolic character as ordinary communications, but it is able to articulate this symbolic meaning in ways that are not common. By dramatizing, emphasizing, or clarifying the vagaries of situations or ideas, artists bring out meanings that may be obscure or little appreciated. Hence there is really no new creation in art, but only new and more insightful ways of expressing collectively constructed meanings, grasping the significance of situations. It is clear from the study of art too, that the term "meaning" is not to be construed too narrowly. Emotions are engaged by the artist. Collective emotional responses to symbols are as much a part of this as are cognitive responses. Art not only makes things cognitively clear; it also makes plain the emotional consequences; it knits together a complete human response to an act or idea. For example, the artistry of the novel unfolds human predicaments and shows the consequences of making certain decisions. It shows how individual responses affect the whole course of events, and it commonly heightens the reader's sense of involvement by cleverly engaging his interest. In short, a good novel draws the reader into the ongoing action, gives him an account of it, and simultaneously presents him with a description of the consequences of the actions, the circumstances leading to these actions, and the personal and social connections among actors and consequences. A novel does this with imaginary characters; fiction becomes art in the symbolic, representational nature of the human conduct displayed, situational analysis, and moral dilemmas.

3. Language

To the pragmatic philosopher, ordinary language does for its users what artistic representation does for the artist. Communication is the

---

[4] For a secondary treatment, see Hugh H. Duncan, *Communication and Social Order* (New York: Bedminster Press, 1962), pp. 55 ff.

manipulation of "significant symbols" that portray action and its expected consequences. Meanings for symbols arise in the context of action, and it is said that symbols have "intersubjective" meaning when all involved get the same understandings of acts and intentions from a given gesture. Although mistakes are possible, they are made less likely by the fact that meanings are closely associated with the collective experience of those who use the symbols. Persons sharing experience find the means to communicate symbolically about it to each other on the basis of their common insight derived from it.

It is clear from this that meaning is not based on private experience. Meanings are not invented by persons to describe mental events. Meaning is in action; action is symbolized as an aspect of the personal adjustment process by which people interact; the content of communication is the meaning derived from action.

D. The act; social conduct

Up to now, action and behavior have been mentioned but not discussed directly. From the description of language and symbols, it should be clear that action, to the symbolic interactionist, is something quite special. Yet there is a problem to solve that is of the pragmatists' own making. If human action is not to be accounted for by determinism (as with forms of sociologism and cultural determination), or from inside (via the infinite buildup of reflex arcs), and if it is to be regarded as coming about in a symbolic context of meaning, and if it is directed as it proceeds by the person doing the acting, the question of *what causes action* must be faced, and there is a need to describe how communication and language play a part.

The pragmatists settled on the concept of *impulse* to help solve this problem. Impulses are not instincts. "Instinct" denotes an innate force which has a one-to-one correspondence with some activity, as with nest building of birds. Birds do not learn to build nests; they just know how, innately. The force causing the bird to build is apparently inflexible. It is not symbolic. Impulses, on the other hand, are subject to modification, and they are rather more diffuse. But they still arise as a matter of "human nature." The question of why man does anything at all is not up for discussion. It is assumed that some active principle gives rise to activity. The important problem is the direction and control of that action. "What processes control action?" is a more significant question than "Why is there action?"

Mead uses the term *conduct* to indicate social behavior in the ordinary sense, and it will be wise to adopt this usage now, because the more general terms "behavior" and "action" can mean nonsocial activity. Conduct is behavior that is being controlled by the actor toward goals, or with reference to emotions, and so on. Remember that we are to avoid determinism. Pragmatists think that conduct starts as impulse that the person is not aware of, or notices only dimly. Although a given piece of conduct may be of exceedingly short duration, say, the pronunciation of a word, it is analytically separable into a succession of parts. The first part arises in impulse, which brings out some action. This action, once it becomes manifest, enters one's consciousness as a recognition of oneself in action. But note: Such self-recognition is an aspect of memory, because, analytically speaking, what is now in consciousness has already happened as a result of impulse, even if it happened only an instant before. When impulsive action and recognition are completed, the formation of conduct becomes possible. The symbolic representation of what has occurred opens the way for modification of action-in-progress. The actor can now see the probable result if the action were to continue on its present course. If he does not like that result, modifications can be made. This is something like a situation in which a person starts talking. When he notices that what he hears himself say is not just what he "means," he starts again, lengthens the speech to include modifying clauses, alters it to indicate something different from what it appeared to mean at the beginning, and so on. The sentence is a piece of conduct constructed in stages by stringing together pieces of action, by monitoring those actions as they come out, and by constantly making adjustments toward the end product of a completed bit of conduct.

Note the central importance of symbols in social conduct. Conduct is possible because a person is able to grasp the meaning of his own gestures (his impulse-related acts) and direct their course. Similarly, those sharing the symbols may also grasp their meaning. Thus ongoing conduct, continually regulated by an adjustive process, constructs itself as it emerges.

Imagery has the additional property of being able to call out action, which can end up as conduct. Such imagery can be habituated, say the pragmatists, so that more or less predictable action will be called out by a given symbol. But note that this is just the beginning. This does not mean that conduct resulting from a presentation of imagery will be predictable from the image alone. Stimuli and the first reaction to it are purely stimulus–response behavior. In this, man does not differ from the rat. But in the symbolic representation of that action as memory, in the eventual modification of the action into directed conduct processes that symbolic representation makes possible, man and rat differ very much. At the heart of the difference is the symbol and language as a symbol-organizing technique for transmitting meanings.

E. The self

A concept is required that is capable of organizing the pragmatists'
ideas about human conduct, symbols, and communication, and that
locates these activities in the person. The concept *self* performs these
duties. A self is not possessed as a matter of inheritance or biology.
Rather, self arises in the context of symbolic associations with other
people. People are capable, through their use of symbols, of having a
self, but the self is not something that is carried about until used. It is
an integrating self-conscious quality that becomes actualized in performing conduct. When action arises from impulse, the actor, seen by
himself as an object, is the self.

In addition, the word "self" has come to mean the physical possession of the impulses and the sensory machinery that initially give rise
to conduct. Self must contain these features as well; one tenet of
pragmatic thinking on social life is that self-directed conduct is really
the marriage of impulse and controlling factors. This seems confirmed
by the self-consciousness all feel, but none can know in others.
Cooley begins his discussion of the self in this context.[5] But he soon
makes clear that what he means by the self is really only partly
private. The other part is the inward representation of others' wishes
and valuations in whose company the self is acting or has a history.
Hence the thing impressing us as being our private self is really in
some measure a property of the group, made by it and partially under
its control. The term "self" indicates a kind of group reality that
arises in interaction and becomes attached to a particular person.

This kind of thinking about the self accounts for the pragmatists'
early interest in psychology, face-to-face groups, and small-scale sociology in which the contours of social conduct are personal and perhaps intimate. Symbolic interactionism is still largely a perspective
appropriate to social psychology, rather than to larger-scale studies.
Part of this concern for small-scale social analysis is derived from
fascination with the self for its own sake. Thus Cooley explores the
self by describing it in various characteristic phases, such as vanity,
honor, pride, and so on. All these he understands to be aspects of the
congruity between a person and his surrounding situations in which
these feelings arise.

This fascination with the self deserves further attention. In Dewey's
Psychology[6] several chapters are devoted to "feelings," by which he
means experiencing the self in mood, attitude, and temperament.
These explorations are indeed unified by the pragmatic philosophical

[5] Charles H. Cooley, *Human Nature and the Social Order* (New York: Schocken
Books, 1962), pp. 186 ff.
[6] New York: Harper, 1890.

tradition. However, it appears to have been an early characteristic of interactionists, just as it is a characteristic today, to become interested in the experience of selfhood quite apart from whatever philosophy might underlie the concept. The self assumes a central position in symbolic interactionists' perspective largely because of the inherent richness of the idea. And as we shall see, additional sociological concepts, such as society, interaction, minded behavior, and so on, really come back to the self as the touchstone that unifies the whole depiction of social life.

F. Self as object

Putting aside all the fascination of the self as an intriguing part of subjective human experience, we must turn now to the objective part the self plays, for it is as an object that the self is viewed as a unifier of personality and human relations.[7] No matter how much an abstraction of both social and personal elements, the self tends to be experienced as a coherent, firm entity, and it comes to impress others in this way as well. In this solidified form, the self can become an object in another's experience. It becomes a target toward which communications are directed and the perceived part of the acting person. This self-as-object enters relationships between people, or between the self as knower and the self as known. Here the English language sometimes obscures the analysis. The self can take its own "self" as an object, so that meaningful gestures can be directed toward it, just as they can be directed toward other persons. Getting outside the self and looking back at it, so to speak, allows for the possibility of viewing the self as others do. Taking this objective, exterior view of one's self allows for a kind of verification procedure. While having such a view of the self, it is possible to compare one's own inner feelings about identity, conduct, and so on, with the apparent evaluations of others. Thus an adjustment process can proceed from the viewpoint of another. The same verification procedures are opportunities for change, because finding discrepancies between the other's evaluations and one's own offers the chance to accept or reject the other's views. When the self arises in a person, it is this objective-yet-subjective monitoring of one's own conduct that is the mechanism for fitting together one's intentions, feelings, and actions with those of other persons in a workable, organized way.

From this line of argument, we see the connections between the pragmatic philosophy of symbols and art, language, the mind–body problem, the self, and the act. Conduct is built up toward objects that

---

[7] Mead, *Mind, Self and Society*, pp. 135 ff.

have significance for the person. The way to know this significance is to have meaningful ways of denoting essential features. We have to define the objects. Hence what matters is not the inherent character- istics of the objects, but the relatedness of the objects to the knower. This is also true with respect to the self, when it becomes an object to itself. The person has not so much a given "nature" from which all his activities spring and by which they can be explained, but a capa- bility for adjusting and defining his world, taking on features of it as needed for action, and gaining his "content" from the surrounding definitions of objects, including himself.

Mutuality in interaction is derived from these principles. A true sociology based on them must say that interaction cannot be ex- plained as deductions from first principles about the nature of social systems or of persons, but rather it must describe the working out of suitable interrelations between individuals, all engaged in precisely the same process of definition and conduct toward the self and others. In fact, the key word here is "process," rather than "structure" or "nature." The interactionists mistrust social structure, institutions, and the like, when these are given as explanations for conduct. Most interactionists would agree that something like these structures exists. But they would say that reference to them as a means of explaining conduct misses the point. Structures and institutions, for the interac- tionist, become just more objects to be adjusted to. They do not assume prominence among all objects; they are not more significant.

IV. George Herbert Mead

Mead was not a sociologist, but a philosopher with an interest in social processes. As a philosopher, he was occupied by questions like the mind–body problem, the nature of consciousness, the bases of human rational powers, and the interpretation of what man is. His viewpoint was fundamentally that of the pragmatic philosopher. He was impressed with the philosophical works of James and Dewey, but he was not exactly a follower of anyone. It is simplistic to say that all philosophers of a given school think alike. Mead wanted to make use of pragmatic philosophy in rather a different way from the others. Fundamentally, he used pragmatism to interpret the mind. How did people differ from other animals? If we all start out as creatures capa- ble of responses to stimuli and impulses, how was it that people end up with mental facilities that seemed to go beyond those of clever apes? Mead did not forget the mind–body problem. It was insufficient merely to name the rational facility, call it "mind," and then say that people had it, and that was that. To do so would be to "solve" the problem by giving it a name. This trick pragmatists in particular could see through at a glance. Mead intended to tackle the mind problem along lines set out by the pragmatists in their studies of symbols, their philosophy of communication and of art; and he wanted to stay within the critical spirit of pragmatic philosophy. He was not trying to compose the simplest possible theory in order to get on with studying social behavior, as Homans did years later. Mead found that his philosophical concerns carried him into the world of social psychology and sociology, and for this reason he has come down to us as a social theorist.

For an influential thinker, Mead did not actually write a large amount. It is hard to grasp a sense of his development in the sociological field because we must use mainly the published lecture notes of some of his students.[8] For all we know, editing may have rearranged certain parts, emphasized points, and neglected others. We are not sure we are studying Mead as Mead would have had us do. But in those lecture notes, we do have Mead's conclusions. His main ideas are clear enough.

Mead knew that to answer his main question about the nature of mind, he would have to criticise the existing theories of mind.[9] Additionally, he would have to develop his own to replace the old ones. Pragmatic philosophy concerning the meaning of symbols involved him in a discussion of the social group, and in a theory of communication. Finally, there would need to be an account of the possessor of "mind" – an account of the process of mind arising and the communication processes involved. There would have to be a discussion of the nature of the self. Although it is not clear in what order these basic ideas came to Mead, or exactly what his mode of solving preliminary problems was, the three main facets of his work centered on mind, self, and society.

A. *Psychological parallelism and behaviorism*

Mead was most familiar with the psychology of Wundt with its physiological orientation.[10] This psychology consisted very largely of the study of perception and of experiments that investigated stimulus–response associations with muscle movements. In fact, emotions, feeling, mood, and the like, were regarded as being analogous to muscular movements; they could all be triggered by appropriate stimuli.

When the question of consciousness was raised among psychologists of this persuasion, answers usually came in the form of what

[8] *Mind, Self and Society* is itself such a set of notes compiled from the lecture notes of several students.
[9] *Mind, Self and Society,* pp. 1–7, 42–50.
[10] Ibid., pp. 42 ff.

Mead called "parallelism."[11] Consciousness could be accounted for by physical responses to stimuli. Running parallel to the bodily course of events was consciousness, which, in this viewpoint, was the coming to awareness of what the body was doing. Consciousness was parallel to action in the sense that it followed, side by side, wherever the physical organism took it. But it was always consciousness "of" bodily action; action stood in a prior and superior position. This line of argument demoted consciousness and swept it away entirely as a psychological problem. It was a way of saying that, eventually, behavioral psychology would explain even consciousness by physiology; but until it did, consciousness would be allowed to run subservient and parallel to the really important thing – bodily response and external stimuli.

This parallelism, to Mead's way of thinking, contained errors as well as a certain appeal. In the first place, it emphasized in empirical form the mind–body distinctions the philosophers had debated. The parallel account of consciousness is based on a philosophy that analytically separates mind from body (falling into all the philosophical traps by doing so). It then treats these abstractions as separate entities. Mead was suspicious of this from the start. Yet it was clear that "body" was certainly responding to stimuli, and that there was no empirical way to cause "mind" to do the same. Were these psychologists right? Mead thought the mind–body distinction was indeed wrong and that he needed to find a way of deriving mind from body while giving mind a more prominent place. In a way, fighting physiological psychology on its own ground, he would have to show that mind was indeed a behaviorally responsive entity that could influence action just as material stimuli could do, and that could be empirically accounted for, not only with the lame assertion of spiritual force, an inborn rational facility, or the like.

Mead begins, then, with a critique of physiological psychology. In his behaviorism we see the answers starting to form up – answers that were central in the subsequent construction of *Mind, Self and Society*. In the first place, to Mead, behaviorism was a kind of correlational enterprise. It tried to show the correlation between an individual's experiences and the conditions under which these arise. Mead criticized making an arbitrary division between the activities of the central nervous system and what we call "consciousness." In any case, if consciousness runs parallel to bodily processes, any physical or emotional conditions correlated with bodily responses are also correlated with conscious process. Therefore, consciousness and physical activity are simultaneously explained as responses to empirical

[11] Ibid., pp. 18 ff.

stimuli. Mead says behaviorism needs to find a language to express such responses so we can recognize that experiences of mind are explicable by reference to the conditions giving rise to them.

In Mead's critique of physiological psychology, we see the main features of his alternative.[12] His willingness to accept the main paradigm of psychology and seek stimulus–response patterns shows his uneasiness with abstractions that go unresearched. However, Mead would not go along with this psychology in denying a real role to conscious processes, for he knew that to treat consciousness as a residual parallel category is to ignore it. Consciousness is just as much a fact as is a muscle twitch. Mead tried to unite consciousness with empirically based psychology as a correlational technique. Bringing these two together led him to conclude that conscious mind could be accommodated to behavioral psychology by concentrating on the ways mental powers arise in people during their activities in groups. Mead focused on consciousness arising under certain conditions, the self as object of stimuli, and the centrality of communications.

B. Mind, gestures, signification, and meaning

Mead's discussion of mind is actually devoted primarily to an account of symbols and communication. He did not intend to elaborate states of feeling, the meaning of intelligence, insight, or other standard topics often associated with "mind." Rather, he was interested in suggesting how the concept of mind should be understood. Mead begins by discussing symbols and communication among animals, and then shows how the human process differs from this.

Looking back, Mead noted that imitation was a key feature of thought about linguistic behavior, suggesting that one animal simply does what it sees and hears others do. The imitation argument holds that one person observes others who make certain sounds in given situations. The observer connects the sounds made by others to features of their situation, and then makes a similar association with respect to himself. This explanation of language is not sufficient. Perhaps something like this occurs, but in fact human communication could not be explained in this way. Communication could not be merely imitative, because one person would only imitate another and the conversation could never get off the ground. What is the kernel of truth in the imitation argument? It is that a symbol, a vocal gesture, or some other kind of signification, comes to stand for a complex relationship between the person using the symbol and some feature of his world. What is this complex relation? To begin with, the amount

[12] Ibid., pp. 61–7.

and diversity of stimuli around us are always very great indeed. This large amount of stimuli is not all represented by one gesture. A situation holds many things that are not actually very important, and a situation could have more than one kind of significance, depending on other circumstances. Thus Mead concluded that symbolization in gestures must necessarily be selective. We pick out aspects of the situation that are of particular importance. It is the selected part that is symbolized.

Selection raises a problem that is quickly solved in pragmatic philosophy. Which aspects of an environment will be associated with a given gesture? It is the relationship between the symbolizer and the environment that is the key. The meaning of a gesture is in the action made toward it by the symbolizer, or the action in response to it. For example, it is because of an overt act with respect to a particular object that the term "chair" has to do with sitting down on something. This explains why extremely diverse objects may all be indicated by the word "chair" when the intended action is basically the same. Similarly, the word "chair" may mean something entirely different when the relationship is different between it and the symbolizer, as in the case when "chair" indicates discussion leader or committee head. We tend to say that, in the second example, the word "chair" is used symbolically, whereas in everyday speech we do not think of the first usage as symbolic. But to Mead, they are both symbolic in exactly the same way. Both denote a relationship between a symbolizer and an object.

Recall also that all objects are not tangible things. In the previous example, "chair" referred to a social position as well as to a thing. In referring to a social position, it denoted features of a situation particularly relevant to some action. It is not important whether the person in the chair (the group leader) is tall or short, dark or light, Polish or Australian. The point is that the term denotes an intangible and abstract quality about a situation to which it is important to refer with a symbol. Abstract as this is, it is still concrete in that the relationships denoted are experienced. Relationships to objects lend meaning to their symbols. The *mind* enters this discussion not as an entity but as a process, "minded behavior," as Mead sometimes called it.[13] Minded behavior is the concrete action associated with symbol use. Mind is not an abstract thing unconnected with action or physiology. It is an associational quality that depends on the processes of selective attention and perception to organize action with respect to objects.

Raw gestures are the sounds, movements, or other productions that can carry meaning, but this does not suggest that all gestures do carry

---

[13] Ibid., pp. 124–34.

it. A gesture is not significant if it communicates no intelligence either to a hearer or to the gesturer himself. But *significant gestures* are another matter.[14] These are the symbols that, as Mead says, call out a similar response in both the hearer and the gesturer. Significant gestures are the basic stuff of linguistic communication. A sound one associates with fear or hope that also indicates fear or hope to another is a significant gesture because the same thing is indicated to both. This calling out is a matter of similar experience, imitation, and stimulus–response learning. At this point, Mead is still discussing something he considers appropriate to both animals and humans, although he believes that animals make far less use of this than men do. Calling out a response is a matter of dragging up old associations to a symbol and, in a way, of having a memory of one's predicament at the time when this symbol was committed to memory. One's predicament refers to one's relationship with certain selectively perceived aspects of the environment at the time. Significant gestures call up associations primarily as aspects of relationships.

To understand *meaning* as Mead did,[15] it is necessary to recall something of the pragmatists' philosophy of art. Meaningful communication is symbolization that collapses aspects of the present with both the past and the expected future. Viewing paintings is a matter of looking at the present, but "seeing" the consequences and the associated feelings and motives as expressed by the artist. This bringing into the present both the genesis of a thing and its consequences is what Mead had in mind when he said that significant gestures bring together the symbol that stands for the act with the intended consequences of that act. Another way of saying this is that signification through symbols indicates a whole, a completed thing that has not yet occurred, or that is just in the process of emerging. Human communication emerges from this analysis as something very subtle. Significant gestures carry a content of meaning that tells about the speaker, and also about his expected responses to himself, as well as his mental idea of the appropriateness of what he says to the situation he is in.

We must now complicate this somewhat by making a qualification. Recall that "conduct" is the process of directing action as it emerges from impulse by the use of adjustive mechanisms. So *signification* is the process of symbolizing and then adjusting the meaning with additional symbols as they emerge, to indicate an intent. A flow of symbols starts in impulse, just as an animal cry starts in impulse. This cry brings forth associations in the person who then, perhaps while the cry is still in process, performs adjustment on it to redirect its meaning to better indicate intent. A series of these symbols, all rooted in

[14] Ibid., p. 68.
[15] Ibid., pp. 75 ff.

the associated experience of relationships between speaker and situation, ends up as an indication of the expected consequences of the situation for the actor.

Recall further that persons have the capacity to indicate to themselves, as well as to others. They hear themselves speak as others do, and make the adjustments necessary to express themselves. This is Mead's idea of mind as minded behavior; it is behavioristic in the sense that it is always rooted in stimulus–response associations and perception, and it is minded in the sense that as soon as a symbol emerges, it does not go to completion without having been interpreted and directed. It is possible for me to direct symbols, rather than simply emit them, because I can tell from my experience whether or not the symbols I find myself emitting are indicating the intended consequences. When the hearer understands by a set of significant symbols the same consequences and situated actions the speaker intends, then the symbols are called *meaningful* by Mead, and communication is established.

Implied by the foregoing is an additional element of mind – reflective intelligence. Thought is recognition of the significance and consequence of ongoing, already progressing acts. This viewpoint does not set mind over against the acting organism, nor does it demote mind to a mere accompaniment to action. Reflectiveness of mind suggests that mind is always in the process of arising as the need for mental activity occurs. It is always later in time, analytically speaking, than the action it cognizes. Reflective thinking is coming to a consciousness of what has been and measuring the consequences of this action for the future.

C. Self

Mead's view of the self follows directly from his ideas about mind and communication. One could say that the self is another way of applying exactly the same points about language and communication and then drawing another set of conclusions.

1. The "I"

Symbols arise in impulse, and are later directed. Because of this sequence, Mead found it useful to divide the concept of self into the "I" and the "me" to indicate the two phases of conduct: the arising in impulse, and the consummation in directed action.[16] Use of the "I" has not been consistent among the pragmatists, although Mead, James, Dewey, and Cooley all found need for some kind of "I" and

[16] Ibid., pp. 173 ff.

"me" to distinguish between phases of the self. For Mead, the "I" is the aspect of self attached to us as our individuality. We identify with it, as he says. It is also true that, in learning how to act, a person acquires attitudes and behavior patterns from others. These are first present through imitation or as stimulus–response activities not yet under the control of the person, or, as Mead might have said, are not yet in his consciousness. Then the I enters the picture. It is the I that becomes aware of these actions and attitudes. The self's arising is the process of the I's acquaintance with the behaviors the person emits. Hence Mead says that it is the I with which we identify, because we see that it was ourselves who acted. But I comes in as a "historical figure" who has already acted.[17] This is the reflective nature of consciousness, of mind. Having arisen in self, the I reacts to already performed behavior. It affects behavior again not in forethought but as corrective or adjustive action. Sometimes the I is also identified with impulse alone and not with reaction to other impulse. If the genesis of a given action is needed, it can be found in the I.

2. The "me"

The "me" is the other half of the analytically divided self.[18] It is here that Mead locates the forces of the outside world as they affect the person. A me is a set of "organized attitudes of others which one himself assumes."[19] From others we learn that given attitudes are appropriate for given occasions. It is the me to which the I reacts, because it is the me that commonly guides the behavior of a socialized person. It is also the me of which a person is aware when thinking about himself, because, following Mead's terminology, the I only enters consciousness as a me.

Surely this is confusing. The point is that we do not experience the I, but only what the I has become in past actions. At the present instant of experiencing the self, the I is already doing something else we are not yet aware of. Hence we observe that we have just acted with regard to a behavioral standard that we ultimately gain from others. The I has entered consciousness as a me of recent vintage.

It was predictable that confusion would arise over the place of the I and the me in Meadian social psychology. The words themselves tend to come so fast upon each other that the meanings become confused. However, if the basic philosophy behind them and the main points about the origins of significant symbols are kept in mind, the sense of the I and me concepts can be easily worked out. Also, it is well to

[17] Ibid., p. 174.
[18] Ibid., pp. 192 ff.
[19] Ibid., p. 178.

keep in mind that Mead intended the terms "I" and "me" simply to be ways of naming the phases of the self as it is generated in action. Mead's problem was to develop a way of talking about the phases of the self that distinctly separated the operation of self-action that was not yet conscious (he called this the I) from the influence of others in actual consciousness (this he called the me). Finally, Mead needed to show the relationship between these two in any conduct.

3. Acquisition of self; role-playing, role-taking, and the theory of stages

In discussing how individuals become capable of communication, self-recognition, reflective thinking, and the like, Mead shifted away from an analysis of the fully formed person toward a developmental account of how selfhood arises. Mead may have been influenced by Darwinian thinking, because there is in Mead's account a kind of developmental thesis.[20] But actually there is little of Darwin here, except the historical viewpoint. Mead has no species analogy, struggle, or natural competion in mind; instead, he sees cumulative development through which persons become capable of interacting symbolically as adults.

(a) The stages of self-development. Some commentators find three stages in Mead, some four. Mead himself mentioned only two: the *play stage* and the *game stage.*[21] By detailing the requisite conditions for reaching the play stage, three stages can be identified; by dividing the game stage into two parts, four stages are possible. No matter how many stages are involved, the idea is that self-development must reach a point where it is routine to experience oneself as an object. This entails taking the viewpoint of another toward the self. From that imaginary exterior standpoint, one views the self as it is and becomes aware of its appearance to others.[22]

By "play," Mead means acting as though one were someone else. The play of young children is unstable and mistakes are the rule. It is not possible for the child to know the role of its own father in any depth, for example. In early play, certain parts of the father role might be grasped. The child may refer to himself in the third person, as his father would refer to him. When a sentence such as "Johnnie is a bad boy" is spoken by Johnnie himself, it suggests he has grasped the fact that he is an object that can have certain qualities (goodness

[20] Charles Morris, Introduction, ibid., p. x.
[21] *Mind, Self and Society,* pp. 152 ff.
[22] Ibid.

or badness) when viewed from another's point of view. Of course, Johnnie's father behaves in a very complex way toward Johnnie. The fact that Johnnie understands something of himself from his father's point of view does not mean that he is fully capable of performing father roles. Nevertheless, Johnnie eventually comes more fully to take in the complexities of his father's role and to know the feelings and motives that lie behind his father's conduct.

To the symbolic interactionists, role-playing is this incomplete or perhaps superficial placing of oneself in the role of another. The idea of playing a role suggests that the role is not truly "me." To *play* a role is to have sufficient insight into it to act overtly as though one were someone else. But the typical attitudes of this role will not have become incorporated into the player's natural repertoire. As Johnnie plays father, he might also play fireman or some other superficially adopted role. As he does so, he learns fundamentally two things. The first is how the other person is expected to act in that role. This can include insight into how such persons typically feel as well. If a little girl is sad because her doll is sick, we suspect she understands that sadness and sickness are related in the grown-up roles concerned with such things. More important, from the viewpoint of social theory, this kind of play teaches the distinction between me and not-me. For in the process of playing, taking a make-believe position, role expectations are dramatized. To the extent that a person must mentally strip off what he is in order to enter the role he knows he is not, he is required to know how he differs from the role he is playing. There are both superficial and profound ways of doing this, and with practice, the child comes to have a greater insight into others' roles and, concomitantly, a greater grasp of his own being.

Note here that self-insight comes through taking another person's view of the self, and not from introspection or contemplation alone. This is consistent with the pragmatists' assertion that selves grow up in contexts of symbolic communication that form the new selves; it is not the other way around. Although persons do, of course, have influence on group action, the genesis of personhood is explained by the group. But also, such social formation involves learning self-insight, which sets the individual free to make his own judgments. This idea cuts a middle course between social determinism and the errors of extreme individualism.

One feature of the play stage is that the player normally has only one alternative role in mind at a time, or perhaps a composite mixture of various roles. These enter consciousness during play as only one exterior point of view. It is rather like looking in a single mirror and seeing one's own face. But there may be other mirrors. A multiple mirror can show the face from several angles at once. In the *game stage,* Mead has something like this multi-mirror analogy in mind.[23] In a game, several players act in concert, and game-players must grasp the organized and united roles of all the players in order to understand their own action. Playing shortstop in baseball has to do with fielding, throwing, tagging runners, and so on; but it also has to do with the organized and more general relationships between infield and outfield. "Infield" is an abstraction, for there are no "infield" players, but only basemen and shortstop, pitcher, and catcher. The role of the infield is an abstracted derivative of all the jobs of all the specific players who occupy positions in the infield. Thus to occupy adequately an infield position one must understand the team as an abstract unit. This calls for a generalized knowledge of how team partners will probably act. To know individually the expectations for shortstop, second baseman, first baseman, and so on, does not add up to a knowledge of what infield play is. Infield play is, in fact, the interrelations of all of these acting as a unit.

Mead thought this abstracted way of viewing the self from a *generalized* exterior point of view developed in the *game stage.* The self as a reflection of others' attitudes takes on a more complete, rounded form, and it assumes an abstract three-dimensional quality. The game differs from mere play by requiring the exterior perspective of an aggregate of other persons. Play leads to game, and game leads to depth of understanding.

Role-playing is the key concept in this description of the developing self. The more profoundly one accepts a definition of self derived from the viewpoints of others, the more such roles are taken as one's own. This more complete, enduring acceptance of external viewpoints on the self is called *role-taking.*[24] In play and games, there is a continuing make-believe quality that is useful in learning and self-identification. But role-taking suggests more than play and means something that is the opposite of make-believe. Whereas role-playing instructs the developing self, role-taking identifies the self. The person, say the interactionists, comes to develop so well rounded and consistent a set of self-definitions through role-taking that he finally comes to see himself as wholly consisting of the person portrayed in the reflections. His own conduct then tends to confirm these impressions. In a stable system of others' definitions and self's definitions, the self emerges as a patterned repertoire of conduct that is "me."

However, according to Mead, the self is not passive and receptive, as the foregoing description might suggest. Accepting others' definitions of oneself does not make one have that self.[25] The additional

23 Ibid., pp. 158 ff.
24 Ibid., pp. 150–2.
25 Recall the *active* nature of the "I."

ingredient Mead calls for is the "realization" of self in action.[26] Taking the role, as opposed to only playing it, means doing it. This follows, of course, from the basic pragmatic philosophy of knowing the self only in reflection. Taking a role means doing it and observing the self in action while grasping other's interpretations about the self. Taking a role is an active process, with reality, not imagination, the arbiter.

Finally, role-taking and self-realization are bound together in Mead's scheme by the concept of the *generalized other*.[27] This idea develops from the concept of the other as the viewpoint from which the self is seen objectively. The other became the general viewpoint of an organized collective in the game. It becomes, in abstract form, the basis from which to evaluate the self's performance. Although the generalized other is composed of concrete evaluations and the attitudes of real people, it is portable from situation to situation in the "mind." Hence it is actually more stable and consistent than any actual set of others. Sometimes the generalized other is equated to the superego or to society. These terms might suggest something powerful and unyielding in control of the individual, but Mead simply means a generalized set of attitudes and values actively worked through in the invention and completion of conduct.

D. Society

Symbolic interactionism has concentrated its greatest weight of argument on the ideas of self, communication, individuality, self-attitudes, and self-change. But in addition to this, Mead stood ready to give an account of *society* in terms of his theory of the self and the mind. It is, of course, based precisely on the same key ideas as the mind and self, and the same processes are central. Just as the self was implicit in Mead's idea of mind, so society is implicit in Mead's understanding of mind and self. It is sometimes said that symbolic interactionism does not describe society in a convincing way. Indeed, in the critical section of this chapter, such an argument will be advanced. But it is worth remembering that the interactionists have let this challenge go unheeded and mostly unanswered because of their essential interest in other things, rather than for lack of resource to argue the case. It is because interactionism could pose at least some description of society that it qualifies as a sociological perspective. With the discussion of society, Mead comes to the conclusion of his sociological work, having drawn up his theoretical picture of man, society, and the man-society relation.

---

[26] *Mind, Self and Society*, pp. 200 ff.
[27] Ibid., pp. 160 ff.

Mead's main principle in his theory of society is that communication involves the participation of one person in the life of another.[28] This point goes back to the theory of mind – the assertion that mind arises in communication. The point is that whereas society was a prerequisite to the development of selves, so persons with these selves are the explanation for society. This argument is frankly tautological, and will be regarded by logicians with a jaundiced eye, but to the interactionists the truth of the whole idea shines through. They do not attempt to build a theory of the genesis of society or to discover its origins in some state of nonsociety, but to describe a historical process that is still going on. Interactionism does not speculate about how the first society arose that was capable of producing the first selves, as it were. It tries to understand social organization by applying the communications theme.

Symbolic communication involves the appearance of one self in another through the mechanisms of role-taking and reflective thinking. Hence the concept of intention (the symbolic representation of an act together with its consequences) when mutually applied to several people suggests that their communication will entail mutual adjustment. The mutual adjustment process, in this context, is often called "self-criticism" by Mead.[29] By this he means that the conduct of the self is fitted to the conduct of others. An integrated action unit results. Furthermore, Mead says that this is not merely a method of regulating individualities that might otherwise be on collision course. Two arguments apply here. One is that individuality is really the personalization of generalized community attitudes; the second is that there can be no conduct at all without community attitudes and a generalized perspective from which to sustain each person. Being involved in a mutual adjustment process is to be self-criticizing. Regulating one's conduct by reference to collective society is to live the only life possible. This general conclusion comes close to those of other theorists, although the others have often worked from different premises. But the important thing is not that different theorists reach similar conclusions, in this case at least. The important thing now is to notice that Mead's idea of society is rooted in the pragmatists' solution to the philosophical problem of mind and body, that a stimulating new series of ideas has been constructed to reach a conclusion that everybody already knew – men live in societies.

More specifically, we can note some of Mead's thoughts about society. For example, let us explore his idea of *institutions*. Following from the concept of communications, conduct is mutually adjusted. If these multiple conducts are geared to a common purpose, and remain

[28] Ibid., pp. 200–9.
[29] Ibid., p. 255.

stable for some time, Mead calls this an institution. Institutions are not things, but a certain lasting and specific quality of interaction. Note that an institution is not really a "common" response, even though *Mind, Self and Society* uses this term.[30] Mead has in mind mutually supportive and additive social relations organized around interests that all share. For example, the educational institution does not involve everybody in classroom teaching, but in a variety of lines of action with a root purpose. Mead would say that a general grasp of the root purpose comes from each person's ability to take the roles of others in the system; each can see his own conduct fitting into the larger organization, the general aims of which all share. Mead sees institutions as flexible and "progressive," changing with changing definitions of situations or the changing nature of the institution's problems and the like, although he recognizes that institutions do appear to have an ability to become rigid and inflexible. He does not carry out an analysis of how institutions could do this, if their nature were as he says, but nevertheless he believes that, inflexible or not, institutions do change. Individual creative acts of common purpose win out over ossification.

Mead is not pitting the individual against society here. This should be obvious by now, but Mead clinches the argument by pointing out the fusion of I and me in society.[31] He says that, when persons are engaged in collective action toward common goals, their consciousness of the sharp distinction between self and other becomes blurred; effort in common brings out an extremely close identification of the person with the group. In this kind of action the me is so completely in concert with other people's me's that the individualistic I weakens. Actually, it is not a matter of suppression of the I; rather, similarity of conducts makes it appear so. The impression of a separate I recedes in favor of a common me. Hence the most complete identity of individual and society is in extreme cases of commonality, in which the most profound examples of the other appearing in the self occur.

V. *Mead's influence*

Mead's work had an immense long-term influence on sociology. It was novel and insightful, and complemented work already in progress. Yet Mead's thought did not immediately become a major force in sociology. Rather, it remained a minor theme, finding particular use among persons interested in special areas such as collective behavior, fad and fashion, or social psychology as it applies to face-to-face groups.

[30] Ibid., p. 261.
[31] Ibid., pp. 273 ff.

Mead's influence grew and developed steadily over time, largely through the efforts of his students. Although the fundamental points of what is today symbolic interactionism have not changed a great deal since Mead's seminal work, the job of rounding out the perspective, applying it more universally, and filling in certain gaps fell to Mead's followers. Of particular importance in this work of turning a Meadian perspective into a more fully developed sociology were three areas of concern: (1) A better account of "society" was necessary if symbolic interaction was to become a general perspective for sociologists. (2) A full-fledged methodology appropriate to Mead's thought needed to be worked out and defended. (3) A richer conception of motivation was needed. We shall see that the issue of methodology is yet unsettled among followers of Mead, and that it divides into a striking duality. Some take a particularly operationalistic line, seeking empirical tests for explicitly defined concepts, whereas others who claim Mead as their mentor insist that such methods cannot be used with Meadian theory. An account of society on a more equal plane with the detail and richness of self has failed to appear. The problem of motivation still remains, although it has been addressed specifically and some dark spots have been brightened.

A. Herbert Blumer

Blumer was Mead's student at the University of Chicago. Because of this close association, Blumer is often regarded as the natural heir to leadership of the field. Of course, Mead had other students, but Blumer has taken a leading role, making his career as a sociologist by elaborating and extending what Mead said. Blumer made his most significant empirical contribution to the field of collective behavior. But to the theory of symbolic interactionism and its methodology, his contributions will probably be more lasting. These are: (1) a description of how symbolic interactionism regards society and (2) a criticism of sociological methodology with a view to showing the appeal of symbolic interactionism as a theoretical stance.

In his methodological work, Blumer has sharply criticized the scientific approach to research and substituted a somewhat different angle on the relationship of theory to data. The discussion of society as symbolic interaction is more conventional Mead. Let us take a look at each of these contributions in turn.

1. Blumer on society

As academics go, Blumer appears to be a man of few words, at least in print, although these words are not wasted. His discussion of society as a topic does not cover many pages.[32] And to a great extent, it repeats the main points of symbolic interactionism – interpreting action in progress by capturing the meanings persons attach to their conduct, taking the role of the other in gaining an objective view of the self, constructing action as an intelligent response. Out of this come three basic points that deserve attention. First, society is best thought of as a vast series of individual selves fitting together their individual lines of action. This means that the symbolic interactionist does not imagine persons to be caught up in social structures. They are not participating in something they do not make for themselves, even though the resultant actions may become habitual and what other sociologists might call structured. Secondly, Blumer makes the point that situations (concrete times and places for practical conduct) are the features of social life that people must define and the contexts in which they must align their activities. Hence abstract institutionalized values or norms of action do not play a central part for Blumer. It may be true that institutionalized norms are features of action manifest in situations, but the components of the immediate situation, and not principles of behavior, guide persons in their choices concerning how to conduct themselves. Of course, this point is a broadside aimed at theories of social action that emphasize culturally legitimate norms as a basis of social life. But what must be kept absolutely clear is that Blumer does not deny such institutions exist. Rather, he relegates them to a rather minor role in explaining social conduct. Thirdly, Blumer insists that a cognitive grasp of the situation is a necessary condition for social conduct in it. Before a situation becomes meaningful, and hence before it is possible to act toward it, a person must understand it insofar as he sees his place in it and the likely consequences of any action he might be contemplating.

Cognition, situation, and mutual adjustment, then, form the basis of Blumer's model of society. It resembles very much his idea of a social movement, or his framework for understanding public opinion and its fluctuations. Although institutionalized action does occur, he sees it as a matter of expedience. Persons would be in a muddle if they had to construct all their activities from scratch. Instead, they adopt sweeping definitions of situations. These labor-saving definitions are Blumer's picture of institutions or of social structure.

But more should be said about structured social relations. Indeed, institutions could be an all-important feature of situational definition. Obviously, legally defined behavior proscriptions, for instance, set boundaries within which situations must be defined, unless action is taken surreptitiously. (This in itself is one way of taking cognizance of

[32] "Society as Symbolic Interaction," in Herbert Blumer, *Symbolic Interactionism: Perspective and Method* (Englewood Cliffs, N.J.: Prentice-Hall, 1969), pp. 78–89.

legalities bearing on a situation.) Blumer is not downgrading institutions, but he is trying to take away the priority and necessity he feels other social theories allocate to them. Even though institutions can and do profoundly affect action, they do so not because of their existence as another order of being, apart from human action, but simply because they condition the situations in which individuals have to construct their personal conduct.

2. Blumer's critique of scientific method in sociology

In a series of papers Blumer has shown an abiding interest in the methodology, even in the philosophy, of science, and in the methods specifically appropriate for social science. Blumer feels that what he calls *variable analysis* is particularly unsuited to sociology because it is incompatible with the processual buildup of conduct and the mutual adjustment process.[33]

By "variable analysis" Blumer means the designation of some factor in a situation for particular interest, either as a cause or as an effect, so that this factor receives special attention. Blumer argues that in doing this several mistakes are made. First, the situation in which the variable is important is unnaturally construed. By designating what he is interested in, the scientist makes a legitimate claim to examine the situation for certain features, but he makes an assumption in doing this. The assumption is that the action proceeds according to a predefined idea of variables, and that the resultant conduct can be accounted for in terms of the variables examined. Blumer says that this kind of reasoning might approximate a scientific posture, but that "science" is not the result. A preconception is placed between the observer and the action that does not allow the observer to contact the reality; he notices only the variations on certain preselected scales, measures, or indicators.

Associated with Blumer's rejection of variable analysis is the more important theoretical point that action is mediated symbolically and that variables and constants designated beforehand cannot pick up the subtleties involved. The interpretation of action is all-important to the symbolic interactionist, and a particular variable might in fact have many interpretations for those actually experiencing it. Hence indications from test scores and the like are quite beside the point. In the absence of knowledge of how the participants interpret the action picked up by the indicators, no explanation of action is possible.

For example, it may be that a birth control program is statistically related to the birth rate in a given city. But what Blumer would

[33] "Sociological Analysis and the Variable," *American Sociological Review*, XI (December 1956), pp. 683–900.

consider key features of the situation are not yet known. These would be the symbolic meaning of the program, the type and style of its presentation, whether or not it was viewed as an insult or a threat to a given subgroup or social class, whether or not some persons used the program's information to have children more often instead of less, and so forth. For Blumer, no indication as derived from rigidly controlled variables can capture the meanings of the actions people take, and hence, in spite of all the research findings piling up in sociological journals, little progress toward cumulative understanding of conduct is being achieved.

Finally, Blumer is struck by the vagueness of even the most rigidly and precisely defined variable in sociological analysis. He makes a forceful case for the point that sociology has gone on for years talking about key ideas like community, solidarity, and norm, when in research these things are subjected to unstable and imprecise measurement. The result is that research is not cumulative; various findings allegedly concerned with the same idea are not comparable and insight into conduct remains at a low level.

It must be emphasized here that Blumer has hit upon one of the continuing paradoxes in sociological methodology, and he is trying to turn it to account for symbolic interactionism. The paradox is that although we might wish to know action in its fullest sense, in order to know any of it we must define our concepts about it precisely and rigidly. Doing this in research practice forces the use of methodologically stable indicators for concepts – things like tests, controlled observations, measurements, and the like. In short, all the tools that move sociology toward scientific research actually move it away from what Mead and Blumer consider centrally important: the shifting, adjusting, interpreting, symbolically mediating nature of social conduct. To become more scientifically precise is, to Blumer, to become less capable of capturing reality as it is.

Blumer's solution to this problem is to refashion the idea of the *concept*.[34] In scientific methodology, concepts must be clear, precise, and stable. In sociology, Blumer claims they are not. The reason they must be so in science is that standard use in research requires it. Blumer believes that if sociology abandoned the traditional objectives of science, the rigid strictures could be put aside as well. If variable analysis were not required, then the necessity for concepts to have empirically reliable indicators would also disappear. The result would be concepts as "sensitizing" agents for the researcher. A sensitizing concept is not something that can be built up by rigid definition. Rather, it is an idea that enters the researcher's mind as an abstract

[34] "What Is Wrong with Social Theory?" in Blumer, *Symbolic Interactionism*, pp. 140–52.

principle. He knows, for example, that a person's interpretation of events is to be considered important; so he will look for what he considers "interpretations" without any preconceived idea of what he will find. Through practice, anticipations and predictions might indeed be possible, but these will not be scientific in the ordinary sense. Rather, the researcher's commonsense experience will come out via his familiarity with the situation. The concepts of sociology, then, amount to a universe of discourse having fairly stable meaning among those who know the language, because "knowing the language" means experiencing the conduct indicated by the concepts. It does not mean knowing the abstract derivation of the concepts logically or by definition.

Perhaps it is obvious that Blumer's viewpoint on the proper nature of sociological concepts is uniquely a product of his own theoretical stance, derived from Mead and the pragmatists. Conduct is a matter of stringing together acts while monitoring the developing meanings, shifting actions so as to impart or derive meanings from situations. Hence the interactionist regards normal actors as requiring "sensitizing" concepts. It is natural, therefore, to urge these onto researchers whose main mission is to place themselves mentally in the shoes of the actors they observe.

It then follows that a committed symbolic interactionist ought to practice what he preaches by developing sensitizing concepts in social science. The natural sciences by contrast do not deal with entities that have the capability to interpret their own actions; hence the concepts of social science should differ fundamentally from those of natural science. From this it follows that the objectives of social science are different, the methods are different, and the results are different. And finally, the nature of scientific knowledge about the social world will be different from any other kinds of scientific knowledge.

B. Symbolic interactionists as positivists

Blumer's view of the proper approach to sociology was based on meaning and interpretation. There could be little predicting and no scientific explanation of behavior without doing violence to these main points. Therefore, Blumer wished to reconstitute the concept, making it into a sensitizing principle, allowing it to remain devoid of specific behavioristic content. His contention is that no other concepts are even possible in social science.

But Blumer's argument rests at least in part on showing that, until now, no sociological positivist has done a satisfactory job of setting out stable behavioristic categories, nor has anyone succeeded with such categories in building perfect theory. So far, many sociologists might agree with Blumer. But if the objective of sociology remains to seek these categories and to order them theoretically, Blumer's criticism can be answered by saying, "Because it has not yet been done does not mean that it cannot be done."

1. Operationalism applied to symbolic interaction

If the objective of sociological theory is to remain explanation, and not just sensitization, then the problems faced by other theorists will arise for symbolic interactionists. One such problem is how to establish empirically verifiable indications that what symbolic interaction theory says is true. This question really breaks down into two distinct but related questions: (1) What, precisely, does symbolic interaction theory say that is of empirical importance? (2) How can experimental operations or observations be made applicable to these assertions?

Manford Kuhn has tried to show that symbolic interactionist theory drawn from Mead as well as others can be construed to mean actually nine separate, subtly different theoretical ideas.[35] Mainly, these differences arise from ambiguities about the actual point in conduct when interpretation occurs, the time relationship between an event and its effect on the self (which might be instant or occur over a protracted period), and the question of indeterminacy of the results of action. "Indeterminacy" refers to the question of whether a given event always has the same kind of effect on the social action it influences.

Blumer had much to say about the variable in social science. But Kuhn argues, hoping to justify a more rigorous methodology, that there is really no alternative to variable analysis. The divergence between Blumer and Kuhn on this point would be less serious if symbolic interactionism were another kind of theory, one that did not involve the subjective experience of the acting person. But the fact is that this is a key feature of interactionism. Kuhn puts it succinctly: "It is most difficult to establish generalizations valid for human behavior without methods wherewith to make precise checks on intersubjective perceptions of events."[36] It is indeed most difficult, but it is just this problem that anyone attempting positivistic methodology faces with symbolic interactionism. It is precisely the subjective experiences and interpretations of events that make symbolic interactionism what it is, and these are least accessible to positivistic methods. Blumer said it was impossible. Kuhn says it is possible, but difficult.

---

[35] "Major Trends in Symbolic Interactionism."
[36] Ibid., p. 74.

2. The problem of nonempirical concepts

It is ironic that a sociological perspective based on pragmatists' mistrust of metaphysical notions should contain so many central points offering no possibility of empirical verification. Take, for instance, the dichotomy of the I and the me. No matter how much one is sensitive to the proposal that action develops through an internal conversation of gestures, initiated through impulses released by stimuli, the I cannot be researched empirically because it is not there. Although the nervous system may be investigated positivistically, the I, in and of itself, cannot. It is not an entity, only a concept. Of course Kuhn is frustrated by concepts that have no empirical referent. Hence positivistic symbolic interactionists simply forget about the I and concentrate instead on the me. The me is troublesome enough, but in principle it may be empirically investigated because it refers to the internalized expectations one holds for oneself. These expectations are, in turn, derived from the behaviors of others displayed toward the self, and these can be observed. Correlations can be found between the way others conduct themselves toward a person and the way that person behaves in their presence. Hence the concept of the *reference* group has assumed importance in Kuhn's version of symbolic interactionism.[37] Although the concept of reference group is implied by the "generalized other," the concreteness of an actual group whose activities can be observed tends to take the question out of the theoretical sphere and place it in the empirical world.

In addition, scientific use of symbolic interactionist principles implies a tough decision on the question of determinacy. If one accepts the argument that situations are indeterminate in their consequences, for whatever reason this is accepted, the result is the same: There can be no scientific characterization of such situations. Similar causes are not expected to lead to similar results. But determinacy as a principle has been found in symbolic interactionism, at least by implication and ambiguity, and positivistically minded interactionists find that they must accept this principle as a basis for going ahead with positivistic research. They have no alternative, except to abandon their efforts. Emphasizing reference groups, and applying the principle of determinacy while neglecting the I, the self emerges as the personal manifestation of a series of me's, displayed in a predictable way as a result of internalizing others' expectations.

Following through on this version of interactionism, a schematic diagram of any social action develops in which the self plays a central

[37] "The Reference Group Reconsidered," *Sociological Quarterly*, V, 1 (Winter 1964), pp. 5–21.

part as the acting manifestation of externally determined self-attitudes. Conduct is explainable because it is self-constructed action, meaningfully interpreted as the behavior appropriate to the situation in which the action occurs. And this meaningful interpretation is in turn explained by the self's having been formed as the internalization of external expectations. Essentially, a given bundle of me's makes a self, and selves of a given kind act in given ways in given situations. Hence, working backward, action is explicable as a manifestation of self, which is in its own right a product of community attitudes. Clearly, the same general approach to action is found here as in Mead's dictum that action is both personal and social, in a complex mix of community-determined attitudes and self-constructed conduct. The differences lie in the fact that the nonempirical I is gone, and with it the elaborate vision of the process of action construction. Additionally, action construction as uniquely interpreted responses to situations has been narrowed to become the action that is predictable, knowing the determinant me's for a situation. Thus we see that the problem of nonempirical concepts is solved by scrapping them. Those for which a positivistic case can be made are retained, along with the general form of the theory, with a slightly altered concept of the self at the center.

C. The question of motivation

It has been noted by many that symbolic interactionism is a theory of social psychological importance but lacks a convincing account of *motivation*. Of course this is a serious problem. Motivation is important, perforce, in a theory heavily weighted with concern for the individual, because the reasons why action is taken, why there is some particular action and not another, are questions that go straight to the heart of social science. If we are to make a theoretical perspective emphasizing the creative conduct of individuals, and if we are to account for institutional structures by reference to individual lines of action, then the theoretical explanation of these lines of action is paramount.

It is not strictly true to say that symbolic interactionism had no theory of motivation from the very beginning. In Mead's concept of impulse, for instance, there is the assertion that action originates simply because people are active beings. Mead's point in raising the question of impulse is to show how action that is just "there" is shaped into guided conduct. In other words, he was interested in discovering the mechanism by which conduct is formed and in describing the process by which this occurs. He was assuming that there would be a basic activity of some kind. But there is more to the problem of motivation than this. In addition to the question of why there is action at all, which Mead ignored for the obvious reason that there simply is action, there is the question of what gives action its direction? What forms its goals?[38]

It is important to note that a description of the ways in which conduct might be formed and controlled does not amount to an explanation of why some particular line of conduct is selected. For example, Mead's central point about social life's being the fitting together of persons' conduct according to generalized expectations raises a blunt but important question. Why should anybody care about the "generalized other" or, indeed, any other? It is something to account for group life by showing the mutual adjustment process, but this is not the same thing as an explanation of why it is this form of collective action and not some other.

In Miyamoto's paper on motivation in symbolic interaction theory, the self plays a central part, as it ought to do.[39] Because it is the self that can experience itself as an object and act toward itself, it is this that is the central figure in conduct. Miyamoto's key question is this: By what criteria could the self be expected to evaluate its own actions? If an account of the criteria could be given, then an account of motivation would be implied, because we would then know the important dimensions of any action concerning decisions to choose or reject that action. Miyamoto borrows initially from Parsons's "modes of orientation," noting that, in principle, three modes appear to answer the question of how selves are judged. These are the *evaluative, cognitive,* and *affective* modes. The evaluative mode concerns questions of "good" and "bad"; the cognitive concerns questions of "definable" or "nondefinable"; and the affective concerns questions of "gratifying" or "not gratifying." Miyamoto reduces to three what was essentially an infinity of possible criteria for self-evaluation.

In addition to this, Miyamoto draws on more traditional symbolic interactionist concepts to describe three *perceptual settings,* or fields of activity in which the three criteria of self-evaluation may be applied: (1) the self as an attitude object; (2) the self as a task-performing object; and (3) the self as a role-performing object. The self as an attitude object may receive evaluations that refer to its general qualities – it is kind or harsh, quick-witted or dull, and so on. Task-performing objects are objects that do specific things. Miyamoto suggests that the self is evaluated in part relative to specific tasks that a person performs. In

[38] This is a completely analogous question to that confronted by Parsons in his rejection of the randomness of ends assumed in hedonistic utilitarian theory.

[39] "Self, Motivation and Symbolic Interactionist Theory," in Tomatsu Shibutani, ed., *Human Nature and Collective Behavior: Papers in Honor of Herbert Blumer* (Englewood Cliffs, N.J.: Prentice-Hall, 1970), pp. 271–85.

the third perceptual setting, the self is evaluated with reference to its occupation of a specific social position, a broader concern than that of task performance.

Returning to Mead for inspiration, Miyamoto notes that it is only in the communal context that a person can survive. Hence it must be as a matter of survival that the self comes to view itself as desirable (evaluative mode), definable (cognitive mode), and gratifying (affective mode). It is required that the self regard itself in these ways, because these are the ways others, who hold the key to survival, will see it. Hence motive is construed as a tendency to evaluate possible actions according to the effect they might have on the self's desirability, definability, and its ability to gratify.

Of course, desirability, definability, and the ability to gratify are not always of equal importance to the survival of the self. It is for this reason that Miyamoto introduced the different settings of action (attitude, task, and role). These settings tend to place one or another of the self modes at a premium from time to time. The point is that whatever is at a premium in the situation, in the setting of the action, must be maximized by successful selves. Of special interest here is that by trying to systematize the criteria of motivation, Miyamoto has taken a long stride toward the conclusion that organizational necessity plays a large part in determining what action will be taken. This stride is away from the intense individualism of previous symbolic interactionist theory.

VI. Research and symbolic interactionism

The symbolic interactionist perspective has typically encouraged sociologists to do field work, often observation rather than active experimentation. A large amount, and wide variety, of research has been carried out using, in some way, the main principles of symbolic interaction as points of departure. Much of the field work has been inspired by the notion of concepts as sensitizers and therefore tends to be somewhat impressionistic. But such work can be coupled with other methodological tools, such as questionnaires. One branch of symbolic interaction developed a special series of tests devoted to describing the self.

Being in principle a social psychological perspective, interactionism has led its adherents to select research topics that avoid social structure, institutions, social evolution, or similar subjects. Instead, the emphasis is on personal performances or feelings. For example, the standard alternative to the functionalist portrait of deviance is drawn from interactionists' interpretation of the process by which a person takes on deviant attitudes toward himself and how these spawn deviant acts. The wider problem of behavior change has been addressed from the interactionist perspective, as in studies of the professionalization of medical students,[40] the rehabilitation of convicts, the analysis of status passage and ceremony, and the like.

Interactionism makes contact with certain branches of psychiatry as well. Mead's interest in the process of self-acquisition is similar to medical interest in how socialization goes wrong, or how the processes can lead to painful results. Thomas Scheff's *Being Mentally Ill: A Sociological Theory* is an attempt to explain the influence of social interactionist factors in convincing persons, or confirming them in their fears, that they are indeed physically sick with mental disease.[41] Numerous research studies with normal children have focused on role-learning topics, sex-role identification, and the like.

Behavior as it occurs in particularly interesting situations has also been a topic of interactionist research. Schools have come in for study, sometimes to find how different participants in a situation define it. Policeman–suspect interaction, the doctor–patient relationship, courtship and love, family relations, old age, and generation-gap studies have all been done. These tend to point out salient features of the situations that make the action itself of professional interest, and then describe the conduct in terms of interactionist factors. Related to this is some of Goffman's work, which reports more often on everyday life instead of particularly novel or crucial situations.[42]

Obviously there can be no criticism that symbolic interactionist theory does not inspire empirical work. However, some questions can be raised about the exact relationship between the perspective and the research. The question of the applicability of interactionism goes back to Blumer's criticism of the scientific method, and his refashioning of concepts into "sensitizing agents." The basic problem is this: How do we know that my sensitivity to the situation is the right one? And if mine differs from yours, how do we decide who is right? In liberating interactionism from a firm, stable hold on specific definitions, admittedly for a good cause, the perspective runs the risk of enfeebling itself as a research base. Related to this point, research with this perspective tends to be the elaboration of ever-different situations and activities, with a consequent lack of emphasis on relating these works into a coherent view of whole societies.

Aside from the fact that interactionism could come apart at any time through different practitioners' drawing divergent conclusions from the

---

[40] Howard S. Becker et al. *Boys in White: Student Culture in Medical School*, ed. Ann Green (Chicago: University of Chicago Press, 1961).
[41] Chicago; Aldine Publishing Co., 1966.
[42] Goffman, *The Presentation of Self*, and also, *Behavior in Public Places: Notes on the Social Organization of Gatherings* (New York: Free Press, 1963).

interactionist approach, there are associated problems of a more technical nature. For example, in planning a research project, the researcher never knows exactly what he is looking for, and hence he can never fully equip himself to follow up action in all the directions it might lead.[43] Researchers are faced with a constant series of snap decisions in the field – whether or not to count some incident as central or peripheral, important or trivial. There is also the question of when enough data have been collected. Obviously, people do not finish their performances and ring down the curtain. The analogy to drama obscures the fact that situations do not come in discrete, defined packages, and that there may be several situations relevant at a given time in the lives of the participants. The actors' conduct is never finished; nor is the imperfect record of it kept by the observer. This problem usually calls forth a solution in terms of time, effort, and expense, rather than on the basis of clearly defined research goals.

Of course, it is the awareness of problems like these that causes some interactionists to take a more rigorously positivistic approach to research. But here many of the same problems crop up. What are the actual dimensions of a situation? Upon which behaviors should research focus, and how? A more rigorous methodology is easier to defend against questions of reliability or bias, for example, but it does not solve all the problems.

There is a sense in which these general criticisms apply to all sociological research, from all theoretical angles. But it is still true that method is a particularly serious problem for the interactionists because the nature of the concepts and the general looseness of the perspective emphasize questions of standardization, reliability, and unique observation. Imprecise definition of concepts is a count on which Blumer criticized alternative theoretical viewpoints, but making a concept into a "sensitizing instrument" does not solve the problem of precision either, even if it does change the research aims.

A. Using sensitizing sociological concepts

Fred Davis has given a classic example of insightful symbolic interactionist sociology.[44] His aim is to elucidate the process by which people experience and project impressions of themselves – the self-identity issue that is so central to symbolic interactionism. His particular research interest is visibly handicapped persons. Identity pro-

---

[43] See J. Kitsuse's discussion of behavior imputation as a case in point in "Societal Reaction to Deviant Behavior: Problems of Theory and Method," in Howard S. Becker, ed., *The Other Side: Perspectives on Deviance* (New York: Free Press, 1964), pp. 87–102.

[44] "Deviance Disavowal: The Management of Strained Interaction by the Visibly Handicapped," in Becker, *The Other Side,* pp. 119–37.

jection and management by such persons are sometimes problematic because there may be a suggestion made by normals that handicapped persons are "deviant." Handicapped people might be significantly different from normals, and pose a special problem of interaction management. Even if the "deviance" is imposed, as with wheelchair cases, the stickiness of interaction flow and the uneasiness that may beset both the normal and the handicapped can become an impediment to even the most superficial social interaction. Davis's intention is to describe some of the problems involved in management of self by handicapped persons and the process by which visibly handicapped persons disavow the "deviant" definition of themselves. Davis's paper fits snugly into the mainstream of interactionist literature; it is organized around the concept of self and how selves are thrust into situations in which they must cope.

Additional features make this classic interactionism. The settings in which Davis is interested are typical. He wishes to describe everyday face-to-face interaction that is prolonged enough to establish a relationship, but not so old as to be governed by norms of extreme familiarity or deeper sentiments. The interaction cannot be too stylized; if it were, the interactional dynamic would be restricted by formality. However, the interaction cannot be completely unpredictable. That is, the normal rules of behavior and etiquette ought to apply, because these give a general boundary and set a tone for a developing situation.

Obviously, these strictures are not rigid. What Davis is trying to say by delineating the kind of interactions he wants to describe is that these are the normal bounds within which most social interaction occurs among people who are neither intimate nor total strangers. A rather loose and undefined set of behavior rules governs activity, but considerable room for novelty and impression-management exists. Here individuality has its fullest room to develop as it constructs interaction via controlled self-projections and interpretations of self.

What is Davis's specific research problem? He wishes to understand how visibly handicapped people subtly erase the impression that they are "deviant" from the minds of those they contact socially, and replace this with a delicately balanced definition of themselves that acknowledges their essential normality, yet clearly denotes their limitations. Davis says it is almost always obvious to the handicapped that they are being defined as deviants. Davis's discussion of this points up the interactionists' emphasis on symbolization of attitudes as key features in interaction. He notes that the way handicapped people know how they are being defined is by reading the signs left by faux pas, revealing gestures, slips of the tongue, and inadvertent remarks, as well as by the pace and flow of the interaction itself. These are all symbolic of a set of attitudes that defines the situation and the relationships of the people in it. Much has been said about language in this chapter, but this should make it clear that the interactionist means far more than words and sentences when he uses the idea of symbolic communication.

Davis notes that the handicapped person is always potentially threatened in his social interaction, because the handicap itself may become the exclusive focal point, cutting off opportunities and restricting the relationship. Additionally, the sympathy most people feel for the handicapped might actually overflow its normal bounds, overcoming the normal restrictions on everyday feelings. Smothered in sympathy, the handicapped person may actually be prevented from engaging in normal activity. Finally, the handicap can pose a threat to the person's being defined as normal in most other ways, and this, coupled with the ambiguity that accompanies it, is at best a nuisance to handicapped people, and at worst a barrier to their forming normal social relationships and definitions of themselves.

Davis notes from his interviews with the handicapped that the process of deviance disavowal has three stages. The first of these makes use of everyday manners by causing them to work in the handicapped person's favor. In early stages of interaction, it is common to accept people as they would like to appear, and to make no reference to obvious departures from that. This "fictional acceptance" is a possible starting mechanism for interaction. However, the second stage is more delicate. If interaction is not to end in waves of sympathy, or stumble over the handicap itself, the handicapped person must manage the interaction so that it facilitates role-taking concerning the normal aspects of self being projected, yet clearly denotes the limitations posed by the handicap. If this is successful, says Davis, the psychological effect on the normal person is the receding importance of the handicap, to the point where it disappears from consciousness for normal interactional purposes. One of Davis's informants called this "breaking through." The breakthrough is acceptance of the preferred definition of self. This definition forms the basis from which role-taking is performed in the ensuing relationship. "Crippled" or "blind" cease to be the salient features of the person, and more normal dimensions of definition, such as "knowledgeable," "attractive," "witty," may take over to provide a potentially expansive relationship. The final stage of this process, Davis notes, is an institutionalization of the favored definition of self for most purposes, and an accompanying normalized recognition of the limitations placed on the relationship by the handicap. When this process is complete and successful, a disavowal of the "deviant" self-definition has been made and it has been replaced by a more normal one.

We have already noted how this research report is typically symbolic interactionist in its emphasis on self-definition, the centrality of the self in the process of role-taking, and the subtle use of communication. Additionally, we should note Davis's research style, which was to interview a small number of handicapped persons and ask them general questions about themselves and how they managed social interaction, following these questions further as the opportunity presented itself. No controlled questionnaires or battery of tests was administered. Similarly, Davis's natural tendency is to conceptualize mutual interaction as a process. He says that deviance disavowal by handicapped persons is a process that passes through stages on its way to completion. It simply is not in the interactionist's repertoire to view Davis's research question as answerable by a specific set of normative prescriptions, morally legitimate role expectations, or the like. The interactionist is more likely to see all questions of identity, situation definition, and interaction stabilization as processes, developing in time through the alignment of individual conduct in a mutually acceptable pattern. This parallels Mead's insistence on the progress of stages in the self-formation sequence, and it echoes Blumer's emphasis on society as the fitting together of individual actions in a never-ending adjustment process. Finally, it is worth noting again that all this is viewed by the interactionists as a symbolic communications process. Davis gives examples of the projection of attitudes and the denial of deviance proceeding via inadvertent noises and inappropriate sympathy, and via management of self-projection using norms in a way that will work to the best advantage of the person involved.

B. Empirical investigations of the self

A continuing puzzle in most sociological research is the subjective versus the objective point of view (see Chapter 2, section II). Whereas sociological theory often implies the subjective point of view, as symbolic interactionism does, the methodology employed to discover subjective facts is usually external and objective. All divining of other people's subjective states is in some sense objective, because understanding comes to the observer via external cues, reports, situational behavior, and the like.

Davis, in the sociological work just described, followed Blumer's dictum about research. Davis applied none of what modern sociologists would call "empirical" tests, and he had no particular hypotheses. He had no structured research techniques or specific procedure for working on his data after they were gathered. But, as we have noted, there is an alternative approach to research on symbolic interactionist theory, one that takes the major points raised by the pragmatists about self, communication, and society, and applies more structured procedures to them.

Kuhn's name is linked with this attempt to research symbolic interactionist theory more systematically.[45] His thinking runs something like this. The self is at the center of sociological theory. The self is formed in social interaction by internalizing various self-attitudes from the others with whom one comes in contact or of whom one is somehow aware. In fact, for research purposes the self may be conceptualized as a more or less stable set of attitudes about one's own identity. Because attitudes, in Kuhn's view, are tendencies to act, the self-as-attitudes argument leads to this conclusion: If we knew in sufficient depth the identity of a person as he knows himself, then we might have adequate information both to explain his activities and to predict his future action. If we could not predict in the individual case, then at least some tendencies or proclivities could be made clear, some alternatives eliminated. Further, Kuhn has discovered that Mead's statements concerning the self are not wholly consistent and are in some ways ambiguous. The I–me problem is of interest here. While the I plays a theoretical part in the analysis of conduct, the me is the internalized attitudes of others that give action its shape and direction, its social coherence. Therefore, if the question simply is, "How do we conceptualize the self for research purposes?" then the self as a set of attitudes is the answer–the me. Kuhn has argued both that the self ought to be conceptualized as a set of attitudes, for reasons of clarity, and that "others" from whom the self-attitudes are derived have received less attention than their importance calls for. His own work has followed up these points.

Kuhn faces the question of the subjectivity of self by asking people for their attitudes toward themselves. This is an objective attempt to discover subjective identity. Kuhn's Twenty Statements Test (TST) was developed for this purpose. Fundamentally, the TST is simplicity itself. Kuhn gives people a paper with twenty numbered blanks on it and asks them to quickly write down their responses to the question, "Who am I?" as though the responses were to oneself and not to an impersonal research worker. Analysis of the results makes the TST of interest to symbolic interactionists.

In a series of papers based on the TST, Kuhn reports that he first found the results of his test divided into answers that were either "consensual" or "subconsensual." The consensual category includes all those items of identification that are obvious to others, or that could be obvious. Things like religious membership, sex, class membership, and so forth, are in this category. In the subconsensual cate-

[45] See M. Kuhn and T. McPartland, "An Empirical Investigation of Self-attitudes," *American Sociological Review*, XIX, 1 (February 1954), pp. 68–76.

gory are those items of identification that we think are more "private," such as happiness or sadness, optimism or pessimism, and the like. Later, Kuhn reported that further studies with the TST put salient self-attitudes into five categories: social group and class identifications, ideology and belief, interests, ambitions, self-evaluations. Note that the basic dichotomy of consensual and subconsensual still remains.

As confirmation of Mead's basic idea, Kuhn found some interesting things. One was that, in making the twenty statements, most people thought of their consensual identity first, and only later went into their more private (perhaps less communally validated) world to identify themselves by subconsensual statements. This is readily interpreted. Supposedly, people gain their identity through contact with others. The theory of the me says that self-attitudes are a product of what other people think of us. These self-attitudes of most importance to us will be consensual ones. The tendency to think of some self-attitudes first and rapidly is Kuhn's *salience factor*. Salience refers to readiness to identify oneself. The more quickly an identifying attitude comes to mind, the more salient. Typically, consensual identity is more salient.

So far, so good. Most sociologists following Mead would have predicted this. Interactionist theory tends to suggest that all persons in all situations gain their self-attitudes externally. However, Kuhn has demonstrated (and this is the importance of this research) that not all people think of the consensual category of self-identification first, and that people vary a great deal in this depending on their age, sex, amount of schooling or training, degree of involvement with groups, and so forth. Furthermore, with a standard tool like the TST, the degree to which people vary from each other can be gauged and correlated with their other characteristics. Kuhn interprets these variations more or less in line with the interactionists' general theoretical perspective.

For example, measuring religious salience by noting how soon people make religious references about themselves, and how often they make them, Kuhn has shown that persons having "standard" religious affiliations (Roman Catholics and members of established Protestant churches, for example) have a lower religious salience in their identity than those of more sectarian faiths, and all these have higher religious salience than do nonbelievers. Another interesting finding is that sex identity apparently increases with age, up to at least middle age. At any age, females identify more by sex and kinship relations than do males of the same age, and females identify less by race than do males. As one would expect, occupational identification varies directly with years of involvement with the work.

These findings with the TST are important in understanding symbolic interactionism because they clarify an area left relatively untouched by the theory in its original state. Taken alone, the findings might be trivial. We do not really care, theoretically speaking, if Protestants or Catholics identify more by religion than do Jews. The theoretical importance of this lies in the qualification it places on the theory of the self. The Meadian hypothesis about self-acquisition is that one takes his cues from others by taking the role of "other," finally coming to an understanding of the "generalized other." Kuhn's work fills in some details. Where there is great heterogeneity, selective factors enter into self-identification that are predictable by other sociological facts such as age, sex, religion, and nationality. This is something that symbolic interactionism, in its enthusiasm for the individual and his uniqueness in situations, has tended to undervalue. Similarly, it has tended to ignore institutions, social class, and religion. Kuhn's simple demonstration that factors like these have considerable influence on the development of self has reemphasized the value of more standard sociological categories. He rediscovered structured social relations, but within the context of symbolic interactionism.

Yet, as Blumer would say, the subtleties are missed in Kuhn's work. It is not possible for Kuhn with twenty statements to conclude that he "knows" a person to the extent some other interactionist, using other techniques, would say that he knew him. But here is where the arguments between objectivists and subjectivists miss each other. Kuhn is trying to give a theoretical description of the self as self-attitudes and to describe the relatedness of these to sociological factors. Most other interactionists are researching relationships and the formation of them. The focus of Kuhn's work is on the self directly, whereas for most other interactionists the focus is on the uniqueness of the relationship and less directly on the self as a determinate entity.

VII. Conclusion and criticism

In appraising symbolic interactionism in sociology it is necessary to recall again that this is a perspective and not, strictly speaking, a theory, even though individuals might make stronger claims. Nor are the interactionists' theoretical efforts usually toward the standard aims of scientific explanation and prediction. Parsons claimed in mid-career that his work was actually preliminary to the building of real theory; Homans has claimed rigorous deductive theorizing for the exchange theory principle. But the interactionists still basically eschew scientism in sociology, opting instead for more interpretive forms.

Nevertheless some criticisms of the interactionist tradition may be offered that do not ignore the interactionists' real intentions. To begin, we should go back to Mead, particularly to his concept of language, because it is language more than anything else that unifies interactionist work. An adequate account of language should stand behind any derivations from Mead. But it is curious to note that most modern interactionist literature does not really pay close attention to what Mead said about language. Normally, the point simply is made that language is important, and that people use it to adjust their activities. There is usually no more inquiry into basic principles than that.

Mead's concept of language is behavioristic in tone and intent. Linguistic expression is the causing of a symbol to represent action and the consequences of action. Today, we might call this the "sign" function of gestures—a verbal gesture is the sign of a certain kind of event in certain circumstances. But what is intended by most modern interactionists is not this at all. They usually mean far more interesting things than Mead's theory of language could account for. How does one know, for example, that one situation is like another? If this is requisite knowledge for the use of a gesture to represent actions and consequences, then some principle of transference or generality of gestures should be found in the account of language. Mead attempted to answer this problem by pointing out that perception is selective, and that signifying is a selective process; but of course the question arises, "On what principles or from what basis does this selection occur?" Mead's work leaves this question unanswered.

A more serious problem with the Meadian view of language centers on the question of novelty in language, and the related question of language structure. Mead's treatment of language is so behavioristic that it closely associates experience of action with given gestures. But it is surely true that most people have never before heard the sentences they utter every day. The sentences are new and will probably never be said in exactly the same way again. Similarly, situations are new, even if similar to old ones. The deeper point here is that Mead gives no suggestion of how hearers of language could know the significance of gestures when the hearers' understandings have been built up in dissimilar situations, with other people. Add to this the fact that the language being spoken is not likely to have been heard in the same way ever before, and the Meadian view of language starts to look quite inadequate.

Criticisms like these lead up to a basic point that modern linguists would make at the outset: Language is a structured way of communicating. Mead's rendition of how language comes to exist and how it works might provide an explanation of how words become attached to conduct, but he suggests nothing of how strings of these words can convey thoughts across situations, across time, and between people who use words in infinitely various ways. It is indeed the structure of language that allows this to happen. Everyone knows that a child who is completely innocent of the rules of grammar can speak sentences in his native language that are formed more or less correctly. He will say, "Ginger is a horse standing in the field." He would never say, "Horse standing is field Ginger a in the." The same words are used in both "sentences." The child knows both the words to express his observation and the grammatical structure for the formation of an adequate English sentence. The real significance of communication by way of language is in the determinant structured usage of utterance. Mead's concept of language does not account for this.

Also missing from Mead's concept of language is an account of purely abstract terms and usages. Mead's overriding concern to link gestures to action caused him to neglect important classes of terms that do not refer to action at all. Purely abstract concepts such as "beauty" or "justice" have no concrete referents. One can say, "That canary is beautiful." The term "beautiful" is not used in the same sense as a concrete term, as in, "That canary is yellow." The difference is that "beautiful" refers to an abstract quality, not an empirical attribute of concrete things. As anyone knows who follows theatre, film, or music, concepts like "beauty" are far from being concretely applicable with precision, accuracy, and decisiveness. Language conveys more pure abstraction than most people realize, and a firmly behavioristic account of it can hardly serve as a characterization of everyday speech.

Another question related to Mead's idea of language is the paradoxical relationship between the individual and the ongoing group. It is true that Mead did not wish to spend time on such questions, but it may not be idle to ask how the individual comes to play so small a part in developing the meanings of gestures, and how the *group* (made up of individuals) has the power to generate meaning and implant it into the group's members. Locating this power of meaning formation with the abstract group, while not making individual members more significant, remains a problem. Lest it be argued that Mead did not mean this, recall his insistence that the self's reflection coming from other people in the community, making up internalized me's, was the necessary requirement for group action and presumably the existence of the group in the first place. Particularly if the I is neglected, as it tends to be in some interactionist work, this makes the person a bundle of me's constructed by his group, and very little more. The group becomes exterior and logically prior. A kind of crude sociologistic fallacy is the result, in which the individual is smothered in group determination. In fact, it was probably Mead's intention to enhance the place of individualism in theoretical thinking, but emphasizing group importance as a means of explaining individualism only leads to paradox.

More generally, we can note again that interactionism consistently fails to give an account of social structure. Rather, it usually takes structured normative relations as given parameters from which to begin, as Davis does in his discussion of deviance disavowal. What Davis says is that persons use norms to their advantage as best they can. But should the sociologists not also wish to know why there are these norms? Saying they are simply agreements among people who have worked out livable relationships flies in the face of the fact that, among many, normative rules are a direct constraint, and that, for many others, an extreme feeling of powerlessness and alienation toward normative order exists. It may be true that, given prior normative order, people work out modes of coping; but this does not amount to an explanation of social structure – rather, it assumes social structure as a prior condition of coping.

This leads directly to the question of motivation. Miyamoto has given a symbolic interactionist account of motivation, suggesting that group requirements are at work that have heretofore been neglected by the interactionists. We would wish to know why people consistently choose to act in given ways in certain situations, instead of in all the other ways they might possibly have acted. The reasoning drawn from Mead is that the community standpoint is taken into account, and the person acts to fit in. But why wish to do that? Miyamoto's answer is that successful activity depends upon the individual's decisions to act so as to maximize his effectiveness. Miyamoto wishes to cast this in terms of group approval, but how far is this from saying that expectations are laid down by others because they wish to have tasks performed? This is close to saying that acceptance is contingent on performance. And this is very close to saying that people require certain activities because they are crucial, either to existence or to well-ordered social affairs in the community. If this is what Miyamoto implies, then he is saying that fitting in with the wishes of the group is in reality a matter of defining the individual's place according to some criterion set abstractly by the group itself. This removes the question of motivation from individual will and places it at group level, where efficiency, survival, orderliness, or some other structured criterion is the basis for decisions on motivation. This takes symbolic interactionism a long way toward recognition of its relatedness to structural theory, rather than enhancing its view of itself as an alternative.

There is also the possibility that symbolic interactionism, as advocated by Blumer, runs the risk of removing all specific subject matter from sociology. Subject matter is an old question that has gone out of fashion. When sociology was establishing itself, debates were sometimes held on what unique subject matter sociology could rightfully claim that was not history, political theory, philosophy, and the like. Blumer's position on the nature of sociological research, and on sociology as a collection of sensitizing concepts, makes this question relevant again. If sociology is simply another language in which to talk about social intercourse, and "doing sociology" is simply the mastering of that language as a way of describing observations, then in fact there is no particular subject matter – such as social structure – for sociology to claim. Sociology would again face the question of whether or not its insights compare in quality and resolving power with those of other disciplines.

On the positive side, it is clearly true that some of the most fascinating sociology is in the symbolic interactionist tradition. People are probably naturally interested in themselves, and the story of how oneself is of crucial significance in society is bound to be interesting when the story is told with flair and a modicum of human insight. Such telling is almost exclusively the province of the interactionists. Sometimes it is said sociology's studies and findings are trivial. Indeed, some are and when they are dull as well, the effect is devastating. But the interactionists have a knack for seeking out and describing relationships of theoretical importance that can be of practical interest, too. An example of this is the work on professionalization of medical students done by Becker. Here is a study that to some extent unmasks the high professionalism of the medical profession, and that is informative about how doctors come to regard their patients, how they judge the importance of cases, how they come to differ from other people in attitudes toward disease, suffering, intimate exposure, and so forth.

Is there no sense, then, in which symbolic interactionism can be said to "explain" social life? It does not do it very successfully by rigorous deductive methods, or by establishing covering laws and advancing hypotheses. Yet as a method of making one understand by telling a tale in terms of a perspective on human affairs, all the while asserting that this perspective is really "the way it is," interactionism achieves a "soft" explanatory style that is valuable to sociology in its own way.

KEY CONCEPTS

perspective	play stage
self	game stage
other	social conduct

234 *Symbolic interactionism*

pragmatism	me
mind	I
society	parallelism
role-playing	variable analysis
role-taking	perceptual settings
language	sensitizing concept
significant gesture	salience factor
TST	reference group

TOPICS FOR DISCUSSION
1 Debate the various merits of the positions on symbolic interactionist research taken by Blumer and Kuhn.
2 In what ways did the pragmatists reject metaphysics in their attempts to understand the mind? What had this line of thought to do with behavioral psychology?
3 Answer the question, "Who am I?" in twenty statements and then compare answers to see whether consensual or subconsensual statements appeared first in most cases. What is the significance of your findings?
4 Think through the process of self-acquisition and then discuss the necessary sequence of events leading to significant self-change.
5 Describe the theoretical reasons why motivation is said to be inadequately explained by symbolic interactionist theory.
6 What are the main features of a perspective in sociology, and why is this term applied to symbolic interactionism?

ESSAY QUESTIONS

What is the controversy about determinacy of self-attitudes? Discuss the debate and come to conclusions about which side of the dilemma seems correct.
How does the research work by Kuhn and others with the TST help show the relationship between symbolic interactionist explanation and more traditional structuralist sociology?
How is the idea of "minded behavior" different from the idea of "mind"?
What questions would you have asked if you were doing Davis's research on visibly handicapped people? How would these have improved the result?
Discuss role-taking and role-playing by showing the theoretical differences between the two.
Why does the I only enter consciousness as a memory? Discuss the theory of the I and suggest, if possible, ways of doing research on it.

FOR FURTHER READING AND STUDY

Becker, Howard (ed.). *The Other Side: Perspectives on Deviance*. New York: Free Press, 1964.

Blumer, Herbert. *Symbolic Interactionism: Perspective and Method*. Englewood Cliffs, N.J.: Prentice-Hall, 1969.

Cooley, Charles H. *Human Nature and the Social Order*. New York: Schocken Books, 1962.

Goffman, Erving. *The Presentation of Self in Everyday Life*. New York: Doubleday, 1959.

Huber, Joan. "Symbolic Interaction as a Pragmatic Perspective: The Bias of Emergent Theory," *American Sociological Review,* XXXVIII (April 1973), pp. 274–84.

Kuhn, Manfred. "Major Trends in Symbolic Interactionism in the Past Twenty-five Years," *Sociological Quarterly,* V, 1 (Winter 1964), pp. 61–84.

Lindesmith, Alfred R., and Anselm L. Straus. *Social Psychology*. 3rd ed. New York: Holt, Rinehart and Winston, 1968.

McCall, George, and J. L. Simmons. *Identities and Interactions*. New York: Free Press, 1966.

Manis, James, and Bernard Meltzer (eds.). *Symbolic Interaction: A Reader in Social Psychology*. 2nd ed. Boston: Allyn and Bacon, 1972.

Mead, George H. *Mind, Self and Society*. Ed. Charles Morris. Chicago: University of Chicago Press, 1934.

The Philosophy of the Act. Ed. Charles Morris. Chicago: University of Chicago Press, 1938.

Miyamoto, S. Frank. "Self, Motivation and Symbolic Interactionist Theory," in Tomatsu Shibutani (ed.), *Human Nature and Collective Behavior: Papers in Honor of Herbert Blumer*. Englewood Cliffs, N.J.: Prentice-Hall, 1970.

Shibutani, Tomatsu (ed.). *Human Nature and Collective Behavior: Papers in Honor of Herbert Blumer*. Englewood Cliffs, N.J.: Prentice-Hall, 1970.

Stone, Gregory, and Harold Faberman (eds.). *Social Psychology Through Symbolic Interaction*. Lexington, Mass.: Xerox College Publishing, 1970.

7   Ethnomethodology

I. Introduction

The newest development in sociological theory is ethnomethodology. Because it approaches theoretical questions in untraditional ways, some would even deny that it is theoretical. But because ethnomethodology does imply theoretical questions and achieves a new (if somewhat radical) sociological viewpoint, while going to the heart of the sociological enterprise, it demands treatment as a theoretical position. Ethnomethodology appears to reject theorizing about social structure. But no matter how much we might wish to remove theoretical concerns from investigations and descriptions of everyday life, it is impossible to do so.

Ethnomethodology contains a great deal of philosophy and meta-theory, but almost no intermediate-level theory. The ethnomethodologists find it important to reject preconceived ideas of the nature of social order, for example, those found in functionalist or exchange sociology. They would regard such generalized descriptions of action as entailing regrettable and avoidable prejudice that distracts attention from more useful work. Thinking of social behavior as exchange, for instance, subtly prevents us from thinking of it as anything but exchange, and imposes a narrow, not particularly accurate, concept of social action. Far better to discover what the participants in social action think they are doing. Find out from them how they account for their behavior, what rules they follow, and why. Such a commonsense idea of sociological work, which seems so nontechnical, is in fact deceptively subtle, and filled with theoretical, even philosophical, difficulties. Ethnomethodologists are aware of this and spend considerable effort making plain the basis of their viewpoint. It is this commentary on basic assumptions that we can rightly regard as the meta-theory of ethnomethodology. And, in fact, this is not really so different from our approach to other theories.

Perhaps ethnomethodology is a "perspective." It is not a deductive theory, and it is probably not a pattern theory. It is difficult to place in the sociological scene because of the unique position it takes on the ontological status of social order. Ethnomethodologists tend to say that social order does not "exist" – or at least it is not "out there" in the same sense as other theorists think it is. If it does not exist, although social relations remain the subject of study, no natural property of the social world exists about which to ask objective scientific questions. Therefore, there can be nothing about which to write social laws, from which to derive invariant patterns. All science assumes an order in its subject matter, which it becomes the business of scientists to describe and explain. If no assumption of existential order is made, then the program of action for the "social scientist" must change quite drastically; his focus of interest shifts from "causes" of social order to appearances, his idea of rules followed by ordinary people becomes a concept of the ways people produce and sustain appearances, his explanation of social encounters shifts from exchange, sanctions, socialization, and the like, toward techniques by which people acquire and use the ability to get along, facilitating each other's action in understandable ways.

II. The rise of ethnomethodology

Perhaps it was predictable that ethnomethodology, with its special idea of social order, would arise in the second half of the twentieth century, accompanied by the breakup of previous world orders, the disintegration of previously unified nations, the relaxation of moral constraints as the foundation of social systems, the triumph of individualistic ideologies. Historically, ethnomethodology might be regarded as another reaction to sociological functionalism which stressed the importance of structured, rule-dominated social relations, culturally sanctioned norms, and the constraining conditions survival placed on social action and social systems. Functionalism lays such heavy stress on society as an action system, making demands upon persons and collective groups that cannot be refused, that it inevitably raises the question of the individual. Exchange theorists noted this and rejected the sociological program of functionalism; interactionists had long been calling for a different picture of the persons who were supposed to be the "actors" of functionalism. But some, who were later to become the proponents of ethnomethodology, asked yet another question. At first, this question was simple and limited in scope: What kind of real human being must the functionalists be talking about? Once we get past the superficial complaints against the functionalists' oversocialized concept of man, some very interesting social and psychological problems remain. If a social rule is to be followed, how do people know when it is in force? How do they know what actions are appropriate to it? How do they know how to act in accordance with it? Do they ever act contrary to the rule while remaining convinced they are following it? How do they judge others' actions according to a behavioral norm? How do they decide when and how to enforce rules? Is there a difference between the public and private selves regarding rule following?

Such questions as these are derived from this problem: By what mechanisms do persons in concrete situations apply behavior norms to their own conduct, and use such norms to understand the actions of others, toward the end of maintaining order? Perhaps it is becoming obvious that this question leads the investigator away from sociologically exterior and prior constraints on social action–away from the Durkheim to Parsons tradition–and directly to the study of individuals as social units, rather than action systems. This alternative tradition goes back beyond Weber and the concept of *verstehen*. It encompasses phenomenology, following through eventually to Alfred Schutz and his searching criticism of rationality.

Schutz says that in daily life, what we call "rationality" is in fact supported by various nonscientific assumptions that must be made so that rational-appearing conduct may proceed. Such a line of thought could take the inquiring mind in many directions. One of these is into the study of language. Because it is obvious that behavior norms are enforced, transmitted, and taught linguistically, the relationship between what we say and what we do takes on theoretical importance. Perhaps saying *what we do* also somehow communicates *why* we do it, and *when*. These additional aspects of descriptions are not often communicated directly, or perhaps even consciously. There is something about the context of our thought and actions that give these additional messages. Returning to Schutz, we find the phenomenologists saying that certain nonlogical assumptions of everyday life support multifaceted communications about everyday actions. People say and hear more than the actual meanings of the words and sentences they use. They accomplish this, and routinely expect to do so, because they make unanalyzed assumptions regarding context and meanings. Both speaker and hearer "fill in" meanings from their own minds to augment and complete interpersonal communications.

Before we go on to explain this more fully, let us take the next step that completely severs ethnomethodology from traditional social science. If actions are understandable because they correspond to nonverifiable, private, and perhaps unconscious assumptions, and because people fill in meanings not actually communicated, how can there be objectively recognizable social order? Perhaps there is none. At any rate, it is not necessary to assume some general property of orderly social relations to explain conduct. If it is not necessary, do not assume it. Simply describe the ways people communicate and draw on their own experience to sustain the mutual impressions of order they create. This is the radical break. Throwing out the preliminary general assumption of social order implies the total rejection of social science principles, its theories of action, and its methodologies. Of course, ethnomethodologists have to supply alternatives, which they have tried to do. This radical departure from the basic idea of social science partially accounts for the cold reception ethnomethodologists receive from the sociological community.

Having broken away from traditional sociological theory, ethnomethodologists are at liberty to replace it as they wish. But typically, ethnomethodologists do not proclaim that there is no order in social life. Contradictory though it may seem, they are impressed by interaction that proceeds along predictable and seemingly orderly paths. But in such interaction, ethnomethodologists see a different challenge. They normally regard orderly social affairs as created and sustained appearances that in no way derive from abstract sociological properties of interaction. Their point is that everyone sees things this way. Ethnomethodologists try to discover how ordinary people go about acting in such a world.

If social action is not conduct predictably the result of sociological factors combined with basic human motives, then what is it? Here the ethnomethodologist would like to trade places with his subjects, and let them tell him. Everyday people are always asking each other just that question. And they routinely find answers by processes resembling those social scientists might use. Everyday action progresses smoothly, and appears orderly, because people tell each other, in many ways, that the things they do and think are appropriate and necessary.

III. Attitudes of daily life and the ethnomethodologists' program

We must now return to Schutz's analysis of human rationality. It is the basis of the argument that appearance, and not higher-level order, actually characterizes human relations. Schutz compared the ideal scientific attitude to attitudes of daily life.[1] His comparison shows that people typically do not apply scientific rationality to everyday judgments. Indeed, doing so might be impossible. People do not usually act in the spirit of rationality that includes, among other things, always knowing all alternatives for every action choice, and all the outcomes of each, having a means to compute the values of various alternative actions, and knowing the rules of procedure by which rational choices must be made.

[1] This discussion follows H. Garfinkel, "The Rational Properties of Scientific and Common-sense Activities," *Postivism and Sociology*, Anthony Giddens, ed. (London: Heinemann, 1974), pp. 53–73.

A. *Attitudes of everyday life*

Schutz's idea of the way people normally do act in everyday situations shows that they usually do not act scientifically; that is, they do not judge themselves and others according to attitudes that lead to accurate scientific knowledge of the world. Instead, they behave according to the following nonlogical assumptions that actually make practical action possible.

1. Typical action entails the *belief* that things and people are what they appear. This is in contrast to the scientist's unlimited and continuing doubt. The scientific attitude always allows for the logical possibilities that all data are not yet known, all interpretations not yet made. Action based upon such an attitude is never decisive and, in purest principle, should never be taken; certain scientific knowledge is never achieved. But the everyday person acts toward his world based on the belief that things and appearances are what they seem. This belief produces mental closure around events, facilitating action, but at the cost of some unwitting closed-mindedness.

2. Another assumption concerns the relationship of the "plain man" to actions and others. He assumes that his activities make a difference to the world he lives in, and that he is affected by the actions of others. This is contrasted with the attitude that requires the scientist to think and observe from a theoretically remote position – to avoid interfering in, and interference from, the actions of his scientific subjects. Whereas the scientific attitude requires suspension of involvement with subjects, the everyday attitude is just the reverse. Familiarity through involvement is exactly what the everyday person seeks. His practical interest in the world supports his assumption that his activities make a difference, not the scientists' assumption that his activities make no difference.

3. The everyday person assumes events have a temporal sequence that he knows from experience. He expects things to happen according to familiar steps, and in known progression. He usually regards sequences as causes. Further, he assumes that his time perspective is entirely public, and the same for everybody. The scientists' attitude toward time is different. If he reasons from scientific laws, he expects them to apply across time and place. Scientific laws are "timeless" in this respect. Also, he may think of cause in many ways that have nothing to do with apparent sequence, or causes may operate on a time scale that the everyday man does not know or grasp.

4. The "plain man" assumes that "forms of sociability" exist for him, and that these are in some way under his control. He believes there is a difference between his private and public self, and that he can decide which public self he will display. This amounts to belief in

forms of sociability, because such a belief supplies a rule by which the everyday person groups his experiences. He knows which experiences properly go with whom, and he knows from experience how his actions will probably be received in each form of sociability. This contrasts with the scientist's attitude toward social action. To be objective, the scientist remains outside the roles being enacted. Whereas the scientist views social life from the "outside," it is precisely and only from the "inside" that forms of sociability can be known and utilized.

5. Everyday persons assume something about language that has plagued the social scientist from the beginning. The "plain man" supposes that daily life is conducted according to a common world of intersubjective communication. This is a *belief*, and one the scientist is obliged to resist if he is to retain his objectivity and skepticism. Everyday life contains millions of instances in which one person assumes others know what he means when he speaks, and assumes he knows what is meant when he hears. This is an essential background assumption for all human interaction. It is the basis from which it is possible to "fill in" meanings not actually spoken, and to grasp the general meaning of a specific statement. This has been called the "et cetera" assumption people routinely make when they act as if they knew the generic kind of action being spoken about in specific terms, and as if they knew *all* about it.

B. Ethnomethodology's program

Schutz's critique of rationality appears to prove that everyday reasoning could never produce scientifically accurate pictures of the world. A corollary to this is that people in their familiar routines of daily living do not behave with the "real world" in mind, but produce impressions of social order and facilitiate others' doing the same. Ethnomethodologists argue, therefore, that formally and rationally reconstructed theories of social organization must be rejected, and a new program for sociological study must be developed.

Rejecting formal sociological theory is easy. Ethnomethodologists can simply deny the explanatory value of such theories, while not necessarily denying the observations upon which the theories are based. Developing a new program for sociological study is not so easy, and has tended to emerge in small pieces as the research literature appears. But in principle, ethnomethodologists know very well what they want. The aim is to regard social routines in exactly the same way a normal participant in them would, and then to discover upon which kinds of mental attitudes, presumptions, and actions such routines depend. We have just seen that doing this entails using a logic foreign to the scientific spirit. Therefore, it cannot result in formally deductive theories. Speaking in particular about social organization, Bittner puts the point clearly:

> We must emphasize that our interest is in outlining a program of inquiry, not in producing a theory of organization. It has to be this way because the inquiry cannot get under way without first employing the very sensibilities that it seeks to study, i.e., the common-sense outlook. At the very outset, the phenomenon of organization comes to our attention in just the way it comes to the attention of any normal member of our linguistic community. Even as we turn to the investigation of the common-sense presumptions in which it is imbedded and from which it derives its socially sanctioned sense, other common-sense presumptions will continue to insinuate themselves into our thinking and observation. The important point in the proposed study is that we must be prepared to treat every substantive determination we shall formulate as a case for exploring the background information on which it in turn rests.[2]

Earlier in this chapter, we noted that ethnomethodology is considered by some to be antitheoretical. Perhaps we can now see the reason for this charge, and that this is exactly what ethnomethodologists want. They begin with what can only be called a theoretical account of the human being in everyday situations. But because people do not usually behave according to scientific procedures, the ethnomethodologists draw the conclusion that we cannot use rational scientific theory to begin to grasp the meaning of human behavior. Also, no scientifically formulated or assembled theories of human conduct should result from ethnomethodology. Its theory remains at the meta-theory level, while the lower levels of abstraction are relatively vacant. Ultimately, we reach the concrete level, where ethnomethodologists do most of their work.

And what kind of work do they do? In principle, there are three types of study that have come to form the ethnomethodologist's program of research. One type is the acquisition of social and cultural knowledge, and the study of its distribution and maintenance. In its most ambitious form, this is a full sociology of knowledge, which takes all knowledge as its subject, and could in principle form an account of all culture.[3] However, this kind of study usually proceeds more piecemeal. Here we often see the terms "accomplishing" or "acquiring" used in a unique way. For example, in "Accomplishing

[2] E. Bittner, "The Concept of Organization," in R. Turner, ed., *Ethnomethodology* (Harmondsworth, Middlesex: Penguin, 1974), pp. 76–7.

[3] Cf. P. Berger and T. Luckmann, *The Social Construction of Reality*. (Garden City, N.Y.: Doubleday, 1966).

Ethnicity," Moerman[4] describes the ideas and acts in the experience of belonging to what anthropologists might call a tribe, even though the externally observable traits of tribalism have faded or become confused. He points out that belonging is an "accomplishment" that consists of grasping unique meanings and successfully identifying with them – an aspect of sustaining and projecting a tenuous facet of orderly social relations. Similarly, the term "acquiring" refers to learning routine procedures by which an appearance of order may be produced and sustained, as in Cicourel's classic paper, "The Acquisition of Social Structure: Toward a Developmental Sociology of Language and Meaning."[5]

In addition to treatments of social knowledge, ethnomethodologists have been busy describing concrete encounters, which is perhaps where their greatest strength lies. For example, Wieder's "Telling the Code"[6] describes the use of the "convict code" by the staff of halfway houses. It is classic ethnomethodology. The convict code consists of a set of maxims about how convicts should behave toward each other and toward "straight" people. It contains admonitions not to tell on each other, never to admit wrongdoing, to share, not to trust staff or "straight" persons, and so on. It is in describing the use of the code by the staff of a halfway house that Wieder's ethnomethodology is put to use. He says the staff regard the code as a generalized way to make sense of inmates' activities, which when judged by normal standards might be quite bizarre. The staff use the code, a shared background of information, as a method making sense, in much the same way that everyday people use other such codes. In this way, activity that would look chaotic to an outsider is considered perfectly normal, legal, and not disruptive to regular routine. Here we see Wieder describing what to his mind is *not* an instance of inherently orderly activity, but instead, an instance of the *appearance* of order (which to others looks like chaos). This is produced and maintained by the nonlogical use of shared knowledge by insiders who interpret behavior as though it made sense according to some orderly framework.

A more active strategy in ethnomethodological research focuses on the ways people decide that the activities of their peers are acceptable and understandable. In fact, research of this kind probably started ethnomethodology on its way. Harold Garfinkel made a study of ju-

4 M. Moerman, "Accomplishing Ethnicity," in Turner, *Ethnomethodology*, pp. 54–68.
5 A. Cicourel, *Cognitive Sociology*. (Harmondsworth, Middlesex: Penguin, 1973), Ch. 2, "The Acquisition of Social Structure: Toward a Developmental Sociology of Language and Meaning."
6 L. Wieder, "Telling the Code," in Turner, *Ethnomethodology*, pp. 144–72.

rors.[7] His task was to listen to jurors' conversations and deliberations to see "what makes them jurors." In other words, what did people do, to which common understandings did they refer, to judge acceptable behavior in the role of juror? This question is more complicated than it sounds. There is no school for jurors. The whole point about being judged by one's peers is that *laymen* make the decision of guilt or innocence. Even though they are swayed by men of the law, and instructed by the judge, they make the final decision in their own way, somehow causing the evidence, courtroom performances, and common sense to coalesce in an accurate decision. At the time, no name had been given to Garfinkel's type of question. He later named it "ethnomethodology" in an attempt to describe the fact that he was interested in the folkways used by laymen to reach social decisions.[8] The case of the jurors became a prototype for other ethnomethodological study.

An aspect of the research with jurors was that Garfinkel was to interview them (after he had heard tapes of their conversations) to see how they would describe their deliberations to an outsider. Here is an important technique of ethnomethodological research that has been enlarged and copied in various research settings. In listening to the jurors' tapes, Garfinkel was searching for the everyday understandings that "made people jurors" according to their own lights. Later when he talked to them, they were placed in a different frame of reference – being interviewed by an outsider. How would they depict their activities as jurors to one who (they presumed) did not have inside knowledge of it? The work with jurors put Garfinkel in an effective position to see how depictions of activities actually compared with those activities performed by insiders. Such knowledge was useful in showing how it was *depictions, accounts,* and *explanations* that were important to the interview sequence, and not necessarily strictly accurate reports of what happened which might be governed by a general behavior rule, such as "always tell the truth." Out of this kind of early work came the research strategy that was widely copied by ethnomethodologists – that of intentionally disrupting an ordinary interaction sequence to observe the effects of shifting background assumptions and frames of reference. The results of such studies generally are that *any action* appears chaotic until it can be accounted for according to a recognizable everyday form. Such results stress appearances while reducing the explanatory value of socialized behavior rules, master motives or processes (such as exchange), and social structure.

[7] H. Garfinkel, *Studies in Ethnomethodology.* (Englewood Cliffs, N.J.: Prentice-Hall, 1967), p. 110 ff.
[8] H. Garfinkel, "The Origins of the Term 'Ethnomethodology,' " in Turner, *Ethnomethodology,* pp. 15–18.

Research such as Garfinkel's, Wieder's, and Bittner's all regard the subjects as doing their own social methodology. All of us, they claim, are everlastingly "doing methodology" in an effort to discover the assumed bases of orderly appearances and the expected bases from which to project our own actions. Because this is the case, it is only natural that academic sociology should start at a similar place with the assumptions and procedures of everyday methodology used by everyday people. The "program of inquiry" Bittner was later to call for is being fashioned by ethnomethodologists in the field.

IV. Ethnomethodology and language study

The study of language became woven into the ethnomethodologist's program. Some, such as Garfinkel, concentrated on field studies and the philosophical background derived from phenomenology (particularly Schutz); others took an academic interest in language, its composition and acquisition. Cicourel's name is most closely associated with this aspect of the field. Language has an obviously close relationship to all of ethnomethodology, because it is through linguistic forms that messages about appropriateness and mutual understandings are sent among persons who produce and maintain the appearances of order. But this is only to state the obvious. Cicourel had the additional notion that there might be something about language itself – perhaps its structure, its linear organization, its classifications of linguistic utterances – that made social organization possible. Perhaps, in addition to the things people say to each other that make orderly appearing activity possible, there is something about the modes in which they communicate that ensures the appearance of orderly activity.

Such an idea is supported by studies of language-in-use: ways common things and activities are named and given meanings. In discussing the language in which police and probation officers conduct their work, Cicourel says:

> How the activities of the [officers] associated with the court of detention facilities produce information that becomes part of an official file on the juvenile . . . is not understandable without reference to the improvised but "normal" rules and theories utilized by officials. The rules and theories, however, have their roots in commonsense or folk typifications making up law-enforcement officials' stock of knowledge. Without some understanding of everyday categories – the "strange," "unusual," "wrong," and what is "routine," "harmless," "right," – we cannot understand how improvisation necessarily enters into the

picture in making the formal legal and clinical categories invoked by law-enforcement officials work.[9]

Cicourel is saying that the particulars of any incident are somehow combined with the folk wisdom that defines normal practices by which people make sense of their world. This is much the same emphasis we found in Garfinkel's work with the jurors. But although Garfinkel was interested in how the jurors went on from that point actually to make decisions, Cicourel's work leads him increasingly toward finding out how language categories become established initially, and how they respond to everyday use. In his research with police, he has a professional sociological audience in mind. His intention is to show how working legal and theoretical categories are generated from encounters, and how "official" records (which may become the bases of statistical sociology) mask over the complicated and subtle bargaining, negotiation, sweet-talking, and rough handling that actually lead the name of a particular person to become linked with a definition and judgment of action. Comparisons of such records against the ethnomethodology of actual encounters highlights the socially and linguistically organized ways in which acts become categorized, understood, and evaluated.

Language enters into the program of ethnomethodology, then, because it is the medium through which encounters are transacted, and the medium through which persons reconstruct, justify, and explain their actions. "Official" language, as depicted perhaps in police records, is a cleaned-up version of actual talk, which is fragmented, partial, colloquial, often incoherent, almost never in complete sentences, and which probably proceeds by way of many false starts, mistakes, awkward phrases, and so forth. Cicourel finds something very important in the fact that everyday language has this character. The grammar of textbook speech cannot contain such normal language. Its situated context encompasses the unique culture in which such language is spoken. More about this is necessary.

It is impossible to overemphasize how important the following work of Cicourel's is to sociology. It takes ethnomethodology away from mere street work, with a special interpretation of everyday life, and straight into contact with the most fundamental questions of sociology—how is it possible that humans produce behavior norms that they somehow use to control their activities and other people? This may sound like a return to the problem of social order, and in a uniquely ethnomethodological way, it is.[10]

We have established that language is the medium through which

---

[9] A. Cicourel, "Police Practices and Official Records," in Turner, *Ethnomethodology*, p. 85.

[10] The following is based on Chapters 2, 3, 4, and 5 of Cicourel's *Cognitive Sociology*.

people send and receive information on the social world, and by which they come to make judgments about its normality. It is important, therefore, to have an account of how language works. When this account takes shape, the theoretical importance of Cicourel's work becomes clear.

The enduring questions about language have to do with meaning and sense. How do terms gather and hold meaning, and how are these meanings arranged into utterances that can carry across space and time, depositing themselves in the ears of those who recapture the meaning for themselves? How can a finite vocabulary and grammatical rule book produce sentences with unlimited potential to communicate? And how do ordinary people, many of whom are completely unfamiliar with the formal rules of grammar, and most of the words in their native tongue, make themselves understood quite adequately, sometimes eloquently? Questions like these have occupied theoretical linguists for a long time. The branch of this study most important to ethnomethodologists is "generative linguistics," which consists of several subtheories based on the component parts of the sentence, and the arrangements of these components into meaningful utterances.

If a sentence is disassembled into its basic parts, the smallest part is a phoneme. *Phonological theory* concerns the ways phonemes, or speech sounds, go together in language. Some groups are always found together, and others have a limited number of sounds they group with. By analogy, in English, the letter *q* is always followed by the letter *u*. When pronounced, they form *q̄ū,* a single sound, as in "quick." The letter *q* is never grouped with anything else, such as *r* or *j*, and so there is no sound *q̄r̄* or *q̄j̄*, even though these may be spelled from the alphabet. Similarly, there are rudimentary speech sounds that almost always go together or go together with only certain other sounds. Even though the native speaker of a language may be unaware of this, intelligible speech depends upon his assembling speech sounds in specific and unvaried sequences. These sequences – the statements of what goes with what – may be described as the *rules* of phonology, and can be reconstructed by linguists from native speech. It is not important here to go into how this may be done. The significant point is that, to make sense of speech sounds, the speaker must handle phonemes according to implicit rules of composition, which he learns early and well, from those who "teach" him to talk. In fact – and this is important – there is really very little formal training in talking. People pick up their native language for themselves. We shall return to this point.

Syntactical theory deals with the ways words are put together in phrases, clauses, and sentences. Obviously, a word cannot be placed at random among other words and still deliver meaning to a sentence.

Phrases, clauses, and sentences are composed in determinant ways according to rules of composition in much the same way that speech sounds are formed into words. Again, it is not important here to establish exactly how this is done. The point is that, once again, an implicit set of rules governs the composition of sentences, just as rules governed word assembly. The points about native speakers knowing and routinely using these rules apply. Grammar is the name given to the combined rules of phonology and syntax, and in general the rules of grammar must be followed to produce meaningful sentences in any language.

Semantics is the study of how meanings are associated with words in sentences. The idea of a dictionary comes to mind, because it is the book in which the meanings of words are found. But when we look up a word in a dictionary, we usually see that it has several meanings, often quite different, although meanings usually cluster around some central core. And when we come upon a word we do not know, we may have some difficulty choosing its dictionary definition in an unfamiliar sentence to complete a sensible statement.

The point about semantics we need to stress is that the meanings of sentences are nestled in their structure. Normally, we have no trouble understanding the intended meaning of a word, even though it may have several definitions in a dictionary. We instantly recognize the appropriate meaning because of the place the word occupies in the unfolding sentence. We follow the structural logic of sentences, which we have learned to recognize, just as we follow the meanings of specific words, phrases, and sounds. Needless to say, there are rules by which a language user identifies the meanings of words as they appear in sentences.

Grammar and semantics highlight the extraordinary ways languages are organized according to general rules that allow native speakers to produce and understand unique sentences of limitless variety and meaning, using a relatively small number of sounds, words, and rules for their use. It has been suggested that language does this because it acts as a highly organized categorizing system for meanings and sounds. The idea of "generative grammar" is that the syntactic component of language (how words are put together into phrases, clauses, and sentences), is actually composed of a categorizing system and a dictionary, along with a set of "transformation rules." The categorizing and defining parts of syntax generate "deep structures." These organize meanings according to categories. By way of the transformation rules, meanings result in "surface structures." Transformation rules bring out the intended meaning as speech sounds, which are then dealt with according to the phonetic rules, to produce actual speech.

The points to retain about this kind of analysis of language are that ordinary speech is possible because every normal person is capable of this complicated sorting and meaning-assigning function, and that the transformation rules, grammatical and semantic rules are "known" by all native speakers, even though they could never report their knowledge or even guess the complicated nature of hearing and producing speech. Theoretical linguists are often inclined to regard the rules of language as context free, somewhat mechanical in nature, and operative at all times. Cicourel would question whether such rules, especially those of semantics and syntax, are in fact context free. We turn now to contributions to this line of thought, and to the ethnomethodology of language.

A. *Generative semantics*

Impressive as theories of generative grammar are, they appear too academic. They assume complete ideas to be more or less coterminous with complete sentences. A sentence must be complete before it can be analyzed. It must say something recognizable apart from the context in which it was performed or prepared – as, for example, the sentences in printed matter, or those spoken by well-prepared lecturers. But ethnomethodologists, above all people, are tuned in to everyday speech, and they know for sure that almost no ordinary speech is assembled, completed, and refined in this way. In fact, the striking feature of everyday talk is that it is just the opposite. It is fragmented, halting, perhaps incoherent, almost always incomplete, and relies to a considerable extent on context and unarticulated shared meanings and experiences. Cicourel combines knowledge about the character of everyday speech with the theory of generative grammar to produce what he calls "generative semantics."

The idea of generative semantics is this: If intelligible speech requires invariant linguistic structure, yet most speech is not fully organized structurally, something else must be supplying some component of the required orderly structure. Meanings of *sentences* are fixed in linguistic context. But true *sentences* are not often spoken. It seems that aspects of the social settings in which ordinary speech appears lend critical structure to what people actually do say regarding their intentions, understandings of their world, and so on. Using a language without formal training requires composing and understanding ordinary statements – linguistic productions that are usually fragmentary, incomplete, or partial in other ways. This suggests that the child, as he learns his language, is also acquiring a sense of the social structures in which aspects of his language are appropriate. This kind of analysis leads neatly into ethnomethodology's view of social context and orderly appearances. Order is imparted on the spot to situations through talk and negotiations, in ordinary language. Additionally, the order required by language imposes certain categorizing and sorting functions on all who would participate in such situations. Therefore, the world *must* be made to appear orderly so that it may be depicted in language. This line of reasoning leads to something like this: To act we must have a world we can depict to ourselves and others in language; we can only depict a world exhibiting features of resemblance, consistency, coherence, and so forth, because human speech relies on such space-time categories; therefore, orderly settings and contexts of speech are in practice indistinguishable from the rules of speaking, even though such rules can be logically reconstructed and codified. The rules we speak by correspond in language to the rules we live by in social context – they are *used* (not followed) to depict meaning, impart meaning to occasions and actions, cause actions to seem sensible in context. Social structure, then, is "acquired" or "accomplished" in much the way speech is, and it is generative. Just as generative grammar generates limitless sentences from an orderly and limited number of forms, social structure is generative in that its context-linked rules enable persons to take wide ranges of unique personal action that will be regarded as understandable by others.

Cicourel goes on to try to specify the things anyone would have to assume implicitly for a linguistic construction of the social world to be made. These points roughly parallel Schutz's idea of the plain man's assumptions that divide everyday action from rational science. The first is the assumption of a reciprocity of perspectives. This is not the assumption that the world looks the same from everyone's point of view, but that if persons were to change places, the worlds they see would be the worlds of the persons they changed with; this also assumes that any personal uniqueness of viewpoint, no matter from whose standpoint, may be neglected for interaction to proceed.

Another property of the interaction process is the "et cetera" assumption. This is the assumption that allows persons to "fill in" gaps in messages from their own experience. Much talk, being vague, partial, or incoherent, is not really discursive, but instead "indexes" a course of conversation. In normal speech, we often place the phrase "you know" at intervals. When this receives an affirmatory nod or sound, it marks the course of the speech. All is going well, the hearer is following the speaker, the conversation may proceed. Garfinkel calls such exchanges "index marks."

Cicourel lists the existence of "normal forms" of talk and behavior as a necessary presumption. These are the generally expected attitudes, sequences, colloquial expressions, opinions, and various nonlinguistic aspects of interaction that give key messages about how to regard and respond to the persons who send them. Typically, we operate within normal forms. The questions of what activities go with, and are expected from, whom does not arise. If behavior or conversation becomes unrecognizable, and the assumptions of the et cetera principle, for example, become doubtful, there will be an effort to "normalize" the behavior by giving it meaning that fits some recognizable normal form – even if behavior is labeled "crazy," it is a normality that can be dealt with, because "crazy" people are expected to be erratic and incoherent.

There is continuity in everyday interaction because of what Cicourel calls the *retrospective–prospective sense of occurrence*. By this, he means that we usually have to wait to see what meanings to assign to past talk and behavior. The assumption that there is meaning in vague, incomplete, or unrecognizable messages gives a time perspective, and allows a sense of stable social structure to endure throughout interaction sequences. Such meanings normally become clear eventually. If a person tells a joke, the "punch line" usually comes last. But the preliminary buildup is never judged unrecognizable or incoherent, even though such talk would be most bizarre in any other context. When the punch line arrives, the sense of retrospective–prospective occurrence unites the implied meanings of the buildup with the punch line to complete an interaction sequence. Similar things happen in normal speech every day, sometimes over very long periods. The expectation that we will make sense at some future time lends continuity to the social encounters in which yet unknown meanings are uttered.

It is worth noting that talk itself is a necessary component of understandable action. No matter what is said, talk accompanies almost all normal interaction. Therefore, its quantity, pace, flow, punctuation with laughter or other sounds such as "uh huh," give crucial indications of the kind of interaction it is, and whether it progresses normally. This kind of talk is reflexive. It provides a basis for understanding interaction in which it occurs, and suggests expectations members will have about future interaction. Cicourel says that talk is "always folding back upon itself so that the presence of 'proper' talk and further talk provide both a sense of 'all is well' and a basis for members to describe the arrangement successfully to each other."

Finally, Cicourel notes that particular vocabularies go with certain forms of interaction. They provide speakers and hearers with instructions about how to apply the assumptions of normal forms, et cetera, and occurrence. If people are going to "fill in" meanings as interactions progress, the hearer must be cued as to the behavior qualities and settings being described. Vocabularies and speech forms that go with certain kinds of activity help to do this by suggesting appropriate assumptions about context, states of emotion, and so forth.

Perhaps at this stage it is worth stating again how the ethnomethodological concept of interpretive procedures cuts across the traditional idea of society arising around common values and behavior standards. The idea that social order exists because it derives from common values suggests that social action consists of the application of values in concrete cases. And even if it is questionable whether individuals actually apply society's values, the traditional scheme suggests that this judgment could be made only with reference to a common value scheme. Ethnomethodology says that individuals interact in the absence of such a unifying value scheme. Rather, by employing everyday assumptions about the nature of interactions, and by indexing the occasions and situations in which meanings are intended, persons informally negotiate the interactions they participate in. They do so linguistically, and are subject to the generative patterns of both linguistic rules and context-related meanings. Unfolding interaction provides many points at which persons may take different decisions; the variety of concrete interactions provides evidence that some generative system of interaction flow is actually in operation. Rather than interaction as the application of attitudes, values, or motives, situated interaction itself (combined with personality and individual uniqueness) depends on no valuing, shared intentions, or overall basic motive. In this kind of analysis, values become general policies that are always problematic and perhaps rarely shared widely throughout a society, even though they may enjoy some official or legal status. They are not primary to interaction. Rather, values enter social discourse as justifications in accounts of activity and as indexical expressions indicating the kinds of concrete interactions in which they arise. The ethnomethodologist thus rejects traditional concepts of social interaction as orderly properties of social and cultural events at their own level. He does not deny that social order exists, per se. In fact, he studies exactly that. But he tries to show that any number of social orders may result from the interpretive procedures people use in their talk and situated actions. In principle, the concrete natures of these orders are infinite, and not the results of master causes. Rather, linguistically based interpretive procedures are the only preliminaries to interaction. Such a line of argument reduces the "sociological level" of analysis to ashes; the individual becomes limitless.

V. Research procedures

Aspects of normal speech form the bases of two kinds of ethnomethodological research. One has to do with childhood acquisition of the speech and context rules that make normal interaction possible. This amounts to a study of the cognitive learning implied by the term "socialization," and refers to research on how the child gains a sense of context in which to utter appropriate speech. The second kind of research, usually not with children, is simply the extension of the same principles. Here focus normally shifts away from initial learning of social structure to using it. Then the modes and forms of normal speech become the basis for a study of how persons instruct each other in negotiating interaction. Such research concerns the individual as an interpreter of events, using the linguistic assumptions and rules outlined earlier. The ethnomethodologist's position on social order has led to some characteristic research procedures. For our purposes, we may neglect research on acquisition of language and social structure, even though this may be the most basic research of all.

There are, in principle, two research settings that naturally divide ethnomethodological research procedure. Following more traditional divisions of sociology, we may think of the ethnomethodologist as an analyst of social organization, or as an observer of informal social action, chance encounters, and of loosely arranged social action such as walking. (Yes, there is at least one ethnomethodological paper on "doing walking.")[11]

When the ethnomethodologist examines a formal organization, or some kind of encounter in which the procedures for action are prescribed, he has, in principle, two kinds of data. First is the "rule book," lists of procedures, organizational charts, chains of command, stated expectations, and the like. Also included in this data would be the records kept in organizations – police reports, school and medical records, casebooks. All such data share some features. For one thing, these are the codified statements of how people are to act or have acted, including specifications of the related situations, attitudes, decisions, and so forth. These may be regarded as linguistic depictions of activity, and, therefore, they should describe the sanctionable rules by which it is acceptable to judge behavior of its type and make it understandable. Even if such rules are only implicit, it is instructive to know them, because they describe the context of "normal forms" in the ways these would be described to outsiders. Knowing, for example, that honesty is mandatory for salesclerks, implies that a whole constellation of honesty-related behaviors are suitable and sanctionable – such as "looking honest," a straightforward gaze, a clean, neat appearance, and so on.

Of additional importance when examining written records or rules is the comparison they provide to the ways people actually behave.

[11] A. Ryave and J. Schenkein, "Notes on the Art of Walking," in Turner, *Ethnomethodology*, pp. 265–74.

Cicourel has reported on how police come to know their clientele, and how this knowledge is transformed into reports in police records. For example, "acting suspicious" is undefinable apart from the policeman's intimate knowledge of situated actions. Yet being arrested for suspicion of a crime must be justified according to sanctionable rules of police work. This includes showing that adequate and reasonable police activities have taken place, so that "anyone" would regard the reported activity as "obviously" suspicious. Such research into how people use behavior rules to make their actions understandable within some normal form, and justifiable in law or custom, has occupied ethnomethodologists.

Another example of the creative study of organizational rules is given by Zimmerman.[12] He studied persons working in an organization to which clients came for professional help. The receptionist in the organization was instructed to follow rules to help clients find help in an expeditious way. These norms specified questions to ask the client, how to decide which professional to see, and so forth. But the receptionist also had the practical duty to maintain an orderly flow of traffic, keep other members of the organization happy, deal with all variety of clients in all states of emotion and with widely varying personalities. Zimmerman's observations suggest that the rules specified the spirit of the activity and defined the limits of behavior allowed to the receptionist. They also provided readily available excuses and justifications that the receptionist learned to interpret. But in no concrete sense did the receptionist "follow" the rules. She made use of rules in a normal context of encounters and, assuming uncodified normal background behavior, she interpreted abnormalities in terms of them.

Questions about "what everyone knows" and "normal forms" have been empirically addressed by ethnomethodologists. We have already mentioned Garfinkel's early work with jurors. He wanted to know, "What made them jurors?" He asked them questions about how they acted as jurors, the bases of their feelings and thoughts, and the like. Verbal accounts appropriate and sanctionable in law and custom to an outsider were subtly shifted when jurors talked among themselves. By taking note of such shifts, it is possible for an alert interviewer to grasp the contours of various "normal forms," gauging the ways individuals linguistically reconstruct their actions so that those whom they talk to about them will regard them as predictable, normal, and adequate – as orderly.

---

[12] D. Zimmerman, "The Practicalities of Rule Use," in J. Douglas, ed., *Understanding Everyday Life* (Chicago: Aldine, 1970), pp. 221–38.

VI. An assessment of ethnomethodology

There can be no doubt that ethnomethodology is an important and seminal development in sociology. This is so mostly because it concentrates on a class of questions that has been inadequately treated by traditional sociology and gives some very interesting answers. Such questions are: How do role expectations, socialized behavior, and what sociologists have called "structured social relations" find their way into everyday activity? What is the mechanism by which people act out their lives according to the rules of social life? It is unfortunate that ethnomethodology developed so much apart from the mainstream of sociological literature and debate. Both it and traditional sociology would have benefited had closer ties been established sooner. As it is, with ethnomethodology growing in influence, an unnatural division in the field has led some to think of ethnomethodology too much as an alternative to the "structural" sociologies. Ethnomethodology, in its enthusiasm for everyday encounters, has placed correspondingly little emphasis on social structure. But, in fact, some important speculations on the way social structure *works* have been made by ethnomethodologists. If this speculation could be attached to a more convincing description of *why* we have the social structures we do, and why these call forth our particular "normal forms," then some real progress would be made. We shall return to this point.

A. On social order and social structure

Ethnomethodologists have found it convenient to discount or disclaim the existence of social order, even though the subject of their studies is almost always some aspect of socially organized activity. In fact, they disclaim a necessary sociological level of orderliness, or some kind of culturally prescribed constraint system, such as shared value perspectives or contextually fixed actions. This disclaimer takes them out of the Durkheimian tradition of society *sui generis,* existing at its own level of abstraction and influencing everyday actions from there. Once removed from this tradition, it might appear that there is no further reason to seek causes for social orders of particular kinds, or even to consider if and how situations are comparable, or why they seem to arise at given times and places. The ethnomethodologists put the individual at the center of sociological analysis. But even this eventually leads to the problem of social structure. As yet ethnomethodologists have not given convincing accounts of structure, preferring to concentrate on less abstract matters. So it is with some reservation that we must regard the ethnomethodological position on social order. Just as with the symbolic interactionists, ethnomethodologists find it hard to give a sociological explanation of the causes and consequences of order, because they concentrate on individuality. Ethnomethodology simply goes a step ahead to argue that unique situations unfold in unpredictable ways, and to suggest from this that no higher-order causes could possibly be constraining the activity depicted.

In this vein, ethnomethodologists often use the words "social structure" in much the same sense that symbolic interactionists use "situation." The idea that one learns social structure in the same ways, and at the same time, that one learns the lingua franca of society trivializes the concept of social structure into something more or less synonomous with "social setting" or "human environment." Unquestionably, knowledge about social settings is important, even crucial. Nor is there reason to disagree with the proposal that a person's social setting and the language he speaks are vitally important factors in determining the ways he will be judged, and the ways he will regard himself. But "social setting" is not what most sociologists mean by "social structure." Indeed, it is probably true that social settings are generative, in the way that Cicourel suggests, and that the languages of social settings combine with the settings themselves to make orderly social interaction possible. But such an observation raises a question not typical of normal ethnomethodology: Why, despite all the possible variety, is there so much abstract uniformity about social life? In ethnomethodological terms, we might wish to know why there are "normal forms," where they come from, and why they are what they are and not otherwise. Such a line of questioning inevitably leads to a reconsideration of social structure itself, to a different model of man, or both.

Cicourel has already suggested the direction ethnomethodology might go with his ideas on the generative aspects of social situations. In this work, language structure is both an explanatory idea and an analogy. If it is true that the mind can only deal with speech in definite hierarchical ways, and that self-articulation is crucial to social action, then perhaps the orderliness of normal life is in part a consequence of our making sense of things in orderly language. A fuller development of this idea would be exciting, especially if it were to link up with concepts of social structure already found in sociology and anthropology.

In a similar vein, it seems likely that the "plain man," whose mind works in an unscientific way, could provide more than a rudimentary model from which to begin. Schutz's ideas about the difference between scientific reasoning and everyday thought, Weber's formal and substantive rationalities, and Kaplan's logic-in-use and reconstructed logic–all sketch a nonrational actor whose mind requires an orderliness to function. Pareto thought that "verbal proofs" and post hoc descriptions of conduct masked over physically determined action tendencies. Perhaps ethnomethodology will not fasten onto instinct in its description of persons, but a fuller picture of the "plain man" is required if the concept is to be more than straw from which to build a flexible model of the actor.

Ethnomethodologists have added significantly to the research techniques used by sociologists. With their perspective on organizational records and reports, ethnomethodology has reestablished the fact that an interpretive process interposes between events and written accounts–a process that may be more interesting than the events themselves, and a process that must be reckoned with whenever other methodological techniques are used. The methodological canon that results are only as good as the data now assumes the necessary interpretive dimension, no matter what theory is in use. It will be impossible for any sociologist to forget about interpretive procedures again.

Ethnomethodology shares the problem of all the subjective sociologies; the lack of falsifiability. In principle, ethnomethodology is a dogma about how the human mind works when people interact, and when they give verbal accounts. Because this is essentially an untestable dogma, it leaves the practitioner to produce convincing explanations without publically agreed standards of reliability and validity. What if two ethnomethodologists give conflicting explanations? There is no way to adjudicate them. Perhaps two ethnomethodologists give the same explanation, but is this because they "see" the same thing, or because they share a world view that has nothing to do with the action they observe? Questions like this will not be answered by ethnomethodology. How could it? A basic principle of the field says that people make unsupported assumptions about intersubjectivity and the adequacy of communications when they relate events to each other.

A more abstract theoretical problem concerns the methods by which ethnomethodology gains and interprets data. From one point of view, it would seem that ethnomethodology incorporates a cognitive bias. People are asked, in various ways, how they make sense of their worlds; the answers they give are broadly linguistic: People employ interpretive frames in which expected types of actions have a normal meaning; and when something jogs them out of the frame, they find a normalizing explanation. This is highly cognitive and verbal. No action is understandable to normal people until it finds its explanation in everyday terms, even if this explanation is implicit and not problematic. Is this much emphasis on cognitive processes really wanted?

Giving ethnomethodology a foundation in generative grammar, and using this as an analogy to social settings, opens a very interesting and fruitful area of speculation. But this can cut across the cognitive element in ethnomethodology. The rules we speak by may be in our "minds" but hardly in our consciousness. If asked to "account" for normal speech, could the "plain man" give a response that would lead a researcher to discover the rules that organize thoughts into speech sounds? If he hears nonsense, even if it does produce dissonance, can the "plain man" normalize it into meaningful messages? Perhaps the ethnomethodologists are correct to point to the generative functions of speech and social setting as crucial aspects of normal social life. But it *may be* that the significant rule following of everyday life is just as mysterious and unconscious as the phonetic rule following of speech production. It *may be* that linguistic and interpretive methodologies do not pick up important parts of social behavior that operate at some level of unconsciousness or abstraction not reachable by cognitive methodologies. For ethnomethodology, this would be especially significant because in it the main point is that everybody is a methodologist, doing "naive methodology" in an effort to make sense of everyday life.

Ethnomethodology is a young tradition in sociology, and one that has shied away from public display in textbooks and generalizing statements. Instead, we have preliminary statements of the philosophical position combined with concrete applications, and little hardheaded theory between. Most ethnomethodologists appear to think that this is as it should be, because there is really nothing to theorize about except the methodologies by which people get on with life. But perhaps as ethnomethodology answers its critics and bites into standard sociological questions, it will provide an explicit theory of social action. Judging from promising beginnings, this could only be a significant addition to sociological theory.

KEY CONCEPTS

ethnomethodology	social structure
et cetera	generative semantics
verbal account	"what everyone knows"
normal form	intersubjectivity
behavior rule	attitudes of daily life

TOPICS FOR DISCUSSION

1 Compare ethnomethodology and exchange theory by contrasting their objectives.
2 What is so interesting to ethnomethodologists about what people *say* they are doing?

3 How can a rule that we do not *follow* influence our conduct?
4 How many "forms of sociability" are there and where do they originate?
5 Contrast the "attitudes of daily life" with those of the ideal scientific attitude. What are the significant differences?
6 How might ethnomethodology establish theoretical links with other sociological theories?

ESSAY QUESTIONS

Compare ethnomethodology with symbolic interaction regarding the question of social order.

What do you think is the main assumption about human motivation in ethnomethodology?

Describe some normal encounter by listing the unstated assumptions necessary to make it take place.

Compare ethnomethodology's program of sociological research with its depiction of everyday life.

Write an account of a recent encounter that you intend to be read by someone you know intimately. Write up the same encounter for a stranger. Compare the descriptions. What is the significance of the comparison?

FOR FURTHER READING AND STUDY

Berger, Peter L., and Thomas Luckman. *The Social Construction of Reality.* Garden City, N.Y.: Anchor, 1967.

Bittner, Egon. "The Concept of Organization," *Ethnomethodology.* Roy Turner (ed.), Harmondsworth, Middlesex: Penguin Books, 1974, pp. 69–81.

Cicourel, Aaron V. *Method and Measurement in Sociology.* New York: The Free Press, 1964.

The Social Organization of Juvenile Justice. New York: Wiley, 1968.

Cognitive Sociology. Harmondsworth, Middlesex: Penguin Books, 1973.

Douglas, Jack (ed.). *Understanding Everyday Life: Toward the Reconstruction of Sociological Knowledge.* Chicago: Aldine, 1970.

Douglas, Mary (ed.). *Rules and Meanings.* Harmondsworth, Middlesex: Penguin Books, 1973.

Garfinkel, Harold. *Studies in Ethnomethodology.* Englewood Cliffs, N.J.: Prentice-Hall, 1967.

"A Conception of and Experiments with 'Trust' as a Condition of Concerted Stable Actions." *Motivation and Social Interaction.* O. J. Harvey (ed.). New York: Ronald, 1963.

"The Origins of the Term Ethnomethodology." *Ethnomethodology.* Roy Turner (ed.). Harmondsworth, Middlesex: Penguin Books, 1974, pp. 15–18.

"The Rational Properties of Scientific and Common-sense Activities." *Positivism and Sociology.* Anthony Giddens (ed.). London: Heinemann, 1974, pp. 53–73.

Moerman, Michael. "Accomplishing Ethnicity." *Ethnomethodology*. Roy
    Turner (ed.). Harmondsworth, Middlesex: Penguin Books, 1974, pp. 54–
    68.
Scott, Marvin G., and Stanford Lyman. "Accounts." *American Sociological
    Review,* XXXIII, No. 1 (February, 1968), 46–62.
Schutz, Alfred. *The Phenomenology of the Social World*. Tr. G. Walsh and
    F. Lehnert. Evanston, Ill.: Northwestern University Press, 1967.
Wieder, D. Lawrence. "Telling the Code." *Ethnomethodology*. Roy Turner
    (ed.). Harmondsworth, Middlesex: Penguin Books, pp. 144–72.

Epilog

The final pages of this book on sociological theory are an appropriate place to set down some general notes that would have been meaningless at the outset, but that are still of an introductory nature.

As in any living discipline, various practitioners take various viewpoints. The aim of this book is to expose the component parts of various theory groups by describing the ways the key ideas fit together. This entails a concentration on definitions, descriptions of central explanatory mechanisms, and some implications of the reasoning. To grasp the ways ideas work through theoretical statements to produce practical implications, it is necessary to know something of the methodological and philosophical reasoning supporting any theoretical effort. Basic theoretical reasoning is involved in all sociological work, including that which appears to be only practical, because it is by way of theory that we learn to know what to look for and what to expect in social relations. The study of theory as the basic store from which sociological reasoning draws emphasizes it as a necessary intellectual challenge to straight thinking. This can be about practical problems, or about theory itself. But, throughout, the point is to show how theoreticians have challenged themselves with practical or theoretical problems, and how they have followed up these leads by producing highly organized systems of ideas that explain social relations.

Such a viewpoint supports the division of the book into theoretical types—exchange, functionalism, symbolic interaction, and ethnomethodology. Central to each of these groups of theory is something unique to each, which gives identity to the theory growing up around the main core. Diverse theoreticians with similar core ideas make similar achievements, and have similar troubles. In itself, the fact that this happens is worth knowing: Any theoretical path we begin will have characteristic strengths and weaknesses about which some decisions might be made ahead of time.

The viewpoint found in this book is neutral regarding the uses of theory. This book says something about how ideas go together to explain aspects of social relations. It says nothing about which aspects of social relations *ought* to be studied, or *why* these should demand attention. This is an appropriate stance because involvement in normative problems always cuts across theoretical clarity and blurs the distinctions that ideas themselves retain. Apart from academic justifications, normative neutrality in theory discussions is essential to the conduct of intellectual debate among interested laymen and intelligent people generally. It is up to the user to determine *why* he wishes to use a certain theoretical idea. This is not for others to decide in advance, or to tailor content accordingly. Creative use of sociological theory involves the application of new or existing ideas to unique situations, for purposes defined by the user. If he knows something about possible results before he begins, he will be as well equipped as he can be. Therefore, it is necessary that a neutral view of various theoretical alternatives be presented, along with some intelligent critique of each. Choosing for oneself implies knowing what there is to choose from.

This normative neutrality also supports the organization of the book. Alternatively, organization according to problem areas, broad empirical categories such as conflict, or normative intent, allows subtle specification of *what* to think to enter the discussion of *how* to think. Even if some of this happens anyway because various theoreticians concentrate on various problems, a normatively neutral standpoint makes it obvious.

Sometimes students of sociology view theory as a hurdle they must jump before they are allowed to pass on to "meaningful" work. This is unfortunate because they miss the fun of abstract thinking. But more important, such an attitude obscures the fact that the theory of a living discipline is also living – it is changing, responding to critique, making progress, and experiencing failure. Even though the central ideas of social thought are remarkably durable, the combinations, implications, and applications are endlessly changing. It is essential to know this fact and use it if one is to become liberated from dogma. It is heavy labor "following" a theory, or "finding" some theoretical justification for an empirical result. It is far more interesting to look for convergences, differences, implications, applications, and generally to make sense of one's world in various creative ways. The intelligent person does this. Only the intellectual drudge keeps faith with dogma.

Throughout this book there are instances of theoretical success. Each kind of theory does something right; often, quite a little is done right. Yet, by necessity and convenience, if nothing more, the corpus of sociological theory has been divided into blocks that share similar ideas. Is there not some way to "put it all together"? Undoubtedly, the answer is yes. Various theories were devised to explain the same general phenomena. Is it not possible to take a leaf from Parsons's *Structure of Social Action* and find "convergences" among the various current theories that will provide a modern synthesis? This is one challenge to theoretical thinking in sociology.

Name index

Aberle, D., 125n
Abrahamsson, B., 105n
Aristotle, 29, 30
Aron, R., 11n

Bales, R., 129n, 143n–144n, 150n, 154n, 156n, 161
Barnes, H., 11n
Barron, M., 143n
Barry, B., 111n
Becker, H., 11n, 233, 235
Becker, H. S., 168
Bendix, R., 141n
Berger, P., 242
Bierstedt, R., 145n
Bittner, R., 242, 245
Black, M., 143n, 148n
Blalock, H., 29n
Blau, P., 70, 78, 91–3, 95–101, 104–8
Blumer, H., 188–9, 213–17, 222–3, 226, 229, 232–3
Braithwaite, R., 78n
Brodbeck, M., 40n
Buchanan, J., 106n, 110n
Buck, G., 169–71
Buckley, W., 176, 180n
Burnstein, E., 165–6
Burrows, J. W., 42n

Campbell, N., 9n
Catton, W., 175n
Cicourel, A., 243, 245–56
Cohen, P., 43n
Cooley, C., 188, 196, 204
Coser, L., 180n

Dahrendorf, R., 178n
Darwin, C., 11, 117, 206
Davis, F., 223–6, 232
Davis, K., 29n, 141–3, 156n, 165–8, 172, 174, 176, 180, 182
DeVaughan, W., 103n
Dewey, J., 188, 196, 198, 204
Dickens, C., 44n

Dubin, R., 143n, 148n
Duncan, H., 193n
Durkheim, E., 7–11, 59, 117, 123n, 124n, 126, 131, 146n, 168, 174–5, 238, 255

Faris, R., 175n
Freud, S., 49–50

Garfinkel, H., 239n, 243–6, 250, 254
Gibson, Q., 51n
Goffman, E., 13n, 188, 222
Gouldner, A., 69n
Greenberg, M., 103n
Gross, L, 42n, 173n

Heath, A., 107n
Hemphill, C., 173n
Hobbes, T., 123
Hofstadter, R., 6n
Homans, G., 54–5, 58n, 67, 70, 78–93, 98, 101, 104–9, 116, 175–6, 229

Jacobson, A., 169–71
James, W., 198, 204

Kaplan, A., 4, 9, 40n, 50–1, 256
Kelley, H., 87–93, 105
Kitsuse, J., 223n
Kuhn, M., 188–9, 217–18, 227–9

Langer, S., 40n
Lenski, G., 181n
Levy, M., 117, 135–42, 165, 173
Liberty, P., 165
Lipset, S., 141n
Locke, J., 75n
Longabaugh, R., 102, 105
Loomis, C., 168–9, 177
Luckmann, T., 242

MacIver, R., 29n
McKinney, J., 168–9, 177
McPartland, T., 227n
Malinowski, B., 125–6
Malthus, T., 117
Maris, R., 84–5

263

Subject index

Page numbers in italics refer to diagrams in the text.

projection, 49
propositions, Homans', 54, 79–83, 101,
  105; no.1 (stimulus-response), 79; no.2
  (success), 80–1, 84–5; no.3 (value),
  80–1; no.4 (deprivation-satiation),
  81–2; no.5 (aggression-approval), 85–6
Protestant ethic, 48–50
Protestantism, in Durkheim's *Suicide,* 8,
  48–9; in Kuhn's research, 228
psychology, 58, 70, 140, 166, 175–6,
  196–7, 221–3; *see also* experimental
  psychology
public goods, 110; *see also* Blau;
  economic analogy
punishment, 84

quality, 151, *169; see also* pattern
  variables; performance
quantification, 60–3, 89, 102–4, 106–8;
  see also methodology

rank, 75–7, 163; *see also* stratification,
  social
rate of exchange, 74, 82
Rational Man, 5, 43–4, 109–10
rationality, 43–4, 110–11, 145, 238–9
rebellion, 134–5; *see also* adaptation,
  modes of individual; Merton
reciprocity, 94, 107; *see also* exchange
reciprocity, of perspectives, 250
reductionism, 58, 175
reference group, 218; *see also* group; Kuhn
reflective thinking, 206, 210
religion, 138–9, 156–7, 170, 228
requisites, *see* functional requisites;
  functionalism; Levy
research, 60; in ethnomethodology, 252–7;
  in exchange theory, 102–11; in
  functionalism, 165–71; about pattern
  variables, 168; in symbolic
  interactionism, 221–8
retreatism, 134–5; *see also* adaptation
retrospective-prospective sense of
  occurrence, 251
reward, 72–4, 79–80, 82, 84–6, 89–92,
  105–7, 111, 141–2, 155, 156n, 167;
  endogenous and exogenous, 93;
  intrinsic and extrinsic, 93, 104; primary
  and secondary, 86–7; *see also* primary
  reinforcer
ritualism, 134–5; *see also* adaptation,
  modes of individual; Merton
role, 12–13, 21, 31, 41, 50, 118–19, 128–9,
  143, 151, 169, 179, 187, 191, 206–7, 209,
  255; differentiation of, 137–8, 140; *see
  also* systems, social
role-playing, 206–9
role-taking, 206–10, 213, 225–6, 229
Roman Catholicism, 8, 228; *see also*
  Durkheim; Kuhn

rules, 76, 133, 243–4; grammatical, 245–9;
  see also norms

salience factor, 228; *see also* Kuhn
scientific law, *see* law, scientific
scientific procedure, 23–6; *see also*
  methodology
self, 13, 59, 110, 188, 195–7, 199, 201,
  204–6, 208–13, 218–21, 224, 226–7,
  229; as object, 197–8
self-acquisition, *see* stages
self-attitudes, 226–9
"self-criticism," in symbolic
  interactionism, 210
self-esteem, 103, 223–6
semantics, 248–9
sensitizing, *see* concept
sentiment, 146
settings of action, *see* Miyamoto;
  perceptual settings
sexual recruitment, 138–40; *see also*
  Levy; requisites
sign, 230; *see also* gesture
significant symbols, 194, 201–4; *see also*
  communication; gesture; language
situation, definition of, 192, 213, 223, 226
Social Behavior, 78–9, 81, 83–4
social class, 2–4, 24
social debt, *see* indebtedness
social determinism, 27–8, 211; *see also*
  sociologism
social evolution, 31, 122–3, 127, 135, 142,
  161–2, 169–70, 174, 176, 180; *see also*
  evolution; evolutionary universals
social facts, 59; *see also* Durkheim
social order, 70, 237–9, 241, 246, 252–3,
  255
social organization, 45, 91–3, 172, 175,
  241–2, 254; *see also* order, social
social psychology, 87–91, 196, 211, 221
Social Psychology of Groups (The), 87
social relationship, 21, 87–8
social solidarity, 96–7, 138
social stability, *see* stability
social structure, *see* structure
social system, 120, 123, 131, 135–6, 141,
  143–4, 147, 149–50, 154–5, 157,
  159–60, 165, 179, 237; *see also* four-fold
  scheme; Parsons; *159*
Social Theory and Social Structure,
  132n–135n
socialization, 129, 137, 139, 143, 155, 178;
  see also education; role-playing;
  role-taking; stages
societal community, 154n; *see also*
  community; *Gemeinschaft*
society, 41, 153, 168, 209, 212; Blumer on,
  212–14; Levy on, 135–40; in symbolic
  interactionism, 209–11; termination of,
  136; *see also Gesellschaft*

270   *Subject Index*

vitalism, 45
voluntarism, 73, 145, 147, 149–50, 160, 178–9

"we-feeling," 163; *see also* evolutionary universals

"what everyone knows," in ethnomethodology, 240–1, 244, 250–2
will, 25
work, 62, 104, 165–6, 228

Zweckrational, 20; *see also* Weber